IN PETER'S FOOTSTEPS

By the Same Author

CENTERING PRAYER
Renewing an Ancient Christian Prayer Form

DAILY WE TOUCH HIM
Practical Religious Experiences

IN SEARCH OF TRUE WISDOM
Visits to Eastern Spiritual Fathers

JUBILEE
A Monk's Journal

MONASTIC JOURNEY TO INDIA

O HOLY MOUNTAIN!
Journal of a Retreat on Mount Athos

A PLACE APART
Monastic Prayer and Practice for Everyone

M. Basil Pennington, O.C.S.O.

IN PETER'S FOOTSTEPS

Learning to Be a Disciple

DOUBLEDAY & COMPANY, INC.
GARDEN CITY, NEW YORK
1985

LIBRARY OF CONGRESS CATALOGING IN PUBLICATION DATA

Pennington, M. Basil.
In Peter's footsteps.

1. Peter, the Apostle, Saint.
2. Bible. N. T. Peter—Criticism, interpretation, etc.
3. Christian life—Catholic authors. I. Title.
BS2515.P455 1985 225.9'24
ISBN 0-385-19398-X
Library of Congress Catalog Card Number: 85-1541

Scripture quotations are from *The Jerusalem Bible* except where they have been translated by the author from the original Greek

PRINTED IN THE UNITED STATES OF AMERICA

FIRST EDITION

To Paul
and all the other members of
Alcoholics Anonymous
– a constant source of inspiration –
with gratitude

Contents

Forward

Christ is our master and we are his disciples. This is our great privilege.

My monastery at Spencer has been blessed with very special neighbors. Off to the west we have a Buddhist meditation center, and to the south there is a Hindu ashram. There is an excellent rapport among us; we partake of each other's joys and sorrows. We realize we are all seekers, and share a common concern for the uplifting and healing of this world of ours. Our lives exemplify many common values. One of these is discipleship. Our Buddhist and Hindu brothers and sisters have an almost unbounded enthusiasm for their masters. There is no doubt they consider it a great privilege to be disciples. They are tireless in extolling their teacher of meditation. When Achincha comes from Thailand, our Buddhist brethren rise to new levels of excitement. They are eager for us to come to their center to see and hear him; they want to bring him to speak to us at our monastery. And the same is true in regard to Swamiji. In all of this, I cannot help reflecting on our relative lack of enthusiasm and pride in regard to our Master—and he is the Master who made these others masters!

One of the things a disciple needs to learn from a

master is how to be a good disciple. In this regard we could not have a better master than our Lord Jesus. He always did the things that pleased the Father, being obedient unto death, even death on a cross. His meat was to do the will of him who sent him. His whole life and being strained to fulfill the mission he had been given. He set his face resolutely toward Jerusalem. He wept at its unresponsiveness. And he died. "Not my will but yours be done, Father."

Through a filial relationship Jesus brought a new dimension to discipleship. There was, along with a total dedication to the glorification of his Master-Father, a deep love for the Father, a most intimate communion. And he has called us to this same kind of relationship as disciples: I shall not call you servants anymore, because a servant does not know his master's business; I call you friends because I have made known to you everything I have learned from my Father (John 15:15). He prayed that we would be one with him even as he is one with the Father (John 17:21). In baptism, through the power of his cross, he effects this essentially. It is our life's work to learn to think and act in accord with who we are by creation and by the recreation of baptism.

But Jesus' example of discipleship can be overwhelming for us. He *always* did the things that pleased the Father. How often we fail!

This is where Saint Peter comes in. I give him his title of "saint" quite deliberately here. For I suspect when I propose calling Peter a "master of discipleship," you might have some serious reservations. Rather quickly there comes to mind our Lord's stinging rebuke to this overzealous follower: "Get behind me, Satan! You are an obstacle in my path . . ." Or that much more prophetic statement: "Before the cock crows twice, you will have disowned me three times." Even now, this blustery man's oaths that he does not even know the Master sting our hearts. Well might he cry, sob inconsolably—the traitor! Yet it is precisely because Peter—Saint Peter—was such a disciple, one who would fail, and fail miserably, that he is a good master of discipleship for us. Because we too fail. In the end he died for his Master, and greater love than this no man hath, than he lay down his life for his Friend and Master.

We fail. How many times! And we are, in the face of our many failures, tempted to become discouraged, to feel that we can never be true disciples of Christ. We begin to reconcile ourselves to being some kind of borderline Christian, one who will, by God's mercy, somehow slip into the outer reaches of heaven. He heard the dying thief; we can hope he will hear us when we cry out from our deathbeds. But for us there is no hope of being a true disciple. We have all our passions and emotions. We are men and women of the world with family and business to preoccupy us. We even have mothers-in-law to challenge to their very core whatever patience and love we do have. We can't leave all things to follow on the high adventure of discipleship.

Or can we?

I would like to invite you to walk with me awhile along the roads and in the towns and villages of Galilee and Judaea and watch another man—very much a man, a man of flesh and blood, of passion and emotion—as he tries to enter into the way of a disciple. We will watch and listen, and talk about it a bit as we reflect together. In the end, maybe we will let our imaginations carry us to Rome and see a man who has finally learned that God's thoughts are not our thoughts nor his ways our ways as he hangs upside down and sees all creation hanging on the mercy of God.

I must confess I am feeling a bit—or more than a bit —excited as we start out on this journey together. Maybe I am finding something of the enthusiasm of my Buddhist and Hindu neighbors. Come and see and hear our master—a master of discipleship, who will show us how to be true disciples of the one Lord and Master who is God, over all, forever and ever. May he be blessed!

We are certainly blessed ourselves in being called with Peter to be Jesus' disciples, disciples who are called not servants but friends, called to the deepest, most loving, and most fulfilling union. "Peter, do you love me?" "Yes, Lord, you know that I love you." It is, in sum, a way of love that leads not only to perfect love ("No greater love than this . . ."), but to an eternal dwelling place and unending glory: "Father, I want those you have given me to be with me where I am, so that they may always see the glory you have given me because you loved me from the foundation of the world" (John 17:24). "Those who prove victorious I will allow to share my throne, just as I was victorious myself and took my place with my Father on his throne" (Revelation 3:21).

To this, Peter was called. This is something important to remember. It was Jesus who chose Peter: "I have chosen you, you have not chosen me"—and *with* (he didn't leave them behind—at least, not right away) all his faults and failures and human weakness. Peter followed. We too are called. And we too can follow, even with all our faults and failures and weakness. (Who was that saint who for years prayed: "Lord, give me chastity, but not yet"?—the great Saint Augustine!) We can be confident that in the end, that love which is greater than love, *mercy,* will win out. And we too will see and accept the true being of things—even if it turns our world upside down—and know that greatest joy of any true disciple: to be with our Master, no longer serving from afar, but rejoicing in a most complete oneness of consummate love.

This book is meant to be an experience in shared *lectio. Lectio* is an essential element in the monastic life. If you look at the old *horaria* or timetables for the monks' day, you find many periods simply marked *lectio.* It was a time when the monk would sit down with the Word of God and enter into a whole process: *lectio, meditatio, oratio, contemplatio. Lectio,* which literally means reading, is receiving the Revelation through reading the Sacred Scriptures or recalling what has been previously read or heard. *Meditatio* is the process whereby what we have received is interiorized to form our minds and hearts. *Oratio* is our response to this. God has spoken to us. We have heard. We now respond to him. In *contemplatio* our response, rather than some specific words or thoughts or affections, is the response of our whole being in silent presence to God. Contemplation is the consummation of the process, but it does not necessarily have to stop there. As Saint Bernard taught, there is another step, where we go on to share the fruit of our contemplation with others: *contemplationem aliis tradere.* Some of the richest spiritual literature available to us is precisely this, the sharing of the fruit of contemplation of the Fathers and Mothers who have gone before us.

In the rabbinical tradition it is said that Scripture is a *PaRDeS,* which means an orchard. It is full of fruit. *P* stands for *peshat,* the simple, literal meaning of the word. *R, remeg,* is that meaning which is hinted at, the allegorical, the concealed meaning that fills out our experience of the reality something like a dream arising from the lower regions of our consciousness. *Drash, D,* is the searched-out, learned interpretation. And *sod, S,* is the secret, mystical, universal meaning, the transpersonal, the meaning that is hidden in God. In the Christian tradition we find a similar approach to the Sacred Word. Medieval exegesis spoke of four meanings: the literal, the allegorical, the moral, and the anagogical. The first two would be very much the same as in the rabbinical tradition. The moral meaning refers to the response that the Revelation calls forth from us and in us. The anagogical points to the ultimate meaning; it is not unlike *sod.* As we listen to the Scriptures we can be open to all these meanings, seek them out, and let them speak to us.

The Scriptural Texts represent not only the consciousness of the original writer but also, or rather, the collective consciousness of the Christian community. Under the Divine Inspiration he was a mouthpiece of the community *that goes on* in salvation history. We are invited to enter into this consciousness of the living Body of Christ.

We have been baptized into Christ, therefore we are all called to be disciples, friends, lovers, one with Christ in a participation of being and nature beyond anything we can comprehend. In order to be integral, to be true to who we are as men and women baptized into Christ, we must also have the mind of Christ: "Let this mind be in you which was in Christ Jesus." An awesome call! We look for examples among the disciples who were schooled by Christ himself. John the Beloved, the disciple whom Jesus loved, is perhaps the most attractive. But his way is one of intuitive love. It is more to be followed than studied. It can only be learned by experience. Peter, on the other hand, is a wonderfully human fellow who seems a lot closer to us—a good place for us to start to learn to be disciples. The Scriptures are full of information about this disciple of the Lord from the day of his call till, as a wise old shepherd, he shares his heart's concerns with all of us disciples of Christ. The sacred writers do not aim so much to set forth a factual historical record as to present a true image of the person in his precise role in Salvation History. The events recorded by the Evangelists concerning Peter were chosen precisely for the same reason I am writing: to present Peter as disciple and apostolic leader.

As we come into contact with Peter, we really want to open ourselves to the experience: to listen to our own emotions, our own present experiences, to all the components of the scene. We want to note the details and the oddities. We want to allow embarrassment to rise up in us, and also dread. All our associations are relevant. We want to take responsibility, for we have a role in creating the experience. We want to face the demands of the dialectic, allowing opposites to come together. We dare to look at our many selves and ask of each character, why do we create it this way. We want to look at the origins, the unity, and the "now." You are Peter. I am Peter. Each character is you and I. The Body of Christ is a hologram. The whole is in every member. The whole of discipleship is in Peter, in you and in me in potency. It is a question of letting it come forth. We can facilitate this by touching ourselves in Peter. (The word "touching" means to experience something very concretely, incarnationally, in body and soul at the same time.) What Peter once did is also for us to do in our own proper way, the bad as well as the good—for failure is a way to repentance, self-knowledge, growth, and greater intimacy. True, we do want to get to know ourselves, to tell ourselves about ourselves. But we are also afraid. We can only move with our own ability to endure awareness, while at the same time seeking to enlarge that ability. That is why we need to pray for courage when we read Sacred Scripture or a commentary such as this, which is a shared experience of Scripture.

Sacred Scripture, the Revelation, is not something static. Is is a living Word, it is constantly in motion. Like the whole of creation, it is ever coming forth from God, coming forth now in the collective memory of a people. It is coming forth to us, it is coming forth in us, now. It is a new (re-newed) reality, and yet it is the same reality present now. The same, yet wholly new. How will I live it now, today?

I have included the texts of most of the pericopes on Peter to encourage you to enter into them yourself. Under the Holy Spirit, allow them to become your own experience. Enjoy Peter to the full, and fill in the gaps out of your own experience of discipleship.

This chapter is entitled "Forward," not "Foreword." Let us go forward together on the exciting journey of discipleship.

Father Basil

Feast of the Holy Transfiguration, 1984

Called

As John stood there with two of his disciples, Jesus passed, and John stared hard at him and said, "Look, there is the lamb of God." Hearing this, the two disciples followed Jesus. Jesus turned round, saw them following and said, "What do you want?" They answered, "Rabbi"—which means Teacher—"where do you live?" "Come and see," he replied; so they went and saw where he lived, and stayed with him the rest of that day. It was about the tenth hour.

One of these two who became followers of Jesus after hearing what John had said was Andrew, the brother of Simon Peter. Early next morning, Andrew met his brother and said to him, "We have found the Messiah"—which means the Christ—and he took Simon to Jesus. Jesus looked hard at him and said, "You are Simon son of John; you are to be called Cephas"—meaning Rock. [John 1:35–42]

We tend to think that our own lives and our own times are absolutely unique, that no one before has ever been through the things we are going through. But we are all cut out of the same human fabric, we are all part of the whole. One of the fruits of friendship, indeed one of its causes, is that kind of open sharing in which we discover that another is experiencing the very same things that we are. As wise old Solomon said, there is nothing new under the sun.

In recent years we have seen the phenomenon of many young people, and some not so young, heading east, going on a great pilgrimage to find a spiritual master—a guru, a swami, a teacher—one who has found the meaning of life and is willing to teach in a practical way how others can find that same meaning. This pilgrimage to the East in search of a master is nothing new. Back in the fourth century my own blessed patron, Basil, and his friend Gregory Nazianzus left the lecture halls of Athens to search for true wisdom in the East. From Rome the young Dalmatian, John Cassian, did the same. There were many others. And there were women too: Paula, Melenia the Elder, and Melenia the Younger, to mention only a few of the better known. At that time the East meant Syria, Palestine, and Egypt. The same phenomenon was seen in the eleventh and twelfth centuries. As we read the Gospels we find a similar quest going on in our Lord's time. John and Andrew, and Peter also, had left the lakeside of Galilee and had traveled south and east to beyond the Jordan in search of someone who seemed to have some prophetic wisdom, who seemed to have a word of life that could stir up their faith and give more meaning to their lives. They went in search of a seemingly strange man who came from the desert, wearing camel's hair, an ascetic who had a prophetic word. There was courage here, an openness, a questing, a searching. These men wanted a master; they wanted a teacher, a leader. They humbly realized that they didn't have all the answers. They wanted more, and they had the courage to go out and seek it.

God has a profound reverence for us. He knows that the greatest thing he has given us is our freedom, for therein lies our power to love. He will never violate that freedom. He will not invade our lives unless we invite him in. "Ask and you shall receive, seek and you shall find." If we want the Lord to be the master of our lives, we must seek him, invite him.

These young men from Galilee were seeking, were looking for a true master. And they were not disappointed. As John and Andrew stood beside John the Baptizer on the banks of the Jordan, suddenly the prophet raised his arm, and with shining eyes he pointed beyond the crowd to a more distant figure: "Look! Look! There is the Lamb of God." John and Andrew heard that prophetic word and quickly they went in pursuit.

Jesus became aware of his followers. He turned and asked them, "What are you looking for? What do you want?" It is the same question he constantly asks each one of us. He will give us whatever we really want. These young searchers knew what they wanted. They wanted a teacher, and they wanted to stay with him to learn the way of life. So they answered, "Rabbi [which means teacher], where do you live?" Jesus generously responded, "Come and see." So they went and saw where he lived, and they stayed with him the rest of the day. It was already toward evening.

John goes on to tell us that these two, he and Andrew, became at that moment followers of Jesus. Early the next morning, filled with the enthusiasm of a new disciple, Andrew went to his brother Simon: "We have found the Messiah," the Christ, the Anointed One, the great Teacher. Peter too was a seeker, or he would not have been there with his brother and with his co-laborer, John. We do not know exactly what the term Messiah meant to Andrew and Peter at that point. The expectation at that time, especially among the Galileans, was for a Messiah who would not only renew the religious life of the Jewish people, but would lead them to throw off the yoke of the mighty Romans—an anti-Roman nationalist leader was what was generally wanted. Such expectations were certainly very different from those of their newly found Master. Unfortunately, even today we find among those who profess to be followers of Christ, the Prince of Peace, some who think in military terms and would impose their ideas of morality, partial and degraded though they sometimes be, by means of law and military might. Whatever their image of the Messiah might have been, however distorted, the fact is that the disciples came to the Master to learn, to grow, to undergo a transformation of consciousness. We will see a long and sometimes painful process taking place as Peter little by little comes to a true understanding of the meaning of "Messiah," and what that entails in his own life as a disciple who accepts the Messiah in the true sense. For now Peter is open to learn and grow, and that is enough for the Master. It is a starting place. Peter will not be long with Christ before he sees Christ's first sign, the changing of water into wine. Perhaps this miracle was meant to indicate to Peter the transformation that must take place in him and in his thinking before he will be able to serve the Lord effectively and bring joy into the celebration of life.

The way in which Peter was initially called to discipleship tells us something about him. We see constantly in the Gospels that Peter is by nature a leader. It is quite logical to suppose that Andrew is his younger rather than his older brother; Andrew readily accepts his leadership. Yet on this occasion Peter accepts his younger brother's lead and witness. He follows, and he finds. There must be a humble openness in us who would become disciples, a willingness to listen and to follow others who have discovered something, even those who are not naturally leaders, even when we ourselves are natural leaders. True disciples are open to the Master revealing himself through anyone, through any situation, any circumstance. There is such a longing to find the Master, to find the truth, the way of life, that there is openness even to one's younger brother!

For most of us, the call does not come through great visions. There will not be angels coming down to us as to the shepherds, or Gabriel to Mary. There will not be a saint to come to us as Bridget came to Joan of Arc. There will rather be some very familiar person who will perhaps share with us something of his own vision. It can be our own brother, even our "kid brother." How often do we hold back because the call comes through someone we know only too well. This ordinary guy who is just like us, this backslider whom we know only too well, or this person who is anything but a model of virtue, suddenly gets religion and is all enthused. And our tendency? To resent rather than rejoice in his newfound meaning of life. We tend rather to reject than accept and join with him. Peter had the courage to follow this younger brother in his enthusiasm, and thus he discovered for himself that Jesus is indeed the Messiah, the Master, the Hope of Israel.

Peter followed Andrew, who took him to Jesus. John tells us that Jesus "looked hard" at Peter. Simon had leadership qualities. He was a man who was born to lead. And it would take someone who was an even greater leader to call him forth as a disciple. Jesus knew Peter's metal. So he looked hard at him. He looked deeply into him. He spoke to the depths of Peter's soul; he saw the quality, the quality that he, his Creator, had put there, and he spoke to it. "You are Simon son of John; you are to be called Cephas." Saint John tells us that this new name means rock. There are times in the history of Peter when it seems that this was almost an ironical name that Jesus gave to this floundering, fumbling man. Yet the day would come when Jesus would explain to him what his name "Rock" really meant, and then give him the grace and the power to live that meaning to the full. But for the moment it was a significant calling, a moment of profound conversion.

As Jesus looked at Peter, Peter knew that Jesus knew him to his very depths. So he was not at all surprised when Jesus addressed him by name: "You are Simon son of John." Nor, probably, was he surprised that the Master gave him a new name. Peter sensed a turning point in his life. He knew that he was no longer simply Simon son of John. He was now Peter, the disciple of Jesus the Christ.

In the Christian community it has long been the practice at the moment when one first formally becomes a disciple of Jesus to receive a new name. In Christian monasticism it also has been the practice—and still is, though it is waning somewhat in some of our western monasteries—to give the young man or the young woman entering upon the monastic life a new name, for monastic profession is seen as a "second baptism." The practice is waning because we no longer have many true spiritual fathers or spiritual mothers with the prophetic insight to see in the person coming to the monastic life something of what he is called to, so as to give him a name that bespeaks his calling. Parents, in choosing a name for their child who is to be baptized into Christ, should try to reflect deeply in prayer and give a name that will really express in some way the call of their child to be a follower of Jesus and to live a Christian life. Usually it is a question of giving the child a heavenly patron, someone who expresses the fullness of the Christ life and can be a model. If parents truly seek in prayer, they can count on the Holy Spirit to inspire them in the choice of an appropriate patron.

Peter had a new name. It would be a long time before he would really be able to live up to it. As we enter into the discipleship of Christ, the call is to something immensely great, something that is far beyond us; it is a call to a new level of being. It will in fact be a lifetime's labor to come to what we are called to be. We can take heart in walking with Peter, seeing his struggles, his falls, and his rising again. And know that we too can struggle, fall, and rise, and still be disciples of Jesus, and still harbor the hope that in the end we will come to live up to the fullness of that to which we are called.

One of the real struggles of life is this: At some moment—and it is usually at a moment like the one Andrew, John, and Peter are just experiencing, a moment of calling—we perceive an ideal, a vision, something that is big enough to call us forth in all our fullness. It is exciting. It is the sort of thing that leads men and women into monasteries, into missions, into launching a whole new career—a vision of their lives making a difference. And then soon enough our feet are back on earth. We are face to face with the daily, everyday life, with reality in all its drabness and all its shoddiness. A young man enters the monastery, and soon finds that those monks who looked so holy from the visitors' chapel are really very human beings, with the same sort of weaknesses and failures as everyone else. Monks get angry, they can be selfish, they can have bad days, and so on. A marriage partner who used to melt our heart doesn't look so enchanting rolling out of bed in the morning, especially after a bad night. Herein lies the challenge.

There seem to be three possibilities. We can cling to the ideal and refuse to accept the real, spending our lives ever seeking the ideal—the ideal teacher, the ideal place, the ideal circumstances. One day I sat in on an interesting dialogue between two well-known spiritual masters of our times. One of them was a great swami from the East. He had brought the depth of his tradition to America and had used it to open the way for many young Americans. He himself was most faithful in his everyday practice of the tradition that he taught. The other master was a very popular teacher, a Westerner who had adopted Eastern style. He had gone to India and found a teacher there. But he continued on in a tireless quest, seeking to draw from this master and that, willing to experiment with everything he found, always looking for that teacher, that situation, that practice which would finally bring him to a wholly new level of being. The wise swami from Sri Lanka said to him, If a man keeps starting to dig a well and after a few feet stops and goes to start in another place, he will never reach the deep resources that lie far beneath the surface. One must stay in one place and dig and dig and dig. One must be faithful to an ideal and to a practice.

Another alternative that we can choose is to let go of the ideal and be "realistic," accept the seemingly real and settle down in it. The end of this can be totally frustrating, as it is going nowhere. It may be easy to glide with it for a time. But sooner or later we realize that it is a dead end.

The third alternative is to hold fast to the ideal but lovingly embrace the real and live with that life-giving tension which involves constantly trying to bring the real to the ideal.

In his call to discipleship, Peter saw the ideal in Jesus the Master. And Peter's own particular expression of that ideal was prophetically revealed to him in the new name he received: Cephas, Peter, Rock. But he still had to live with and learn to accept the real Simon, the blustery fisherman from the shores of the Lake of Galilee, who was ambitious, who was blunt and overly forthright, insensitive, and cowardly. He had to get to know himself, accept himself, and then, by his Master's teaching and grace, go beyond himself.

On this day John, Andrew, and Peter became disciples. Quickly others joined them. As disciples of Christ, life still had to go on. They had to return to their boats and their nets and earn their daily bread, take care of their families, and fulfill their social obligations. But as they went back to the shores of the Sea of Galilee, everything had new meaning. The openness, the searching that had brought them to the eastern side of Jordan remained. There was a new openness to the potential in life. There was a new openness to the Master, the Teacher, who would help them discover the full meaning of their lives. They came back to their work, their families, their friends with a certain spirit of detachment. They knew that catching fish, and making money, and enjoying friends, and fulfilling their daily tasks were not the ultimate meaning of life. There grew in their hearts a disposition that would enable them to hear God call them to something more, would enable them in part or in full to let go of these ordinary, everyday values of life for something that was more valuable. For some of the disciples of Jesus, life would continue very much as before in its outward circumstances, but there would be a new, deeper meaning, a new freedom, a new joy. There would be more time set aside for reading the Scriptures and for praying. There would be days set aside when they would go off to listen to the Master. There would be a new leaven in their lives. For others, there would come the day when they would be called to lay aside the ordinary values of life in order to follow Jesus in a special way.

This brief pericope on the first call of Peter doesn't really tell us very much about him. In fact, he probably knew very little about himself at this point, but that self-knowledge would grow. Most of us do not know too much about ourselves when we are first called. If our first call came at infant baptism, this is quite obvious. But this was probably true even if it came later in life.

I think of one of the best-known converts in our Catholic community today, Thomas Merton. As a young man he was always a searcher, looking for ultimate meaning in life. He was wholehearted in his search, whether it meant seeking that ultimate meaning in the pleasures of the world, in drink and in sex, or in social concern—he was even a card-carrying Communist—or in listening to an Indian swami. In the end he did find ultimate meaning in the Catholic faith. And he entered wholeheartedly into that faith. He became a monk. Yet even as a monk, at first he didn't have it all put together. He didn't know the true value of God's world, nor even of his own self. He was fortunately blessed with a very wise Father Abbot. Dom Frederic Dunne first made him write his own autobiography so that he could reclaim all the energies, the searching, the desire for life. Merton was then put to teaching—the best way to learn anything is to teach—the patristic heritage. As Merton—or Father Louis, as he was called in the monastery of Gethsemani—studied the Greek Fathers, he discovered a reality of which these Fathers were very much aware. God isn't just to be found in *theoria*—contemplation—of the beyond. God is very present in his creation. They spoke of *theoria physica,* of the presence of God the Word in his creation, of the *logoi.* This all came together for Merton through the experience of a dream that came to life for him a few days later. In a very exceptional letter to Boris Pasternak he tells us about it:

> It is a simple enough story but obviously I do not tell it to people—you are the fourth who knows it, and there seems to be no point in a false discreteness that might

restrain me from telling you since it is clear that we have so very much in common.

One night I dreamt that I was sitting with a very young Jewish girl of fourteen or fifteen, and that she suddenly manifested a very deep and pure affection for me and embraced me so that I was moved to the depths of my soul. I learned that her name was "Proverb," which I thought very simple and beautiful. And also I thought: "She is of the race of Saint Anne." I spoke to her of her name, and she did not seem to be proud of it, because it seemed that the other young girls mocked her for it. But I told her that it was a very beautiful name, and there the dream ended. A few days later when I happened to be in a nearby city, which is very rare for us, I was walking alone in the crowded street and suddenly saw that everybody was Proverb and that in all of them shone her extraordinary beauty and purity and shyness, even though they did not know who they were and were perhaps ashamed of their names —because they were mocked on account of them. And they did not know their real identity as the Child so dear to God who, from before the beginning, was playing in His sight all days, playing in the world.

In this way Merton came to appreciate himself and his gifts and use them to the full. He came to appreciate God's presence in the world and how much God loved the world and everyone in the world, including himself. His contemplation began to flow into a deep, active concern for all that concerns the human family.

Peter would grow as he walked with Christ in the years that followed. He would come to realize that Christ is indeed the Light of the World, and that the disciple's mission is to bring that light to all the human family. As we reflect on Peter's growth, our own consciousness will expand and will undergo a transformation. We will grow and come to know what it is to be a disciple of the Christ.

The Call to Ministry

> As he was walking by the Sea of Galilee Jesus saw two brothers, Simon, who was called Peter, and his brother Andrew; they were making a cast in the lake with their net, for they were fishermen. And he said to them, "Follow me and I will make you fishers of men." And they left their nets at once and followed him.
>
> Going on from there he saw another pair of brothers, James son of Zebedee and his brother John; they were in their boat with their father Zebedee, mending their nets, and he called them. At once, leaving the boat and their father, they followed him. [Matthew 4:18–22]

We do not know how much time elapsed between the first call to Peter and his brother and his friends to become disciples of Christ, and this more particular call that occurred back in their home territory on the banks of the Sea of Galilee. Peter, Andrew, James, and John had returned to their families and their daily labor. But there was a new vision in their lives. They went about their tasks with a new openness to life, to the events of life, to circumstances. They were listening for the Lord in all that they did, all that others said, all that happened. Then one day, as they were busy about their work, the Master appeared in their midst. He spoke but a word, and they left their nets at once and followed him.

We see here how Jesus prepares men, in ways that perhaps at first they do not perceive, for the mission he is going to give them. Jesus called these fishermen to become fishers of men. They could understand his call because of what had gone before in their lives. And they would be able to better fulfill their call as fishers of men because they had spent years as fishermen. They would have learned many things as fishermen. They certainly would have learned patience. How often does the fisherman wait for the schools of fish to come along, sometimes in vain. They would have learned how to adapt themselves to those whom they were to serve as fishers of men. The fisherman has to learn the movements of the fish by patience and discernment, so that he can use their own movement in order to capture them for a higher service. It seems destructive of the fish to capture and kill them so that they might be eaten by men, yet it is in this way that they are raised to a higher level of being. The disciples would learn that it is in dying to our lower selves—which some see only as destructive—that we are able to come to live a higher life, a life that is divine. As fishermen, Peter and his companions learned how to put up with failure and frustration—how often would they fish all the night and catch nothing. They would certainly experience failures as fishers of men. But soon enough, in their close following of Jesus, they would learn something else. Often they would do their very best and still fail, and then suddenly he would turn everything into an overwhelming success. Then they would clearly see that it was not their skill or labor that brought in the good catch or got them safely to shore, but the grace and care of their Master and their God. As fishermen they learned how to sacrifice themselves, to harden their bodies so that they could give themselves tirelessly to their tasks. They learned how to face storm and danger in order to carry their work forward. These men, who were to carry the message of Christ to every corner of the known world, would need such self-giving stamina.

Oftentimes the particular vocation God has in store for us that will give full meaning to our lives comes only after years of fidelity, a fidelity that can involve an endless number of seemingly everyday humdrum tasks.

The whole world, Christian and non-Christian, is conscious of the tremendous work and mission of Mother Teresa of Calcutta. We are filled with admiration, if not amazement, at her untiring outreach to the poorest of the poor, even those impoverished in the most basic human endowments—unwanted infants and the dying. She brings to each a total love because she transparently sees in each the Lord of her life. But how many are conscious of the fact that Mother Teresa spent many years in the quiet, secluded life of a teaching sister? It was those years of fidelity that prepared her to hear and have the courage to say "yes" to a call from the Lord that led her from the security of her convent to the crowded streets of Calcutta.

Pope John XXIII ascended the throne of Peter at an advanced age—"Here I am, an old man and at the top of the heap"—yet almost immediately he inaugurated a radical transformation of the whole Church. This didn't just happen. This good man spent many years virtually exiled to distant outposts, where he was exquisitely faithful to being before all else a good Christian, a humble servant of God and of his fellow human beings. Witness his deeply moving journal.

We have seen two men emerge from long periods of preparation. John the Baptizer had lived in the desert a very spartan life for some thirty years preparing for his moment. His mission would be brief, but it was the most important prophetic mission in the history of the human race. And like many of the prophets, he would quickly seal his witness with his blood.

Jesus, for his part, except for a brief interlude when he came to official manhood at age twelve, followed the daily life of the ordinary pious Jew. Living in a family, he learned to love, to pray, to work, and to take part in community affairs. He seemed to all to be just the carpenter's son. His was a very ordinary life—a life of preparation. But now his hour has come. He emerges, and the heavens open. The Spirit comes down upon him. God the eternal Father speaks out. And Jesus goes forth on his saving mission.

For most of us, perhaps most of the time, life seems to amble or jog along in a very humdrum fashion. Nothing special seems to be happening. But for each one of us God has a role, a unique and important role, for us to play in the working out of Salvation History. If we are faithful to today's call even in what might seem an uneventful daily life, we will be ready for tomorrow's call, prepared to carry out whatever he might ask of us. "Eye has not seen, nor ear heard, nor has it entered into the heart of the human person what God has prepared for those who love him." Saint Paul quotes Isaiah, and adds: "But the Holy Spirit makes it known to us" (1 Corinthians 2:9–10).

Because Peter had been faithful in seeking to know and do God's will, when the astounding summons came to him, he was ready and able to say yes. We do not know for what God is preparing us. Our mission may always be a hidden and interior one. Who knows how much is accomplished in this fragile and needy world of ours by the quiet, joyful, prayerful lives of those who wait in nursing homes? Unfortunately, more often than we like, we see old folks whose days are filled with bitterness. Instead of blessing God and holding the world in caring love and prayer, they are a bottomless well of laments and complaints. What makes the difference? The years of preparation for this final mission in life.

Jesus is sent forth today in the Spirit by his Father to "open the eyes of the blind, to free captives from prison, and those who live in darkness from the dungeon" (Isaiah 42:7). If we do not see the importance of our everyday life as mission or preparation for the mission the Lord has in store for us, let us ask him this day to open our eyes. If perhaps we already seem a prisoner of meaninglessness or hopelessness, let us ask him to bring us out of the darkness into the light of the vision of hope.

We know that, because we have been baptized in the baptism of the Lord Jesus, the favor of the Father rests on us. We are his beloved in whom he is well pleased. We have but to open our hearts, to let ourselves be washed, so that the Spirit may descend upon us with his love and his peace.

* * *

In this small pericope we can also discern something else. We can see that men of very different temperaments can be and are called to the Lord's service. We see this in the very activities that these men were undertaking when they were called. Peter and Andrew were vigorously at work casting their nets into the lake. James and John were sitting quietly in a boat with their father, mending nets. Peter was that active, vigorous doer whose energies, zeal, and ambition have to be harnessed that they may serve his new mission. John was that more quiet man, subject to authority, who would have to learn detachment and be drawn by the strings of love so that he too could give his all to the service of the Master. In Jesus' service there is a place for those who are by disposition very active and for those who are by disposition more contemplative. Such dispositions may well be signs of the role that we are being called to fulfill in the service of Christ and of his Church. Each one will be led forward to a certain fullness. For one, the contemplative dimension of his life will be filled out and flow into a deepened, active concern for the whole body of Christ, such as we have seen in Thomas Merton. For another, who is more actively disposed, it will be the failures and struggles of his active ministry that will teach him the need to ground himself in a deep contemplative prayer life. By his failures and by the watching and waiting during the endless day between Christ's death and resurrection, and during the long days before the ascension, and in the following years as he sat again and again in prison, Peter learned more and more about the contemplative depths of his own life. John too, with special responsibility in the young Church, learned how to go forth from his contemplative rest on the bosom of Jesus to bring the word of life to far-distant places, to suffer for that word, and even to die in exile.

* * *

Another thing that we want to notice here is the fact that Peter is called with others. Back by the Jordan he was with others, his brother and his friends, in his search for a teacher of life. And now, as he is called to apostolic ministry, he is called with them. To be a disciple of Christ is to be called into community. God said at the very beginning of Revelation: "It is not good for man to be alone"—nor woman. The early Christians lived a very communal life, as we see in the Acts of the Apostles:

> These remained faithful to the teaching of the apostles, to the brotherhood, to the breaking of bread and to the prayers. . . .
>
> The faithful all lived together and owned everything

in common; they sold their goods and possessions and shared out the proceeds among themselves according to what each one needed.

They went as a body to the Temple every day but met in their houses for the breaking of bread; they shared their food gladly and generously; they praised God and were looked up to by everyone. Day by day the Lord added to their community those destined to be saved. [Acts 2:42–47]

The whole group of believers was united, heart and soul; no one claimed for his own use anything that he had, as everything they owned was held in common. The apostles continued to testify to the resurrection of the Lord Jesus with great power, and they were all given great respect.

None of their members was ever in want, as all those who owned land or houses would sell them, and bring the money from them, to present it to the apostles; it was then distributed to any members who might be in need. [Acts 4:32–35]

The call to apostolic ministry is usually a call into fellowship with others. The priest is called to be one with the college of priests of the diocese. A man or woman is called into religious community to live and labor together under a leadership that shares the common inspiration of a Founder expressing a particular charismatic aspect of the mission of Christ. Those who are called into a unique mission usually gather others about them to join them in their response to Christ, as we have seen, for example, in the case of Mother Teresa of Calcutta and her Missionaries of Charity.

Because we are weak followers who fall often, it is important that we do have others to help us and encourage us.

Think of what it meant to Peter to be able to come together with the other apostles on that first Holy Saturday. On the other hand, it is important that in our own moments of strength we help others. Even if it is a question of a call to live a deeper prayer, we usually need the support of a group to be faithful. It is a commonplace in the charismatic renewal that if we do not regularly attend prayer meetings, soon enough the wonderful graces we have received from the Lord in the outpouring of the Spirit languish and we will no longer make use of them. In teaching Centering Prayer we always encourage people to begin to teach others and to meet with them regularly for prayer so that they will be faithful in their own daily practice and be supported in it.

* * *

Luke places the call of Peter to apostolic ministry in a different context, or perhaps he is just filling out the context that the other two Synoptics have somewhat passed over:

> Now Jesus was standing one day by the Lake of Gennesaret, with the crowd pressing round him listening to the word of God, when he caught sight of two boats close to the bank. The fishermen had gone out of them and were washing their nets. He got into one of the boats—it was Simon's—and asked him to put out a little from the shore. Then he sat down and taught the crowds from the boat. [We know what Jesus taught on this occasion from Mark 4:1–9.]
>
> When he had finished speaking he said to Simon, "Put out into deep water and pay out your nets for a catch." "Master," Simon replied [We see that Simon has already accepted Jesus as his master, has entered into the

> way of discipleship], "we worked hard all night long and caught nothing, but if you say so, I will pay out the nets." And when they had done this they netted such a huge number of fish that their nets began to tear, so they signalled to their companions in the other boat to come and help them; when these came, they filled the two boats to sinking point.
>
> When Simon Peter saw this he fell at the knees of Jesus saying, "Leave me, Lord; I am a sinful man." For he and all his companions were completely overcome by the catch they had made; so also were James and John, sons of Zebedee, who were Simon's partners. But Jesus said to Simon, "Do not be afraid; from now on it is men you will catch." Then, bringing their boats back to land, they left everything and followed him. [Luke 5:1–11]

We see here, again, a prefiguring of the future mission of Simon Peter. It was into Simon's boat, the boat which Simon commanded, that Jesus stepped and from which he taught. Later it would be from the bark of the Church of which Simon Peter was the head that Jesus would teach the way of salvation across all the seas of the earth.

We see here something, too, of the human graciousness of Jesus. Peter had put himself at the service of the Lord. In the end it would be Peter who would reap the great reward. Our Lord never calls us to serve others, no matter how self-sacrificing the way may seem, without seeing to it that in the end we are the ones who gain the most. (Jesus himself came for us and for our salvation, and yet it is he who receives the greatest glory from his passion, death, and resurrection.) This comes about, though, only if we are open and willing to respond in faith to the Lord. Jesus tells Peter how to find the rich rewards that he wants for him. "Go out into the deep water and lower your nets for a catch." Peter's reason argues that this is not the way. "Master, we have been hard at it all night and caught nothing." The fish are just not running today. Besides, who fishes in the daytime? And yet Peter's openness, Peter's accepting of Jesus as Master, Peter's faith in his Master, enable him to go contrary to his reason, to his instincts as an experienced and successful fisherman: "Master . . . if you say so I will lower the nets." And he caught such a great number of fish that his nets were at the breaking point.

Again we see the importance of community. Peter could not have kept the riches that Jesus had given him if he did not have the support and help of his companions. "They signaled to their mates in the other boat to come and help them. And *together* they filled the two boats until they nearly sank."

One of the things we learn as we go along in the Christ-life is that spiritual gifts and the rich rewards of the Lord, unlike the false rewards of this world, never incline us to pride. Rather, we are humbled and come to realize more and more the immense, complete gratuity of the love of God. One comes to realize more and more one's unworthiness. Peter, seeing how Jesus had so rewarded him for so little, fell to his knees: "Leave me, Lord, I am a sinful man." Even in this statement there is a certain amount of pride. Jesus would take Peter beyond it. Peter speaks as if there was or had to be something in him that merits Jesus' favor. But Jesus' call is completely gratuitous. Jesus would not only give Peter the call, he would give him the grace to accept it gratuitously. One of the great problems we have in the spiritual life is that we constantly want to be able to tell ourselves that we are earning our own way, we are standing on our own feet, we are meriting what we get. But in the end, that can never be the case. This is why Jesus said, "Unless you become as a little child you do not enter into the kingdom." The little child freely accepts all the love, the care, and the gifts which his parents lavish on him. He doesn't have any false illusions about standing on his own feet and earning his own way. We have to humble ourselves and be comfortable with ourselves as children, and accept everything from our heavenly Father as the unmerited gratuity of his overwhelming love. This is indeed humbling. Jesus realized the good will that was in Simon and began to raise him from his fearful, proud self to a truly humble, trusting self. "Do not be afraid." Peter is ready now for the grace of the call to apostolic ministry, the grace that will enable him to leave all and follow Jesus more closely.

Peter's dispossessiveness, at least on the material level, is now complete. It would need more time yet before he would learn to be dispossessed of himself. But the first step has been taken.

* * *

Let me insert a question here. Some time ago the novices gave me a poem entitled "Fish." The first line of it was: "What was Jesus doing while they were pulling in the nets?"

A famous American woman once shared with me the story of her conversion to a living faith. It took place when she was in the House of Representatives. She had just been through a grueling afternoon full of the most tiresome kind of debate. As she reached for her bonnet (it was back in the days when women still wore bonnets), she heard two of the representatives finishing up a conversation. One said to the other, "Well, we can count on the Lord to take care of that." She shot back, "I wish I could say that." The representative was on the ball. He replied, "Go home and read the Gospels the way you would read a bill you are going to vote on in Congress tomorrow, and you will be able to say that." My friend went home, took down the old family Bible and blew the dust off, and began to read Matthew. She read every word, and before the words and after the words and below the words and above the words. She tried not to miss a thing. Before long she was looking for someone to help her understand it all, and was fortunate enough to find an excellent mentor.

As we read these Scripture passages about Peter, we want to savor every word and ask ourselves many questions about what is not being said, what is in between the words. Our Jewish brothers and sisters have the rich tradition of Midrash. Midrash is not a commentary on the words of Scripture in which one explores the various deeper meanings of a word, returning always to the word. Nor is it flights of fantasy. It is rather taking off from a word and finding the fuller meaning that leads on to the next word. It is moving through the Scriptures with the Spirit. The great masters, filled with the Spirit, have shared their experience with their disciples. We each have within us the Greatest of Masters and his Holy Spirit to teach us all things. As we savor the text, we should question the Spirit and allow him to lead us into all truth.

Those of us who cannot encounter Jesus personally in the flesh, as Peter had the great privilege of doing, can encounter Jesus in the Word of Life, in the inspired Word that he has given us in the Sacred Scriptures. For true disciples, such encounters become one of the most important things in our lives. We come with simple and humble faith, something deep within us crying, "Speak, Lord, your servant wants to hear. Lord, reveal yourself. Lord, let me know your love, and then I shall be safe." Scripture study is important. Modern scholarship can at times really help us to break through the barriers of time and culture and language. But there need to be times when we come to the

Scriptures in simplicity and faith, relying not so much on our own knowledge and ability to penetrate the meaning as on the Holy Spirit, who inspired the sacred writers and who now dwells in us. We need to come as children to whom belongs the Kingdom of Heaven. We need to come with the same simplicity and openness that marked the humble people of his time who came to hear Jesus on the hillsides and in the synagogues. We need to be aware of the real presence of Jesus in the Scriptures and open ourselves to a true communion with him. We need to seek from him the words that are eternal life.

So what was Jesus doing while they were pulling in the nets? He who said, The Son of Man came not to be served but to serve (Matthew 20:28) certainly wasn't standing there idle. He had the hardened body and calloused hands of a country carpenter. We can be sure he tucked up his robe and bent his back to the work. It would not have been unusual for a rabbi to work, but Jesus did present a picture of a new kind of Master, one who spoke eloquently to Peter. Peter had been the master of this boat, and his ability as a master had been judged by the catches it brought in. Jesus, obviously not an experienced fisherman, going against all the rules of the lake, has taken command and proves himself a consummate master with a literally overwhelming catch.

This not only spoke powerfully to a fisherman about Jesus as Master, but it re-preached the discourse that Peter had just heard as he kept Jesus' floating pulpit stabilized offshore—restated it in the language of the sea. Jesus had used the simile of the soil for his largely agricultural audience:

> Listen! Imagine a sower going out to sow. Now it happened that, as he sowed, some of the seed fell on the edge of the path, and the birds came and ate it up. Some seed

> fell on rocky ground where it found little soil and sprang up straightaway, because there was no depth of earth; and when the sun came up it was scorched and, not having any roots, it withered away. Some seed fell into thorns, and the thorns grew up and choked it, and it produced no crop. And some seeds fell into rich soil and, growing tall and strong, produced crop; and yielded thirty, sixty, even a hundredfold. . . . Listen, anyone who has ears to hear! [Mark 4:3–9]

Now Jesus, not in word but in living symbol, spoke the same word to the fishermen, and to Peter in particular. This is why Peter cast himself at Jesus' feet. He knew he wasn't hundredfold quality. But Jesus knew his man and what he was to become. Peter himself—yes, he was sinful and not worthy. But Peter remade, or rather continuing in the creation process that had been going on since Peter was conceived—"My Father goes on working and so do I" (John 5:17)—that will be something else. He will not only be worthy, he will be abundantly fruitful. He will bring in not just a hundred, but a hundred and fifty-three *large* fish (John 21:11). All this lies for Peter in the future. But for Jesus God, it is all NOW. For us, discipleship is a patient unfolding, with the daily discovery of the operation of God's creative love in our lives until he has fully refashioned us in the likeness of his Son. This is what discipleship is all about. It is the recovery of a lost likeness, lost in Adam. It is the fulfillment of baptism's promise. It is re-creation. It is a coming into oneness that makes us one with the Son not only in his redemptive mission, where we are to bear abundant fruit and bring in many fish, but even in the inner life of the Trinity, where we are to love and be loved in the unity of the Holy Spirit, who has become our very own Spirit. This is what the call to Christian ministry means. A ministry that is not so grounded in a deep, personal union with Christ in God cannot be truly fruitful and is not worthy of the name Christian. It does not flow out of true discipleship.

The Third Call

> Jesus now went up into the hills and summoned those he wanted. So they came to him and he appointed twelve; they were to be his companions and to be sent out to preach, with power to cast out devils. And so he appointed the Twelve: Simon to whom he gave the name Peter, James the son of Zebedee and John the brother of James, to whom he gave the name Boanerges or "Sons of Thunder"; then Andrew, Philip, Bartholomew, Matthew, Thomas, James the son of Alphaeus, Thaddaeus, Simon the Zealot and Judas Iscariot, the man who was to betray him. [Mark 3:13–19]

We see three successive calls to Peter. First, the call to discipleship when he accepted Jesus as Master and became his follower, but then went on to live his ordinary life, an ordinary life that would be transformed by a new vision and lead to an ever greater dispossessiveness and openness to the Lord. Then there was the call to apostolic mission, when he had to leave behind the things of ordinary life and follow Jesus more closely and more constantly, and dedicate himself to Jesus' mission. Now we come to the third call, a call to apostolic leadership, to be one of the Twelve.

The first calls were calls to follow Jesus. This third call is a call to go forth from Jesus with the fullness one has received in order to bring it to others. The first calls are calls to the inner life, to building up a personal relationship with Christ, to a real life of prayer, to a communion that should develop into a contemplative union, to the development of the contemplative dimension of life, a deep source of life. Only then is one ready to receive the apostolic mission to go forth from Christ but with Christ, always carrying Christ in the depths of one's being, bringing Christ to others, acting out of the power of Christ.

It is very understandable that when we first experience the reality of Christ, the meaning he brings to life, and the immense potential of a heart that is transformed by his grace, we want to go forth and bring this to others. And we can and should do this, to some extent. But to pour ourselves out overzealously in ministry and evangelization before we have grounded ourselves deeply in Christ is a great mistake. We have heard again and again the sad story of burnout, of people who have gone forth with great apostolic zeal into some of the most difficult missions of the Church, especially that of preaching to the poor that "Blessed are the poor, for theirs is the kingdom of heaven." And in short order they have been burned out and have become disillusioned. This happened because they were not grounded in the Source of power, light, and love, and their own little share of these resources was very quickly dissipated. It is very important that those who are preparing for a life in ministry, whether as priests or religious, deacons, and lay persons, be given ample time in the years of their preparation to gain academic knowledge, pastoral skills, and ministerial experience, but also that they be given ample time to develop a deep personal relationship with Jesus, a deep union with him in love, and a deep centering of themselves in the Source of all life and love, the Divine Presence in the depths of their being. Then when they go forth to ministry they will always be sourced, they will always be able to bring to people the infinite creative love of God pouring forth from the depths of their being. Above all others should those who are called to leadership in the Church be men and women who have come to know by years of intimacy him whom they are to proclaim, him in whose name they are to serve, him who is the Source of all that is life-giving.

Luke notes that Jesus issued this call to apostolic leadership only after he had spent all night in prayer to his Father. "Now it was about this time that he went into the hills to pray and spent the whole night in prayer to God" (6:12). Mark details the special qualities involved in this special call. The Twelve were to be Jesus' companions. They were to be sent out to preach with power. They were to have power "to cure all kinds of diseases and sicknesses" (Matthew 10:1—it is very helpful when we are reading the Gospels to look at parallel accounts to get a fuller picture) and "to cast out devils." Matthew places this call later in his Gospel narrative than does Mark. When Jesus conferred upon the disciples this mission, they had already gone through, as it were, a seminary training. They were taught what to say by listening to Jesus' preaching. Matthew has the proclamation of the basic teaching of Christ, summarized in the long discourse that we call the Sermon on the Mount, precede this mission. They had seen Jesus effect many cures—the healing of the leper, of the centurion's servant, of Peter's mother-in-law—many other miracles, many expulsions of the evil one, and even a resurrection from the dead—Jairus' daughter. Finally, they were given a very explicit instruction on how to comport themselves on their new mission. You can imagine how Peter would have carried out the command to "shake the dust from your feet" of a village that did not accept him! (Matthew 10:14). In Matthew we find a very extensive instruction, far more than the Twelve would need on this first missionary journey. It was meant to be a primer for all future missions. Luke rather contents himself with an instruction for this particular initial mission of the Twelve (Luke 9:1–6).

There have been then three calls for Peter, and we will see later that after his denial of Christ and his return to him, in his restoration Jesus again addresses these three "calls" to Peter.

* * *

We are all called. Called first of all in our creation, when we are called from nothingness into life and being for the glory of God. We are called again in our re-creation in baptism—called into an intimate oneness with Christ far beyond anything we can conceive, called to be with him to the glory of the Father in the Holy Spirit. Within these basic calls we are called to partnership, often in the sacrament of marriage, a sign of Christ's union with his Church, or to singleness for the sake of the kingdom. Within these vocations we are called to fulfill other roles among the people of God in the service of the Church or in the service of the whole human family, sometimes successively, sometimes at the same time.

Usually the call does not come in the form of Jesus appearing before us and saying, "Come, I will make you fishers of men." Rather, it comes in the form of interior grace, which enables us not only to perceive the true beauty of a particular mission or way of life, but to perceive it as a good thing for ourselves, a way to live out our life more fully. Then comes the grace that enables us to make a decision to embrace the particular call and to respond to it effectively. Our Lord once said, "You judge a tree by its fruit." The only way that we can be certain about a vocation, a particular call from the Lord, is by the fact that we have been able to respond effectively, for this we can do only by means of his grace. The Lord in his goodness is constantly calling us forth to ever-fuller life. He, in fact, gives us many invitations. He gives us the potential both natural and supernatural to do many things, to fulfill many roles among his people. It is not as though he had some preordained design that we must somehow discover and fulfill if we are ever to find our true vocation. At least, that is not the ordinary case. There are extraordinary vocations. He did personally call the Twelve, and Peter in particular, to fulfill a unique role in his salvific plan. God did send Gabriel to the Virgin Mary, and Bridget to Joan of Arc. He has appeared from time to time to a particular person to give him or her a special call in his Church. But ordinarily it is through the attractions of grace, and the grace to respond to these attractions, that we experience his call, find our vocation, and by the continuing help of that grace come to the fullness of life to which we are ultimately called.

We should not make a great mystery out of vocational discernment. Nor a tortuous process. With and after serious prayer, we should give ourselves a reasonable amount of time to explore our different possibilities and seek adequate counsel. If at the end of such a serious search the matter is not yet clear, we can take it that Jesus is saying to us, You choose what you want to do for me. We must then have the courage to use the freedom he has given us and choose a particular path, fully determined to live it to the full, and generously abandon the alternatives for its sake—something that is not always easy to do. Then we need to say to the Lord, You have left the choice to me. I choose this. I know you have the power to make it the very best, and in your love for me, you are going to make it the very best—for you, for me, for all.

In the end, it is only love that matters. The call is to a way of love, to grow in love. Our "yes," like Peter's, is a commitment to love.

Mother-in-Law

> On leaving the synagogue, Jesus went with James and John straight to the house of Simon and Andrew. Now Simon's mother-in-law had gone to bed with fever and they told him about her straightaway. He went to her, took her by the hand and helped her up. And the fever left her and she began to wait on them. [Mark 1:29–31]

Jesus was becoming well known as a rabbi, a teacher with his own disciples and followers who traveled about with him. Yet he had no intention, nor was there any need, of establishing a sect apart. When he came to cities and towns he went to the regular synagogue services. He remained always a part of institutional religion, he took part in the liturgical prayer of the community. So did his disciples and followers, until the community of the faithful had developed its own institutions and liturgical prayer. Institutional structures and liturgical prayer are in no wise inimical to true discipleship of Jesus. If we follow his example and that of his first disciples, we will be fully part of the institutional Church and will take part in the life of the Church with its liturgical prayer as faithfully as we can.

On this particular occasion, since they were in Peter's hometown, after the service in the synagogue they went to Peter's house. Peter, whom the Church honors as the first Pope, was a married man. We have spoken about vocation and call and have seen how there can be vocations within a vocation. Many Christian communions freely accept married persons for priestly and apostolic mission. In the United States and other countries the Roman Catholic Church has begun to ordain married men who were married and in ministry before their reception into the Church. There can also be second vocations—a call to the ministry of the priesthood after a full married life. Perhaps this was the case with Peter. He had completed his vocation as a husband and father—if ever he were a father—and was now responding to another call from the Lord.

This chapter would be better written by a married man who would know something about a man's relationship with his mother-in-law, what that can mean in his life and in his response to Christ. The only mother-in-law I have ever known intimately was my own mother. She had three daughters-in-law, and I saw how different was her relationship with each of these daughters. I wonder in what ways Peter's relations with his mother-in-law changed when he became a disciple of Christ.

Usually most of our relations come out of what I call "reaction." When we first come into this world we are extremely dependent. We develop our first external relationships with the basic material necessities of life: our need for nourishment, for warmth, and for stroking. As our consciousness expands, we become aware of the people who provide these needs for us. As we develop somewhat further, we become aware of the things we can do, and significant persons usually reinforce our sense of value through our doing. "That's mother's good little boy," when we put away our blocks. "Mommie won't love you if you don't eat your carrots." We come to define ourselves by what we have, by what others think of us, by our doings insofar as they are evaluated by others. We create a false self, a self made up of our responses to things and persons extrinsic to ourselves. These come to determine how we think and act. This is what I mean when I speak of relating out of reaction. Eventually God comes into the picture as the Great One we have to please in order to gain the ultimate things we need: eternal life and the fulfillment of our deepest desires. The false self created by extrinsic evaluation tends to be a very fragile self. It has to be defended and protected at all times. Hence we become very defensive, protective, and competitive; we seek to aggrandize ourselves by putting others down.

What we need in order to attain the dispossessiveness of the disciple of Christ is a real transformation of consciousness. Rather than beholding God as distant from us, the ultimate rewarder of whatever good we manage to accomplish, we need to see him at the center of our being, as our very source. We need to realize that his act of creation is not something done once and for all. At every moment, we are coming forth from the fullness of his creative love.

Remember that scene in the Gospel: One day a rich young man ran up to Jesus and said, "Master, what must I do to gain eternal life?" Jesus answered him and said, "Why do you call me good? One is good, God." He was inviting the young man to witness that Jesus is God. But he was also affirming a basic reality: One is good, God. All goodness, all being, all life comes from God. It is not exactly accurate to say that God made us and everything else out of nothing. Rather, he shares with us something of his own being, beauty, and life. Everything that is, is and is good and beautiful because it shares in God's being, goodness, and beauty. If we see things truly, we see this to be the case. If we truly know ourselves, we know that at the depths of our being is an infinitely loving, creative God who ever more and more brings us forth into being, sharing with us something of his own being, goodness, and beauty. In this love we see our true selves as we are in God and coming forth from him. We know how affirmed and loved we are by him. Coming from this Source, no longer do we have to defend a fragile false self. Rather, coming from our true self, we become a creative source of life for ourselves and for everyone else. We create the relationships that support life. Peter as a disciple would come to know his true self in the love he received from Christ, his Friend and his Master, but also his God and his Creator. And out of that love he would create a beautiful relationship with his mother-in-law. It was because of that beautiful relationship, because of the deep, caring, loving way Peter held his mother-in-law in his heart, that Jesus, when he entered Peter's home, immediately stretched out his hand in healing to the afflicted woman. When we are in touch with our true selves and the power of the love that is within us, we create the kind of relations we want. And because these relations are flowing out of the Source of Creative Love, they are a source of healing and wholeness.

Shortly before, in response to the faith of the centurion of Capernaum who had generously endowed the synagogue, Jesus had exclaimed, "I tell you solemnly, nowhere in Israel have I found faith like this" (Matthew 8:6). Jesus saw in the heart of Peter something greater than faith; he saw concern, love, and care. And to these he could not but respond.

One of the first things we learn from this particular incident in the life of Peter is something about prayer of intercession. We notice that Peter does not ask Jesus to cure his mother-in-law. He had just witnessed the marvelous power of Jesus in the synagogue, where the Lord not only freed a man from a long-standing bondage to an evil spirit, but it seems even raised him to life when the spirit had left him as though he were dead. Peter makes no petition, but Jesus immediately responds. Responds to what? What Jesus responds to, what he hears, is not the words of our lips but the *concerns of our hearts.* We don't have to try to remember to pray verbally for all the different people who have asked us to pray for them, for all the different cares and concerns that have been brought to us or have risen in our own lives. We don't have to rattle off a long litany of needs. If you ask me to pray for you, the important thing is not that I remember you next time I go to prayer, and it will probably do you little good if I just rattle off a couple of "Our Fathers" for you. The important thing is that I place you in my heart and hold you with concern and love so that when I next do go to prayer, Jesus will see you there and will extend his healing and blessing hand.

I think this is brought out in the Gospels not only in this instance, but in a couple of other very important instances involving two great women of prayer, Mary the Mother of Jesus, who ever pondered in her heart, and Mary of Bethany, who chose the better part and sat at Jesus' feet. For one, Jesus worked his first miracle, and for the other, his greatest miracle, before and prefiguring the ultimate miracle of his own resurrection. If the two Marys do express aloud their concern, it is so that we can be in on the happenings. "They have no wine" (John 2:3). At Cana we can see Jesus even squirm a bit. After all, how will it sound going down in sacred history that the first sign the Son of Man worked on earth was turning out more booze for the boys after they had drunk the house dry? Undoubtedly the fact that he had arrived at the party with his band of newly gathered disciples had something to do with the embarrassing shortage. He could not deny the concern of the heart of the one he loved most in all the world. Nor could he deny the other Mary. "The man you love is ill" (John 11:3). He tarried to give them yet a greater gift and sign. And he mingled his tears with hers, sharing her grief, before he renewed the life of her brother.

These Marys did not ask anything from the Lord. It was to their concern that Jesus responded. Peter, in bringing Jesus into his life and into his home, brought him into all his concerns. And Jesus immediately responded to them in his caring, loving, gratuitous cure of Peter's mother-in-law.

Peter had witnessed Cana; it was the first sign he had seen Jesus work. It made a powerful impression on him. He undoubtedly had it in mind when he brought Jesus to his own home that Sabbath morning. He may not have thought precisely of the healing of his mother-in-law, but he knew that in bringing Jesus into his home, it would be blessed in some special way. The home of every disciple should be a place where Jesus is welcomed. The enthronement of the Sacred Heart used to be a popular Catholic practice. Some formal reception of the Lord into a new home and some visible sign of his presence, such as a shrine, statue, or icon, can prove a very real blessing to the disciple. Most disciples will have their hidden sanctuaries of prayer where they go in quietly and close the door and pray to their Father in secret (Matthew 6:6). It is well, though, also to have a shrine where the household can gather for prayer on a regular basis as well as in times of special need or thanksgiving —a shrine that proclaims to all who enter that this Master has been welcomed into this house as the Master of the house because he is the Master of those who dwell therein.

* * *

The healing power of Jesus was now released. Immediately there followed a whole spate of healing, as Mark tells us: "That evening, after sunset, they brought to him all who were sick and those who were possessed by devils. The whole town came crowding round the door, and he cured many who were suffering from diseases of one kind or another; he also cast out many devils, but he would not allow them to speak, because they knew who he was" (Mark 1:32–34).

Another scene in the Gospels indicates how much such a healing ministry cost Jesus. One day, as he was pushing through a dense, jostling crowd, a poor afflicted woman who had suffered many years dared to reach out with faith to touch the hem of his garment. Faith is always rewarded; she was immediately healed. Power went forth from the Lord. Jesus turned around and searched the crowd with his eyes and let it be known that he felt the power going forth from him (Luke 8:43–46). If the Master cannot minister healing comfort without power going forth from him, how much more is this true of the disciple? We find Jesus early the next morning, before anyone else was up, going off into the hills to pray. There he would commune with his Father in the Spirit of Love that bound them in oneness, and touch the Source of the power of his ministry.

If we hope to exercise a powerful, healing ministry, we need to go forth regularly from the crowd, from the insistent demands of ministry, even if it means forgoing sleep and rising early. We need to be alone with our Master, in communion with his Father and ours, in the Love who is the Holy Spirit. We need to return to the Source, know the presence and power within us, and know the bountiful freedom that is ours when we minister out of this Source.

* * *

"In the morning, long before dawn, he got up and left the house, and went off to a lonely place and prayed there. Simon and his companions set out in search of him, and when they found him they said, 'Everybody is looking for you.' He answered, 'Let us go elsewhere, to the neighboring country towns, so that I can preach there too, because that is why I came.' And he went all through Galilee, preaching in their synagogues and casting out devils" (Mark 1:35–39).

We can imagine Peter's reaction when he woke up and found that the Master was gone. There were many reasons for his alarm and concern. He certainly sensed his call to follow Jesus closely, to be a special disciple of the Lord. An affection was growing up between them. Peter was coming to love this man and did not want to be parted from him. There was also another side, I am sure. Peter was delighted the night before when the whole town gathered at *his* door and he was seen to be the great benefactor of the village, for he had brought the Master and all his healing power. Peter did not want Jesus to go away. He quickly roused the other disciples, and they went in search of Jesus. They already knew him well enough to know what he was up to and where he would be found. Soon enough they came upon him secluded among the knolls of the nearby hills, praying to his Father. Peter blurted out his concern: "Everybody is looking for you." Jesus knew and understood the false pride and ambition that still lurked in Peter's heart. He would in no wise nurture it. They would not to go back to Peter's house and make that the center of his apostolic ministry. "Foxes have holes and the birds of the air have nests, but the Son of Man has nowhere to lay his head" (Matthew 8:20). They would go forth to the other towns of Galilee. They would go to the lost sheep of the tribe of Israel. They would bring his healing and his love and his word of life to anyone who would listen. Peter, whose discipleship of Jesus was becoming more important to him than his self-serving love, would humbly follow his Master. He still had a lot to learn.

Putting His Best Foot Forward—Into His Mouth

Called though he was to discipleship, to apostolic ministry, and even to leadership, Peter was still Peter. He was still prone to speak all too quickly. He would be a long time in learning. Fortunately, he had a Master of infinite patience.

The day of the first miraculous multiplication of loaves and fishes gives us a good example of Peter's impetuosity. It had been quite a day! It had begun with the sad news that John the Baptizer, the one to whom Peter and his brother Andrew and their friends had first turned in the hope of finding a word of life, had been beheaded (Matthew 14:13). John was Jesus' cousin. But John meant much more than that to Jesus. The news of his death was shockingly painful. Jesus' immediate reaction was to invite his disciples to go apart with him "to a lonely place where they could be by themselves." But by this time Jesus was too much the man of the hour. The people always had their eyes on him, and news of his movements quickly spread. Jesus' hope to find a "lonely place where they could be by themselves" was quickly frustrated. When he put ashore with his disciples, "a large crowd was waiting" to receive words of life, and healing for their sick. The compassionate heart of Jesus could not but respond. The day was consumed with teaching and healing. Night was soon approaching. The disciples, no doubt with the practical Peter at their head, came to the Lord: "This is a lonely place, and the time has slipped by; so send the people away, and they can go to the villages to buy themselves some food." Jesus' response caught them off guard: "There is no need for them to go; Give them something to eat yourselves." They had already looked to see what they had for themselves. "All we have with us is five loaves and two fish." "Bring them here to me," Jesus said (Matthew 14:15–18).

Jesus proved himself quite practical, and soon had the disciples busily sitting the people down in orderly groups—he knew somebody would want to take a count before the evening was over. Then Peter and his fellow disciples had the astonishing experience of receiving a few bits of bread and fish from the Lord and handing them out, and handing them out, and handing them out, and still having bits of bread and fish. Their growing amazement! They remembered the widow's pot of oil (2 Kings 4:1–7) and the jar of meal at Zarephath (1 Kings 17:7–16). There was indeed a great prophet here, and more than a prophet.

In his busyness and excitement, Peter hardly had time to reflect and realize that five loaves and two fish, when they are our five loaves and two fish, are only five loaves and two fish. But when they are received as a gift from the hands of the Lord —Jesus "took the five loaves and two fish, raised his eyes to heaven and said the blessing. And breaking the loaves he handed them to his disciples"—they are the resources to accomplish anything and everything the Lord wants us to do.

If the disciples had insisted on keeping the five loaves and two fish for themselves, there would not have been enough for a decent meal for them. And they could well have expected friends and neighbors and others, too, to press in on them for a share. Indeed, fights might have soon broken out as each one grabbed for his bit—as in our world today. When our mentality is one of scarcity and selfishness, the end result is scarcity, and oftentimes jealousy, resentment, and fighting. But when the disciples in faith generously turned over what they had to the Lord for the use of all his people, then not only did everyone have enough, but in the end they came away with "twelve full baskets." The generosity of the Lord in response to any generosity we show is pressed down and flowing over.

Yes, it had been quite a day. The banquet was over. All were satisfied—at least in regard to their physical hunger. Other desires could now surface—confused desires, unfortunately, for no one yet understood the Master. Jesus sent his disciples on their way lest they get into trouble, and then he slipped away into the mountains, as was his custom, to replenish his forces in quiet prayer and communion with the Father. He would catch up with the Twelve a little later.

As the Apostles made their way across the lake in their boat, they experienced the difficulty of being without the Lord. They had to battle with a heavy sea and contend with a strong head wind. Things were always easier when he was present. After a long night of struggle, in the last part of the night, the Lord did come. How often it is that the Lord leaves us to struggle as if we have to make it on our own before he comes to our aid! If he comes too soon, we are all too prone to credit ourselves for what he does. It is only when we have a deep experience of our own limitations and helplessness that we can begin to appreciate how truly it is that only by his grace do we accomplish all we accomplish.

Some years ago I was counseling a couple of fine young men who were eager to enter the monastery. Both of these lads were struggling with the problem of masturbation.

And they were really struggling with it. One day, being quite angry with the Lord, I demanded of him why he did not help these men overcome their weakness so that they would be free to follow him in the way they wanted. The next morning, as I was sitting in the spiritual father's room in our guesthouse, a man who had been coming to our monastery for many years knocked on the door. He too had had a long, hard struggle—his was with alcohol. Recently he had struck rock bottom and now, by a great gift of God's grace, he had found his way into Alcoholics Anonymous. With the enthusiasm of a new convert, he began to tell me about this wonderful program. It wasn't my first experience with AA, and I knew what was coming. I sat back, ready to hear the twelve steps. But as he began to recount the first step—a man must admit to himself, to God, and to some other person that he is a hopeless case—a bell rang for me. I realized then what was going on with the two young men I was counseling. What the Lord had taught this man through alcohol, and was teaching others through an angry temper, or a proneness to gambling, or a constant struggle with distractions in prayer, the Lord was teaching my young men through their struggle with masturbation. It is only when we have done our utmost, have struggled with all the energy in us and still have failed, that it finally comes home to us in our guts that we cannot do it ourselves, and that all the good that is accomplished in us is accomplished by God's grace. Once we realize this, God can do anything he wants in our lives because there is no longer any danger that we will take the credit to ourselves. God loves us with an immense love and he has given us everything, even his own Son. But there is one thing that God cannot give us and still be God, and that one thing is his glory. We are so prone to put our own initials at the bottom of the work. But as long as we claim anything as coming ultimately from ourselves, God is no longer God. We have made a false God—ourselves. So the Lord often leaves us struggling through what seems like a long night of the spirit so that we can learn what it is to be without him, what the results are when we try to accomplish things solely by means of our own resources. It is only when we have really learned how limited we are that he then comes in the "fourth watch of the night" and brings us deliverance.

> He made the disciples get into the boat and go on ahead to the other side while he would send the crowds away. After sending the crowds away he went up into the hills by himself to pray. When evening came, he was there alone, while the boat, by now far out on the lake, was battling with a heavy sea, for there was a head-wind. In the fourth watch of the night he went towards them, walking on the lake, and when the disciples saw him walking on the lake they were terrified. "It is a ghost," they said, and cried out in fear. But at once Jesus called out to them, saying, "Courage! It is I! Do not be afraid." It was Peter who answered. "Lord," he said, "if it is you, tell me to come to you across the water." "Come," said Jesus. Then Peter got out of the boat and started walking towards Jesus across the water, but as soon as he felt the force of the wind, he took fright and began to sink. "Lord! Save me!" he cried. Jesus put out his hand at once and held him. "Man of little faith," he said, "why did you doubt?" And as they got into the boat the wind dropped. The men in the boat bowed down before him and said, "Truly, you are the Son of God." [Matthew 14:22–33]

Peter, the commander of the fleet, was still the dauntless seaman. The long struggle of the night had not taught him anything. In fact, he was still buoyed up by the experience of the day before when he saw in his own hands bits of fish and bread multiplied to feed thousands. Jesus' "Don't be afraid" only challenged him. In his enthusiasm he cried out, "Lord, if it is you, tell me to come to you across the water."

Jesus loved Peter, and he knew what was in him. He wanted to encourage this enthusiastic faith. He also knew that Peter had lessons to learn. Without hesitation Jesus replied, "Come."

I wonder if Peter experienced any hesitation once he heard the "Come." The ship was tossing around wildly in a rough sea. Was he so buoyed up, so enthusiastic that he stepped over the side without another thought and went bounding across the water toward Jesus? I suspect so. If he had hesitated for a moment I think his faith would have quickly floundered. For soon enough, "as soon as he felt the force of the wind, he took fright and he began to sink." First his faith began to sink, then he followed right after it. And yet there was that spark of faith. He knew his Master. He still had confidence in him. "Lord! Save me!" And "Jesus put out his hand at once and held him." They walked back to the boat hand in hand. Held securely by the Lord, Peter's love overcame all doubt, all fear.

And those in the boat? They watched the whole wondrous spectacle. They were perhaps not surprised by Peter's outlandish request. They knew him well enough. But they were stupefied when they saw him actually jump out of the boat and run across the water. When he began to sink, that made sense. When Jesus reached out and the two of them walked peacefully and safely toward the boat, a mixture of emotions washed through their minds and hearts. As the Master stepped in they fell down on their knees in awed adoration: "Truly you are the Son of God." Lucky for Peter they were so awed, or he might well have heard some gibes about a fisherman not making a very good fish or a "Rock" that quite naturally sank.

The fact remains: Peter did walk on the water, and he walked on it *with Jesus.* From the moment that Jesus reached out and grasped his hand, Peter knew that Jesus would take care of him. Later he would advise us: "Cast your care upon him for he has care of you" (1 Peter 5:7).

The next day, when the people again crowded around Jesus, the Master challenged them in regard to the bread and sought to raise their thoughts and desires to that Bread of which yesterday's was but a prefiguring. The Eucharist is our constantly recurring multiplication of loaves. But for many, Jesus' banquet of love was too much. Such a communion was "intolerable." "Many of his disciples left him and stopped going with him."

Then, with a heavy heart, Jesus turned to the Twelve: "What about you, do you want to go away too?" Peter, in the power of the faith that he had drawn from the saving hand of Christ, dared to respond in the name of all: "Lord, to whom shall we go? You have the words of eternal life, and we believe —we know that you are the Holy One of God" (John 6:67–69). Job had asked: "Where does wisdom come from? Where is understanding to be found?" (Job 28:12). Peter now knew: "You have the words of eternal life."

This is a fundamental perception for a disciple. The Master has wisdom and is a source of wisdom. He is able and willing to impart it to those who would become his disciples. The disciple of Jesus knows that Jesus is the Source of all Wisdom. He is Wisdom itself. He is the Way, the Truth, and the Life.

This was one of Peter's better moments. How full his

life was of ups and downs—his days on the waves and the luck of the fisherman were perhaps meant to prepare him for this.

"The Holy One of God," his very Son—how quickly Peter would let this realization slip into the back of his mind.

* * *

Peter did not always get off so easily when his mouth got ahead of what his mind should have told him.

> When they reached Capernaum, the collectors of the half-shekel came to Peter and said, "Does your master not pay the half-shekel?" "Oh yes," he replied, and he went into the house. Before he could speak, Jesus said, "Simon, what is your opinion? From whom do the kings of the earth take toll or tribute? From their sons or from foreigners?" And when he replied, "From foreigners," Jesus said, "Well then, the sons are exempt. However, so as not to offend these people, go to the lake, cast a hook: take the first fish that bites, open its mouth and there you will find a shekel; take it and give it to them for me and for you." [Matthew 17:24–27]

For me this is one of the more humorous incidents in the life of Peter. At the same time, it has a very touching element.

Here is Peter, as usual, too ready to speak up. Often enough Jesus has been challenged with his disciples or because of his disciples by the upholders of the Law. So when they come and challenge Peter: "Does your Master not pay the half-shekel?" Peter is all too quick to say, "Yes, yes, he pays." Poor Peter, he doesn't even have a chance to defend himself. When he comes in, immediately Jesus challenges him and calls upon Peter to convict himself. "Peter, now who does pay the tax? The Son or the servant?" Peter's own logic won't let him escape. Then Jesus, without rebuking Peter, with a great deal of understanding, and with powerful pedagogy, sends Peter off to get the tax money. Here he is, the great fisherman, the commander of a Galilean fleet, sent off with a little line and a hook to stand by the seashore to wait for some particular little fish to nibble on his hook. We can be sure the other disciples didn't lose the opportunity to enjoy Peter's discomfiture. As he stood there doing the only thing he could do, trying to wait patiently, he could hear the taunting voices: "Peter, has the fish bit yet?" "Come now, great fisherman, where's this fish?" "Oh Peter, you really are a sight!" Perhaps he did not have to struggle with his rising temper as much as he ordinarily might, diverted as he was by his own reflections on his stupidity and his proneness to put his foot in his mouth.

Finally the little fish did nibble on his hook, and up it came. A very relieved Peter found, as he pulled the hook out of the fish's mouth, that there was also a shekel to be drawn out. The touching part of this story is the fact that Jesus tells Peter to find not just a half-shekel for Jesus' tax, but a whole shekel for his own *and* Peter's tax. There is no other place in the Gospel accounts where Jesus so personally and immediately identifies himself with a human being: "for me and for you." This bit of human delicacy undoubtedly did much to salve the discomfiture that Peter experienced as he sought to learn again and more deeply not to be so quick to speak up out of his own presumptuous spirit, especially when he was taking the responsibility to speak for his Master.

When we disciples speak out to set forth the teaching and the claims of our Master, we must be very sure that what we say is indeed faithful to who he is and to his claims upon us.

* * *

On another occasion Jesus' response to Peter's presumptuousness was not quite so humorous. It seems as though his patience was wearing a bit thin.

> From that time Jesus began to make it clear to his disciples that he was destined to go to Jerusalem and suffer grievously at the hands of the elders and chief priests and scribes, to be put to death and to be raised up on the third day. Then, taking him aside, Peter started to remonstrate with him. "Heaven preserve you, Lord," he said, "this must not happen to you." But he turned and said to Peter, "Get behind me, Satan! You are an obstacle in my path, because the way you think is not God's way but man's." [Matthew 16:21–23]

Jesus had just acknowledged the work of the Father in Peter preparing him for the important mission as the rock on which Jesus would build his Church. Taking heart from Peter's clear confession, Jesus went on to begin to prepare Peter and the others for the dark hour that lay ahead when they would have to see their Master "suffer grievously at the hands of the elders and chief priests and scribes and be put to death." Peter was feeling his oats, having just been praised highly by the Lord. He wasn't ready for the scandal of the cross. So he took Jesus aside and started to remonstrate with him: "Heaven preserve you, Lord," he said. "This must not happen to you." Jesus didn't mince words as he put a pin directly into Peter's balloon. "Get behind me, Satan. You are an obstacle in my path, because the way you think is not God's way but man's."

I think we all at times enjoy the fantasy: Well, if I had been God I would have arranged things in this world a little better. It takes us a long time to absorb fully those words of Isaiah: "My thoughts are not your thoughts, nor my ways your ways, but as high as heaven is above the earth, so are my thoughts beyond your thoughts and my ways beyond your ways." God's ways will not be our ways often enough, and we have to be humble enough to listen, to wait, and to learn. In a word, we have to be true disciples as the Lord patiently teaches us and draws us up toward his level of consciousness so that we can understand, or at least accept in faith and hope, the mystery of the cross. It is only through death that we come to the new life of the risen Christ.

Jesus didn't waste any time in beginning to impart this to his disciples. He immediately went on to say to them, "If anyone wants to be a follower of mine, let him renounce himself and take up his cross and follow me. For anyone who wants to save his life will lose it; but anyone who loses his life for my sake will find it" (Matthew 16:24–25).

* * *

Peter's quickness to speak up was not always to his embarrassment. His blunt questions often provided the occasion for Jesus to teach us basically important things.

Peter was willing to display his mystification at the parables of Jesus—"Explain the parable for us" (Matthew 15:15)—and get for us, who are usually equally mystified, the explanations we need. His question, "Lord, how often must I forgive my brother who wrongs me? As often as seven times?" opened the space for Jesus to proclaim the new dispensation of mercy and love: "Not seven, I tell you, but seventy times seven" (Matthew 18:21–22)—that is, without ceasing. Jesus went on to tell the parable of the unforgiving debtor: "And that is how my heavenly Father will deal with you unless you each forgive from the heart" (Matthew 18:35).

And then there was that far from disinterested question: "What about us? We have left everything and followed you. What are we to have then?" (Matthew 19:27). Surprisingly, this didn't evoke from Jesus a remonstrance, a call to unselfish love. There would surely be many occasions when he would call for that. Well might he have pointed out to Peter that he hadn't left all that much: a few boats, probably leaky, nets that always needed to be mended, and lots of hard work. Rather, Jesus made, not only to Peter but to all of his followers, an offer that is hard to refuse: "Everyone who has left houses, brothers, sisters, father, mother, children or land for the sake of my name will be paid a hundred times over and also will inherit eternal life"—a mighty good investment.

I have a little joke going with the Lord. When I was preparing to enter the monastery, my brother, who was at that time not too keen about my monastic vocation, offered me the opportunity to go to Europe to spend as much time as I wanted doing whatever I wanted before entering. When I spoke to the vocation father about this, he saw it as a tactic to try to divert me from responding directly and immediately to the Lord, and he advised me not to accept this opportunity, but to give it up for the Lord. Contrary to all expectations, in the years that followed, again and again my superiors directed me to Europe, first for studies and then for various activities of the Order. And I keep saying to the Lord, "Really, Lord, I don't want a hundred trips to Europe!"

After responding directly to Peter, Jesus went on to teach the parable of the vineyard laborers (Matthew 20:1–16). It doesn't matter really how much the disciple leaves behind. It doesn't matter whether he was a laborer from the first hour, or the third, or the sixth, or the ninth, or the eleventh. The thing that matters is that when we hear the call we respond and leave everything for Christ's sake, to give ourselves completely to the Lord.

It was Peter who pointed out "the fig tree withered to its roots"—"Look, Rabbi, the fig tree you cursed has withered away"—and afforded Jesus the opportunity to give to Peter, a man whose weakness in faith he had to chide, and to all of us, a lesson on the power of faith. "Have faith in God. I tell you solemnly, if anyone says to this mountain, 'Get up and throw yourself into the sea,' with no hesitation in his heart but believing that what he says will happen, it will be done for him." And the call to pray with faith: "I tell you therefore: everything you ask and pray for, believe that you have it already, and it will be yours" (Mark 11:20–24).

When Jesus spoke of the forthcoming destruction of the great Temple of Jerusalem, it was Peter's question, "Tell us, when is this going to happen, and what sign will there be that all of this is about to be fulfilled?" that afforded Jesus the opportunity to speak at length not only of the coming destruction of Jerusalem, but even of the end times and the signs and distress that would precede them (Mark 13:1–8).

A certain ingenuous simplicity before the Lord certainly has its value. Even if it does lead at times to embarrassment, it can be the occasion, with its openness, to receive from the Lord the important teaching that we need. Unfortunately, all too often we are for putting on some sort of pretense. We want people to think we are wiser than we are, that we understand when we don't, that we have the answers. And in doing this we block the possibility of our Master teaching us what only he can teach. We fail to seek from him the words of true life.

We do not want to imitate Peter's impetuosity, but we

do want to risk his complete childlike openness and trust, for "anyone who does not welcome the kingdom of God like a little child will never enter it" (Mark 10:15). Only those who want to learn and can trust can become in any true sense disciples of the Master.

Prayer

> Six days later, Jesus took with him Peter and James and his brother John and led them up a high mountain where they could be alone. There in their presence he was transfigured: his face shone like the sun and his clothes became as white as the light. Suddenly Moses and Elijah appeared to them; they were talking with him. Then Peter spoke to Jesus. "Lord," he said, "it is wonderful for us to be here; if you wish, I will make three tents here, one for you, one for Moses and one for Elijah." He was still speaking when suddenly a bright cloud covered them with shadow, and from the cloud there came a voice which said, "This is my Son, the Beloved; he enjoys my favor. Listen to him." When they heard this, the disciples fell on their faces, overcome with fear. But Jesus came up and touched them. "Stand up," he said, "do not be afraid." And when they raised their eyes they saw no one but only Jesus. [Matthew 17:1–8]

Tabor remains one of the most beautiful spots in all the land that Jesus and Peter knew so well through constant traversing. Perhaps one reason why I found Tabor so beautiful is that it is the only spot sacred to the memory of Jesus that is safe from the onslaught of hoards of tourists—it is too steep for the tourist buses to climb. It remains a place of sanctuary, a summit of transfiguring beauty.

It was not long after Peter's confession of the Messiahship of Jesus at Caesarea Philippi and Jesus' confirmation that Peter was gifted by the Father with a deeper understanding of who Jesus is that the Lord led Peter, James, and John up this high mountain. I think in this pericope we have a very important teaching on prayer.

First of all, in order to enter into prayer, it is necessary to follow Jesus with faith and confidence, and to go with him to a place where we can be alone with him. Peter and his companions did not know where Jesus was leading them. The way was rugged. But they followed with faith and with confidence. Finally they came to a summit. And *there* Jesus was transfigured.

It was a moment that engraved itself deeply in Peter's memory. Years later, as an old man, he would write to the Churches and remind them, "We had seen his majesty for ourselves. He was honored and glorified by God the Father, when the Sublime Glory itself spoke to him and said, 'This is my Son, the Beloved; he enjoys my favor.' We heard this ourselves, spoken from heaven, when we were with him on the holy mountain" (2 Peter 1:16–18).

The sacred writers struggle for images to bring out the radiance of the transfigured Christ. Matthew says that his face shone like the sun and his clothes became white as light (Matthew 17:2). Mark says his clothes became dazzling white, whiter than any earthly bleacher could make them (Mark 9:3). And Luke says his clothing became brilliant as lightning (Luke 9:29). It was an awesome spectacle. But it was to be made even more awesome. For then there appeared with Jesus the holy Prophet Elijah and the great lawgiver of the people, Moses. And they spoke with Jesus.

For the Jews, revelation was usually summed up in the expression "the Law and the Prophets." Moses was the one who gave them the Law. Elijah was one of the greatest of the prophets, the one who was brought beyond the lightning and beyond the roaring of the storm to the still, small voice that revealed the inner life of God. Both these men had a special experience of God on the holy mountain of the Jews, Horeb or Sinai. And now they appear on this mountain with Jesus. The Old is fulfilled. That to which it pointed, toward which it ever moved, is at hand. What this tells us is that it is through the sacred writers, through the Sacred Scriptures, and through the whole of Salvation History, that we are to come to know our Lord and understand his mission and its meaning for our lives. It is through listening to the Word that we will be led into deep, transcending prayer where the Presence and the love of the Triune God will be revealed to us.

Mark, who is considered to be Peter's scribe, says of Peter that "he did not know what to say" (Mark 9:6). But Peter was never one to be at a loss for words. He knew that he was filled with an immense joy and himself transfigured in this awesome moment of Presence. He wanted it to continue. And so he babbled out something about building three tents. He probably had in mind the sort of tents or fragile little buildings of reeds that the Jews built at the Feast of Tabernacles to remind them of their time of passage through the wilderness.

Luke was probably on the mark when he said that Peter did not know what he was saying (Luke 9:33). As he spoke, the theophany became even more awesome. A luminous cloud, perhaps not unlike the one that descended on Sinai, now came upon this holy mountain and overshadowed them. The disciples found themselves within the cloud. Then the Father spoke. This was too much for Peter and the others. They fell on their faces. No longer could Peter even babble, he was so overcome with fear. The classical Byzantine icon shows the three disciples strewn in different directions, with their sandals flying this way and that. The Lord sometimes has to clobber us pretty hard before we learn that prayer is not a monologue but a dialogue, and it behooves us, as the disciples, to stop babbling and listen. This was the Father's message to the ebullient Peter and his companions: "This is my Son, the Beloved; he enjoys my favor. *Listen to him.*"

Luke tells us that Peter and his companions "were heavy with sleep, but they kept awake" (Luke 9:32). He has a similar report at Gethsemane, but there they didn't keep awake. The Evangelist-Physician sees this as an effect of fear. Sleep is one of the ways in which we try to escape our fears and other negative emotions. In the Garden of Gethsemane Peter did give in to sleep and escaped from his fear and grief rather than staying with his Lord in anguish and prayer. But here on Tabor that was not the case. Here we have some effort to describe the state of contemplative prayer. One of the greatest teachers of prayer that the Christian tradition has ever known, Saint Teresa of Avila, says that when one first enters into a more contemplative type of prayer, one has many misgivings, one wonders if anything is happening, if one is not just falling asleep. Since we are used to passing from the waking state to the sleeping state, when we first begin to pass from the waking state to the contemplative state the only thing we can call up from our past experience is the passage into sleep. It seems similar to us until we become more familiar with the contemplative state, and the great difference between it and sleeping. As the Scriptures say,

"I sleep but my heart watches." On Tabor, indeed, Peter's heart watched and there was given to him a great revelation, the first inklings of the fullness of the Trinitarian mystery. The Father spoke to him and gave him a powerful word of life: "This is my Son, the Beloved; he enjoys my favor. *Listen to him."* This of course is the first and most fundamental principle of all discipleship: to listen to the Master.

When the theophany was over, Jesus himself leaned down and touched Peter with the hand that had become so familiar to him. The tenderness called him forth from his fear. "Stand up. Do not be afraid." Matthew reports that "when they raised their eyes they saw no one but only Jesus." This is a result of contemplative prayer. There develops in us a real connatural sensitivity that becomes aware of God in everybody and everything, that becomes sensitive to the presence of Christ in each of his beloved, that comes to know the whole Christ as a living reality and begins to respond to everybody and everything according to the truth of their being in God.

* * *

As they came down from the mountain, Jesus gave Peter and his companions a very difficult order and one that might have seemed to them very curious. They were to tell no one about the theophany until the Son of Man had risen from the dead. This "risen from the dead" seems to have gone completely over their heads. Instead of asking about it, they asked about Elijah. In his response Jesus again gave them a warning of what lay ahead. He told them that in John the promise of the Prophet's coming before the Messiah had been fulfilled. And then, pointing to the way they had treated John, he told them that the Son of Man would suffer similarly.

Peter and his companions had been drawn into a very

special relationship with Jesus. Jesus' teaching had been opened to them more profoundly than to the people at large. They had seen day after day the power of Jesus going forth, not only overcoming all the weaknesses and ills of human persons, but also conquering the powers of the evil one, of the demonic kingdom. They were ready for a more sublime revelation. And they needed it to strengthen them for the trials that lay ahead, of which Jesus was beginning to warn them. The people as a whole were not yet ready for the full manifestation of Jesus' divinity, and even less so for the awesome mystery of the Trinity.

The true disciple of Jesus, especially the disciple who is called to the ministry, has to learn how to move at God's pace and not at the pace that might be dictated by his own wisdom or enthusiasm. He must respect the way God's grace is working in him and in others, and move in harmony with it. To get ahead of it can only hurt, frustrate, and even destroy the action of that grace in life.

Peter had grown enough now not to be dominated by the very human drive for self-importance. He might have been tempted to vaunt the particular knowledge he had received on the mountain, to pride himself on the special grace that was given to him in the revelation of the transfiguration. But no word of this splendid mystery passed from his mouth until the Son of Man was risen from the dead. In fact, as we see Peter struggle with his own fidelity to Christ in the midst of the Passion, we wonder if the memory of it was obliterated from his own mind and heart. It certainly was there later, as we have seen. It may have been overclouded. So often, in the time of temptation, the light that shone so brightly when we were at prayer seems to be gone. All is obscure. When the time came for an open witness to the Lord Jesus in the fullness of his divinity,

Peter would be able with humble pride to recall that he was with the Lord on the holy mountain.

* * *

We grow both by depth and by expansion. On Tabor Peter was led into the very depths of God in the revelation of the Trinity. He would spend the rest of this life, and eternity itself, plumbing the full significance of what he first caught a glimpse of on the mountain. It was another prayer experience that expanded his conscience and enabled him to see more the length and breadth of the significance of the creative presence of God in the universal call of the Incarnation of God in the humanity of Christ:

> Peter went to the housetop at about the sixth hour to pray. He felt hungry and was looking forward to his meal, but before it was ready he fell into a trance and saw heaven thrown open and something like a big sheet being let down to earth by its four corners; it contained every possible sort of animal and bird, walking, crawling or flying ones. A voice then said to him, "Now, Peter, kill and eat!" But Peter answered, "Certainly not, Lord; I have never yet eaten anything profane or unclean." Again, a second time, the voice spoke to him, "What God has made clean, you have no right to call profane." This was repeated three times, and then suddenly the container was drawn up to heaven again.
>
> Peter was still worrying over the meaning of the vision he had seen, when the men sent by Cornelius arrived. They had asked where Simon's house was and they were now standing at the door, calling out to know if the Simon known as Peter was lodging there. Peter's mind was still on

the vision and the Spirit had to tell him, "Some men have come to see you. Hurry down, and do not hesitate about going back with them; it was I who told them to come." Peter went down and said to them, "I am the man you are looking for; why have you come?" They said, "The centurion Cornelius, who is an upright and God-fearing man, highly regarded by the entire Jewish people, was directed by a holy angel to send for you and bring you to his house and to listen to what you have to say." So Peter asked them in and gave them lodging.

Next day, he was ready to go off with them, accompanied by some of the brothers from Jaffa. They reached Caesarea the following day, and Cornelius was waiting for them. He had asked his relations and close friends to be there, and as Peter reached the house Cornelius went out to meet him, knelt at his feet and prostrated himself. But Peter helped him up. "Stand up," he said, "I am only a man after all!" Talking together they went in to meet the people assembled there, and Peter said to them, "You know it is forbidden for Jews to mix with people of another race and visit them, but God has made it clear to me that I must not call anyone profane or unclean. That is why I made no objection to coming when I was sent for . . ."

Then Peter addressed them: "The truth I have now come to realize," he said, "is that God does not have favorites, but that anybody of any nationality who fears God and does what is right is acceptable to him.

"It is true, God sent his word to the people of Israel, and it was to them that the good news of peace was brought by Jesus Christ—but Jesus Christ is Lord of all men. . . ."

While Peter was still speaking the Holy Spirit came

> down on all the listeners. Jewish believers who had accompanied Peter were all astonished that the gift of the Holy Spirit should be poured out on the pagans too, since they could hear them speaking strange languages and proclaiming the greatness of God. Peter himself then said, "Could anyone refuse the water of baptism to these people, now they have received the Holy Spirit just as much as we have?" [Acts 10:9–47]

Peter went to the housetop about the sixth hour to pray, still observing the regular prayer times of the pious Jew. In fact, for Peter and the other disciples they were becoming the prayer times of the new Christian community. To this day, at least in monasteries, the third, the sixth, and the ninth hour are times when the members of the community leave off their work and come together for prayer.

Peter was still fully human. The sixth hour is near midday, and naturally enough, "Peter felt hungry and was looking forward to his meal." In the few minutes before that meal was served—for minutes of time can be great spaces in the realm of the Spirit and eternity—Peter was to have a mind- and heart-expanding experience. The very heavens were to open to him and he would be brought into the experience of the heavenly Father on the sixth day, when God looked upon his creation and realized that it was good.

Under the old dispensation, the Father took care of a primitive people on pilgrimage by making many basic hygienic laws sacred, as they should be, for we are sacred—the whole of our being and everything that concerns us are the concern of God. But God's loving dispositions for yesterday are not always those for today, nor today's, for tomorrow. We must be ready to move with the Lord of History as he speaks to us through the signs of the times and through his Body, the Church. The practical hygiene that God had raised to the level of the sacramental had unfortunately become too much of the essence of religion for God's chosen people. Like ourselves, they were prone to latch on to the externals, which we humans can manage, in order to avoid the deeper things, which we cannot manage but which rather manage us and lead us into the realms of contemplation, transcendence, and adoration. Peter was to lead the new Christian community into the freedom of the children of God; he himself had to be free. If the salvation that was first of all to the Jews was to be to all peoples, then Peter had to know that all peoples are dear to God. And so in this hour, when Peter was open to God in prayer, he was taught the great lesson that "what God has made clean you have no right to call profane."

We see Peter led step by step by the Spirit according to the needs of the Church. The Spirit had to tell him, "Some men have come to see you. Hurry down and do not hesitate about going back with them. It was I who told them to come." Peter, like all of us, was too inclined to get caught up with what he had just learned. He wanted to stay with this astounding new experience of God. But God wants us always to move on, to share what we have learned from him and bring it into the life of the community. What we receive from God is never just for ourselves; it is for the whole Church, the whole of the People of God. One way or another, we are called upon to share it. Peter went down and said to them, "I am the man you are looking for. . . ." He was ready to go with them.

Peter was not slow to learn: "The truth I have now come to realize is that God does not have favorites, but that anybody of any nationality who fears God and does what is right is acceptable to him." This is a profound truth that we all need to learn and realize fully. If we search deeply in our hearts, I am afraid most of us are apt to find we do harbor there some prejudices, some subtle attitudes in regard to the relative merits or worth or performance of one or another particular race or nationality. We all tend to have our "Samaritans," and see the good found among them as something exceptional. For Jesus and his true disciples, there are only sons and daughters of God —his brothers and sisters, and ours.

How often has the mission of the Church to bring the word of salvation been undermined and even blocked by a certain pride on the part of the messengers, of those called to the apostolic ministry. When I was in India I had lunch in a convent of nuns who had been missionaries in India for many decades and prided themselves on the good work they were doing. There was no doubt much could and should rightly be credited to them. We sat at a long table with a number of Irish sisters, and below them a number of Indian sisters. The Irish sisters thought they had recently made a great breakthrough in acculturation in allowing the Indian sisters to put off the heavy European habits the Irish sisters wore in favor of the *kavi,* the orange-colored sari, that was the native religious garb of India. I had on my way to this convent visited a number of ashrams and so did not find this change at all surprising. It was a step in the right direction. But I was struck by the fact—and mentioned it—that this was the first time I had ever seen Indian women eating with knives and forks and spoons and that it seemed very strange to me. The Indian sisters clapped their hands with joy. They were happy that I appreciated their native culture and their right to preserve it. The Irish sisters were not so happy about my remarks. They thought that they had brought one of the benefits of "civilization" to the Indian sisters in teaching them to eat with these utensils, instead of respecting the sisters' culture and allowing them to eat as their people have always eaten. This is just a very small example. It can be multiplied many times and in many more important areas. The expression given to the theology of the Church has until recently universally required all peoples, in order to embrace Christian teaching, to become Aristotelian or Platonic thinkers of the Greco-Roman tradition. The Second Vatican Council has opened the way to let native peoples receive the simple biblical revelation and express it according to the philosophical concepts that belong to their own culture. The worship of many Christian peoples has also been marred by the almost universal requirement to follow the Roman liturgy. Now we are beginning to allow peoples to take the treasures of their own culture and use them in the worship of the true God just as the first Greek and Roman converts did.

Having seen the great difficulty that some Church leaders in our times have experienced in moving with the breadth of the Spirit in the Church of the Second Vatican Council calling for radical renewal, we are all the more in astonished admiration of Peter. As he readily admits here, he was brought up in a rather strict and narrow mentality that had taught him from the earliest days of his life not to associate with people of other religions and cultures. "You know it is forbidden Jews to mix with peoples of another race and visit them, but God has made it clear to me that I must not call anyone profane or unclean." Peter was ready to learn, ready to let go of his past, ready to move on. And thus he was worthily chosen to be the first leader of the Christian Church, for its call was to be open to all nations, to all peoples, to all cultures, and to all traditions. The Jewish believers who were with Peter were not quite so ready to move, and it took a powerful outpouring of the Holy Spirit with his charismatic gifts to make them realize the new breadth of the Spirit of God among the peoples of the nations. Peter for his part was not slow to proclaim, "They have received the Holy Spirit just as much as we have." When he returned to the apostles and brothers in Jerusalem, he did his best to help them understand what he had learned. He shared openly and humbly the gift he had received from the Lord, even though he knew that many would not receive it and would think less of him for it. But as he spoke honestly and openly, his account "satisfied them and they gave glory to God" (Acts 11:18).

One of the most important fruits of prayer is that it should open us to hear God and allow his grace to bring about in us a transformation of consciousness. If we are stuck with prayer forms, if we are trying to satisfy ourselves and prove our own righteousness in our prayers, if we are too busy saying formulas to stop and create spaces of silence and openness to hear God, then something is radically wrong with our prayer. Prayer is a conversation. In any good conversation we must not only speak, but also listen. We need to develop a habit of listening in prayer, especially since in this conversation the one to whom we address ourselves is the source of all wisdom. How presumptuous it is for us to do all the talking and expect him to do all the listening! But it is not enough just to listen. We must listen with a readiness to respond, even if it means giving up value systems, prejudices, and lifelong traditions and practices. We must humbly realize that no matter how old and wise might be the thoughts and ideas and traditions by which we live, for the wisdom of God they are the nonsense of children. "My thoughts are not your thoughts, nor your ways my ways, says the Lord, but as high as heaven is above the earth so are my thoughts beyond your thoughts and my ways beyond your ways." We must come to prayer seeking to hear God and be led into his ways and his thoughts, and be empowered by the Spirit. Then can we open the way for the outpouring of God's love, grace, and peace in the Holy Spirit. Then can we give effective witness to our fellows that will enable them to step forward into a new consciousness of the ways of an all-merciful and all-loving God.

The Peter who here exclaims, "Certainly not, Lord; I have never eaten anything profane or unclean" is the same Peter who cried, "You will never wash my feet!" But in another sense, it is not the same Peter. The same impetuosity might well be there, but it comes from a humbled and enlightened heart that knows it has yet much to learn. In docility to the Lord, Peter will be led where he does not want to go, but where the Lord wants him to go and where he will be an instrument of the Spirit of life and love.

We see, then, in this brief account of a day in the life of Peter, first of all, the importance of regular times of prayer and fidelity to them. What would have happened if on this particular day Peter had decided to skip the sixth hour of prayer that he usually practiced, if he had not been there to see the heavens open and receive the message of the Lord? We never know what we miss when we omit one of our regular periods of prayer or meditation. We see here, too, something of the expected effects of prayer. True prayer expands our consciousness so that we begin to see things God's way and not just our way or the way of the institution, the tradition, or the laws. Peter's first answer has the savor of the Pharisee about it. "Never have I eaten . . ." He is led to go beyond the law, beyond the security of fulfilling the law, to walk in the way of obedience to God in the Spirit. There is an expansion in his outlook as he sees the whole of creation under a different light. There is an expansion in his activity as he goes forth to be one with Gentiles. And there is expansion in his power as his very words open the space for a great outpouring of the Spirit.

Through fidelity to prayer, and to a prayer that listens, we will learn to hear God and grow with God and be the effective instruments in his hands that he and we want us to be. We will most probably not be favored with any such extraordinary external vision as that reported here, even if we are most faithful to our times of prayer. But as we enter into deep prayer, we will come to know by a certain experience that at every moment we are coming forth from the creative love of God. And not only ourselves, but the whole of creation. And we will know the intrinsic goodness of every human person made in the image of our God. And like our Master, we will want to reach out in compassionate and redeeming love. We will be true disciples.

A Saving Glance

From time to time some of the monks of my monastery visit a nearby Orthodox monastery. It is always refreshing and challenging to come into contact with this fervent expression of our own Christian monastic tradition. As is his wont, the Spiritual Father of the monastery usually presents us with an icon. On the occasion of one of our visits he gave me a very unusual icon. It is simply the head of Christ, but it is Christ in that moment when "he turned and looked straight at Peter" (Luke 22:61), after the cock had crowed announcing Peter's third denial of Jesus. I hung the icon in my cell. I must confess that I have often been tempted to remove it, for each time I look upon it, it is like a stab in the heart. The Lord is now looking at me, and he reminds me how like Peter I am. I think and act as though I were strong, but in fact I am very weak; I let what others think decide my course of action. But the icon reminds me too—which is why I keep it—that no matter how abysmal my failure may be, if like Peter I can have the humility to weep for my sin and stay with the community, I can, by the grace of the Lord's own Resurrection, rise to new strength and courage in his service.

I believe that in that moment when Jesus looked at him, we have a key moment in the life of Peter. Before that moment, he was Simon. "Simon, Simon! Satan, you must know, has got his wish to sift you all like wheat; but I have prayed for you, Simon, that your faith may not fail, and once you have recovered, you in your turn must strengthen your brothers" (Luke 22:31–32). He had been a weak man with whom Satan would all too frequently have his way. But after the saving glance, he was Peter: "You are Peter and on this rock I will build my Church and the gates of the underworld can never hold out against it" (Matthew 16:18). The power of the glance of Christ.

This is perhaps the key element of true prayer, that kind of prayer in which we are truly convicted by the Lord, brought to true conversion, and empowered by the grace of the Resurrection. Saint Paul would later write, "For those who love God all things work together unto good." And another great saint would add, ". . . even sin" (Saint Augustine). When Jesus was seized in the garden, all the disciples deserted him, fleeing through the underbrush and trees seeking to save their own skins. But Peter had the courage to come out of the bush and at least "follow at a distance." He failed, he failed miserably, but at least he was there to receive the healing, saving glance of Christ. When we go to prayer, all too often we try to avoid that glance. We keep busy with our own thoughts, our own ideas, our many words, our liturgical formulas. We avert our glance so that we do not have to see him, we do not have to meet him eye to eye. But there is power in the glance of Christ.

Right up to this ultimate moment of conversion we see the same bravado in Peter. Jesus had sent him with John to prepare the Supper. As we noted before, they are in a way representatives of the two classic types: the contemplative and the activist. They were together in their call. They were sent together by Christ to prepare this meal that he "longed with a great longing to eat with them," to bring to completion his new covenant, the Sacrament of his Body and Blood (Luke 22:18). They would be together with Jesus in the Garden and following him after he was seized. They would be together running to the tomb. At the Last Supper they sat one on Jesus' right and the other on his left.

There is more than one way to follow Jesus. No one is excluded from discipleship. Each can follow according to that temperament and grace which the Lord has given him. No one temperament is of itself better than any other. Each is of the Lord.

> Jesus knew that the Father had put everything into his hands, and that he had come from God and was returning to God, and he got up from table, removed his outer garment and, taking a towel, wrapped it around his waist; he then poured water into a basin and began to wash the disciples' feet and to wipe them with the towel he was wearing.
>
> He came to Simon Peter, who said to him, "Lord, are you going to wash my feet?" Jesus answered, "At the moment you do not know what I am doing, but later you will understand." "Never!" said Peter. "You shall never wash my feet." Jesus replied, "If I do not wash you, you can have nothing in common with me." "Then, Lord," said Simon Peter, "not only my feet, but my hands and my head as well!" [John 13:3–9]

There is one thing very refreshing about Peter's bravado: he doesn't get stuck in it. He is very ready to move and become just as enthusiastic in the opposite direction. This freedom came from his overriding devotion to his Master. His basic enthusiasm was to be a true disciple. As soon as he saw what that called for, he was completely there. Peter was, in some very real way, to stand in the place of Christ in the midst of the infant Church after his Master had ascended into heaven. He had to learn the way of true leadership within the Christian community, the way of service. He learned it. Deep in his gut he experienced swirls of emotional turmoil as he sat there and watched his Master wash his feet, fulfilling the office of a slave in his regard. It would be an unforgettable lesson. Jesus' disciples had all too often argued among themselves as to who was greatest, and vied for the first places in the Kingdom. They would never do that again. They heard deep in their own beings that he who would be first must take the last place.

But all the bravado had not yet been extinguished in Peter. As Jesus went on to speak sorrowfully of the things that were to come, Peter was again presumptuously making claims: "Although all lose faith in you, I will never lose faith. Even if I have to die with you, I will never disown you." And Jesus had to respond with that most dire of predictions: "I tell you most solemnly, before the cock crows you will disown me three times." The words cut deep, very deep. Never again do we hear a presumptuous word from the mouth of Peter. And yet the words themselves were not enough. A lived experience of his own terrible, self-betraying weakness was needed to bring him finally to that self-knowledge that would enable him to grow with a dispossessive humility to all the greatness to which God was calling him.

We all know the sad story.

First there would be the failures in the Garden. Leaving the rest, Jesus took Peter and the two sons of Zebedee with him into a more solitary spot. An immense sadness came over him, and great distress. He said to them, "My soul is sorrowful to the point of death. Wait here and keep awake with me." And going on a little further, he prayed. "My Father," he said, "if it be possible, let this cup pass from me. But nevertheless let it be as you, not I, would have it." He came back to the disciples and found them sleeping. And he said to Peter, "And so you had not the strength to keep awake with me one hour. You should be awake and praying not to be put to the test. The spirit is willing but the flesh is weak" (Matthew 26:36–41). We know this sad scene was repeated a second time, and a third. This "Rock," who said he would even go to prison and to death with Christ, could not stay awake one hour with him in his anguish. Luke adds a very telling remark. He tells us that "Jesus found them sleeping for sheer grief." Sleep is one of the means we use to avoid life, its demands, its anguish, its potentials.

Then we come to the second betrayal: "Judas the traitor knew the place well, since Jesus had often met his disciples there, and he brought the cohort to this place . . . Simon Peter, who carried a sword, drew it and wounded the high priest's servant, cutting off his right ear. The servant's name was Malchus. Jesus said to Peter, 'Put your sword back in its scabbard; am I not to drink the cup that the Father has given me?' " (John 18:2–11). And Luke adds: "Touching the man's ear, Jesus healed him" (Luke 22:51).

Again Peter was playing the role of Satan, trying to stand between Christ and the fulfillment of the role that the Father had given him. An all-too-human love of his Master held him back from embracing who his Master truly was, from being completely one in union and communion with his Master in embracing the Divine Will. In striking out, he did violence to all that Jesus stood for: to healing, to reconciliation, to nonviolence. As Jesus reached out and healed Malchus' ear, he took another step in his all-healing mission.

And Peter headed for the bush.

But the disciple's love was strong, and it brought him out of the bush to follow, at least at a distance. His love was strong—but not strong enough to keep him from the final fall, the final betrayal.

> Peter was sitting outside in the courtyard and a servant-girl came up to him and said, "You too were with Jesus the Galilean." But he denied it in front of them all. "I do not know what you are talking about," he said. When he went out to the gateway another servant-girl saw him and said to the people there, "This man was with Jesus the Nazarene." And again, with an oath, he denied it, "I do not know the man." A little later the bystanders came up and said to Peter, "You are one of them for sure! Why, your accent gives you away." Then he started calling down curses on himself and swearing, "I do not know the man." At that moment the cock crew, and Peter remembered what Jesus had said, "Before the cock crows you will disown me three times." And he went outside and wept bitterly. [Matthew 26:69–75]

It is Luke who adds, "The cock crew and the Lord turned and looked straight at Peter" (Luke 22:60–61). Throughout Luke's account we find a certain tenderness toward Peter. Remember, he was the one who used Mary as his source. It is Luke who tells us that at the very time that Jesus was foretelling Peter's denial, he told him, "I have prayed for you, Simon, that your faith may not fail, and once you have recovered, you in your turn must strengthen your brothers" (Luke 22:32). It is Luke who notes that after one of the disciples (he doesn't mention Peter by name) struck the high priest's servant and cut off his right ear,

Jesus "touching the man's ear, healed him," giving us hope that when in our misguided zeal we hurt others, Jesus in his loving mercy will bring the needed healing. And finally, in the account of the denials he leaves out everything about Peter's cursing and swearing; rather, he has him say simply, "I am not him, my friend."

Is denial a part of discipleship?

Sad to say, for us poor, weak, sinful humans, it is. Inevitably we do fail Jesus, our chosen Master. What is revealing here in Peter, and consoling for us because it is so true in our own lives, is the fact that we fail in the little challenges. Peter had said to Jesus, "Even if I have to die with you, I will never disown you." (And note that all the other disciples said the same.) If in the Garden the soldiers had successfully grabbed hold of Peter and led him off with Jesus, Peter probably would have been loyal all the way to the cross—as he one day would be. But now we see that the gibe of a little serving-girl makes him cower and betray himself, his loyalty, his love, and his Master.

Yes, all we disciples will fail. But then what are we to do?

Peter gives us the example. The moment he realized his failure, the moment Jesus looked at him, "he went outside and wept bitterly." We are to repent. But repentance is not enough. Judas repented, too. He returned his ill-gotten gain to the Temple. But then he went out and hanged himself. Peter, on the other hand, returned to the community. A profoundly humbling experience. Can you imagine his feelings the first time he walked into the midst of the other disciples? He who was to be the leader, he who had made such proud boasts at the Last Supper—and now they all knew it, they knew that three times he had denied his Master. He denied even knowing Jesus, not to speak of being his disciple.

The temptation is very great, when finally we are confronted with our weakness and our failures, to give up. If we do not, like Judas, go so far as to hang ourselves from a tree, we are tempted at least to withdraw from the community, to withdraw from the apostolic ministry, to withdraw from being an engaged disciple of Jesus. How many priests and religious—I have heard the story so often—have entered into apostolic ministry with tremendous zeal, but soon are caught up, more unconsciously than consciously, in a driving activity motivated increasingly by human respect, by the need to be wanted and to be affirmed, by ambitions and temporal goals. More and more they neglect the time they need to continue to deepen their relation with the Lord and to be sourced and strengthened by him. "You should be awake praying, not to be put to the test. The spirit is willing, but the flesh is weak." Sometimes they go on for as much as a decade or more before burning themselves out. Then one day they realize that the very reason they answered the call and entered into the apostolic ministry and the fullness of discipleship has been completely neglected and lost sight of. They are filled with regrets and repentance. But instead of turning back to the community and seeking its help, strength, and guidance to be renewed in the deeper meaning and vision of their call, they throw in the towel and seek another way. Peter returned to the community and so he was ready, he was in place to receive the summons to reconciliation with the Lord.

Mark, who gives us Peter's catechesis to the early Church, makes much of the fidelity of the women to Jesus. They stayed with him to the very end: "There were some women watching from a distance. Among them were Mary of Magdala, Mary who was the mother of James the younger and Joset, and

Salome. These used to follow him and look after him when he was in Galilee. . . . Mary of Magdala and Mary the mother of Joset were watching and they took note of where he was laid" (Mark 15:40–47). The great Peter was scared away by a little serving-woman, but these good women stood fast right to the end. Rightly then was it a woman to whom the Risen Lord first announced his victory over death, a woman he sent to the great Peter to challenge him again to break through his fears into faith. Mary Magdalen "came running to Simon Peter and the other disciple, the one Jesus loved. 'They have taken the Lord out of the tomb,' she said, 'and we don't know where they have put him' " (John 20:2). The man who had received the saving glance was no longer afraid to be known as a disciple of Jesus, to make a fool of himself.

> So Peter set out with the other disciple to go to the tomb. They ran together, but the other disciple, running faster than Peter, reached the tomb first; he bent down and saw the linen cloths lying on the ground, but did not go in. Simon Peter who was following now came up, went right into the tomb, saw the linen cloths on the ground and also the cloths that had been over his head; this was not with the linen cloths but rolled up in a place by itself. Then the other disciple who reached the tomb first also went in; he saw and he believed. Till this moment they had failed to understand the teaching of scripture, that he must rise from the dead. [John 20:3–9]

Mark tells us that it was an angel who directed Mary Magdalen: "You must go and tell his disciples and Peter" (Mark 16:7).

"Yes, it is true. The Lord has risen and appeared to

Simon" (Luke 24:34). That first encounter between the Risen Lord and the repentant disciple who had betrayed him three times is so sacred, so intimate, so special that we are only told that it happened. The details are fully hidden in the hearts of two lovers, a Master and his disciple. The public reconciliation and reinstatement of Peter will come later.

At the root of any true Christian ministry, if it is to be true and effective, must be a personal relationship with Jesus; otherwise the ministry is a charade. First Peter's personal relation with Jesus had to be healed and the healing take full possession of him before he could unhesitatingly affirm it publicly, even three times, and be ready to stand as Christ's vicar, the good shepherd of his flock, the head of his Church.

The Other Side of the Man: The Rock

When Jesus came to the region of Caesarea Philippi, he put this question to his disciples, "Who do people say the Son of Man is?" And they said, "Some say he is John the Baptist, some Elijah, and others Jeremiah or one of the prophets." "But you," he said, "who do you say I am?" Then Simon Peter spoke up, "You are the Christ," he said, "the Son of the living God." Jesus replied, "Simon son of Jonah, you are a happy man! Because it was not flesh and blood that revealed this to you but my Father in heaven. So I now say to you: You are Peter and on this rock I will build my Church. And the gates of the underworld can never hold out against it. I will give you the keys of the kingdom of heaven: whatever you bind on earth shall be considered bound in heaven; whatever you loose on earth shall be considered loosed in heaven." Then he gave the disciples strict orders not to tell anyone that he was the Christ. [Matthew 16:13–20]

Luke, who so often brings special nuances to these occasions, tells us that "when he [Jesus] was praying alone in the presence of his disciples he put this question to them" (Luke 9:18). As we search the Scriptures we find that before every significant event Jesus takes time for prayer. He sought more and more to draw his disciples into this practice. Before his ultimate test there would be a heartbreaking attempt as Peter and the others slumbered in Gethsemane. But they did learn. We find them spending days in earnest prayer awaiting the coming of the Holy Spirit in the epiphany of the Church at Pentecost.

We come now to one of the climactic moments in the mission of Jesus and the consummation of Peter's call to discipleship. Jesus is a good teacher. So he first seeks to clear the space, removing the superficial influences: "Who do people say the Son of Man is?" We are all influenced, perhaps much more than we realize, by what other people say and think. It is only by some conscious reflection on where our opinions or thoughts or prejudices are coming from that we can begin to realize that they are not truly our own. Then we can lay them aside in order to look more deeply into our hearts and see what are truly our own personal convictions, the sources of our life's conduct.

After clearing away other peoples' conjectures, Jesus then put his finger on his own disciples, and specifically on Peter, whom all by this time would expect to be the spokesman. "But you, who do you say that I am?" Peter comes up with the right answer: "The Christ, the Anointed One of God, the Son of God, the Messiah." It is difficult for us who have not lived in and been formed by an intensely religious Jewish culture to grasp the significance of this affirmation, all the connotations that that word, the Christ—the Messiah—held for a pious Jew —the burden of centuries of history, of election, of exodus, of promise, of covenant. Certainly Peter did not understand the full weight of what he had said, especially when he added, "the Son of the Living God." This is why Jesus went on "and gave the disciples strict orders not to tell anyone that he was the Christ."

There were too many false ideas and false expectations with regard to the Messiah. This is very evident from the next scene, when Jesus begins to bring out for the Twelve the fact that the Messiah, the Christ, the Anointed One, is also the Suffering Servant of Isaiah. Peter for one was not ready for this. He was scandalized by it. He was not ready to embrace the mystery of the cross. And so our Lord did not want him or the others to attempt to speak yet about his true identity.

Much harm is done within the Christian community because those who are proclaiming the Word really do not know what they are talking about. If they really did, they could not live the way they do. Like Peter, most Christians have the words but do not understand what they truly mean. We "know" that God is love, but we do not know what this means when it comes to living as a disciple of Christ. Cardinal Newman in his writings makes the distinction between a "notional assent" and a "real assent." We have the notions. We accept them. Christianity for us too often is just that: acceptance of certain notions and ideas. What we need is that "real assent," that profound understanding that calls forth the response of our whole being. As Chesterton has said, "Christianity has not failed. The problem is that it has never been really tried." To live love—that is what Christ did. That is what we his disciples must do to be true disciples. Not parrot formulas. And above all, not try to force our formulas, no matter how right and sacred, down the throats of others. Or persecute others because they won't parrot them with us. Rather, like Christ our Master, we disciples need to lay down our lives with all their certainties and formulas, to embrace our brothers and sisters, and to serve them with self-giving love. But such a life-giving truth cannot come from ourselves.

Jesus told Peter, "It was not flesh and blood that revealed this to you, but my Father in heaven." The revelation of the divinity of Jesus Christ, and his sonship, and his unity with the Father in the Holy Spirit who is Love is not a notion that can come from anywhere except God himself. It is a revelation of the inner life of God. Even the notions, and being able to say "yes" to them, are an immense grace. At the Last Supper Jesus promised that the Holy Spirit, the Paraclete, would come and would teach us all things: "The Advocate, the Holy Spirit, whom the Father will send in my name, will teach you everything and remind you of all I have said to you" (John 14:26).

At baptism we received what have been called the theological virtues, the virtues of faith, hope, and love, by which we are able to believe what God has revealed to us and place our hope in him and love him in a way that is worthy of him. But also in that moment when we were made partakers of the divine nature, there were implanted within us certain dispositions by which we can operate beyond the human mode, even the human mode strengthened with the theological virtues of faith and hope. These dispositions have been called the gifts of the Holy Spirit. These dispose us to allow the Spirit to guide us according to the divine instinct, far beyond what our human mind, even with the help of the virtues, can attain. This is the purpose of a deeper, more contemplative type of prayer. We leave off the thoughts and reflections and ponderings of the rational mind and open the space for the Spirit to operate within us. Through the gifts he will give us a deep experiential sense of who God is and who we are in God and what it means to be disciples of a Master who is Love. It is only when we can let go of our more superficial selves and enter into a prayer of profound listening that we can come to that living and life-giving knowledge of Jesus Christ that will enable us powerfully and effectively to proclaim that he is the Christ, the Son of the Living God, and live in accord with what we are proclaiming. Peter as a disciple had begun to learn to listen. We, as disciples, need to begin to make space in our lives for divine learning by a daily practice of listening prayer. The simple method of Centering Prayer is a good way to begin this.

"You are Peter and on this rock I will build my Church." This proclamation of Peter's special office corresponded to a role that was natural enough to this forceful man from the shores of Gennesaret, and was indeed already being exercised. Peter had a natural gift for leadership, and the other disciples willy-nilly respected it. Grace was building on nature. From whom did the nature come?

Jesus would speak of Peter's special role in relation to his fellow disciples again at the Last Supper, even as he warned of Peter's weakness and failures: "Simon, Simon! Satan, you must know, has got his wish to sift you all like wheat; but I have prayed for you, Simon, that your faith may not fail, and once you have recovered, you in your turn must strengthen your brothers" (Luke 22:31–32). His special role was recognized in the announcement of the Resurrection. The angels told the women, "You must go and tell his disciples and Peter" (Mark 16:7). "And running to the tomb," John showed deference to Peter, for he did not enter, although he arrived first, until Peter had entered in. After the ascension of Jesus into heaven, it was Peter who led the community of disciples in choosing a successor for Judas (Acts 1:15). He became the spokesman for the disciples from Pentecost onwards. His leadership was confirmed with awesome power in the case of Ananias and Sapphira (Acts 5:3), and also in healing—even his very shadow healed people (Acts 5:15). Saint Paul acknowledged the particular preeminence of Peter after his conversion: "I went up to Jerusalem to visit Cephas and stayed with him for fifteen days, I did not see any of the other apostles" (Galatians 1:18–19). Even though he "opposed Peter to his face," he always acknowledged Peter's special call.

I do not want to develop here a theological treatise on the primacy of Peter. What I want to bring out is that there are reasons why the power to bind and loose that Jesus confers here is usually considered to be a special prerogative of Peter and his successors. On Easter Sunday Jesus will stand in the midst of his disciples and he will breathe on them and say, "Receive the Holy Spirit. For those whose sins you forgive, they are forgiven; for those whose sins you retain, they are retained" (John 20:22–23). The traditional understanding of this text is that Jesus is on this occasion giving all the apostles a certain power to bind and loose. This has been seen as the origin of the power that the ordinary priest or bishop exercises in the ministry of the sacrament of reconciliation. However, I think both of these texts can in some way be truly applied to every disciple of Christ. We are all called to be ministers of reconciliation, ministers of Christ's forgiveness in our daily forgiving of one another and of our enemies and of ourselves. The compassion of any disciple's heart is a channel through which Christ's healing, redeeming, and reconciling grace can flow. The hardness of any disciple's heart that withholds forgiveness in some way blocks the grace of God's forgiveness from reaching the hearts of our brothers and sisters.

* * *

As we walk with Peter we see a very weak and fearful man who hides consistently behind the defensiveness of boasting and bravado and who quakes before the challenge of a little serving-girl. We will, though, see this man, in fulfillment of the prophetic naming of the Lord, become a true *Rock* who will without hesitation withstand the threats of imprisonment and be ready to be led where he would prefer not to go. What made the difference? The *Resurrection.* The grace of the Resurrection given to Peter by Christ and brought to fullness by the outpouring of the Holy Spirit enabled this very weak, imperfect human being to become a powerful and empowering disciple. The folly and the victory of Peter can give all of us disciples of Christ cause to hope that we too can enter into the mystery of Resurrection and experience in our lives that same transforming grace.

Resurrection

The spirit in the upper room was very different from what it was some forty days before. Then Jesus had disappeared from their midst, led away by a cohort, and less than twenty-four hours later he was hidden behind the stone slab that covered the door of a tomb. Then the disciples cowered in the upper room, fearful and uncertain—those that hadn't headed out of the city like the two on their way to Emmaus. Forty-three days later Jesus departed again from their midst, this time through a glorious ascension. As he went he left them with a command and a promise. They were now in the upper room, in obedience to that command, and filled with the expectation of the promise.

Gathered with Mary, the mother of Jesus, whom he had bequeathed to the whole Church—"Behold your mother" —they were engaged in a final preparation for the epiphany of the Church.

Jesus had spent much of his lifetime in preparation, living an ordinary life in the obscure town of Nazareth. His immediate preparation for his public ministry was forty days spent apart in prayer. Again and again he nourished his ministry with time apart, especially at night in solitary prayer to the Father. On various occasions he asked chosen ones to be with him, as on Tabor and in Gethsemane. Now the disciples, following the example of the Master, were preparing for a promised event with a period of apartness in prayer—"Go into your room, close your door, and pray to your Father in secret" (Matthew 6:6).

After ten days of preparation the Spirit came upon the disciples in power. It was now time for Simon, who had truly become Peter, the Rock, to stand forth with power and proclaim the Resurrection of the Lord Jesus: "Men of Israel, listen to what I am going to say: Jesus the Nazarene was a man commended to you by God by the miracles and portents and signs that God worked through him when he was among you, as you all know. This man, who was put into your power by the deliberate intention and foreknowledge of God, you took and had crucified by men outside the Law. You killed him, but God raised him to life" (Acts 2:22–23).

We cannot help being astonished. Here—probably in the very Temple itself, for such a large group of Christians—120 of them—could not have readily found room in any other "house" in Jerusalem; but the porticoes of the Temple would have been available to them, and the large crowd of Jews in the courts of the Temple could then easily perceive the powerful coming of the Spirit—here stands the man who quaked before the simple interrogation of a servant girl; now he boldly proclaims the very things for which his Master was put to death less than two months before. And he didn't mince his words, either.

The proclamation of the fact of the Resurrection of the Lord Jesus would become central in all the teaching of Peter. When he performed his first public healing in the Temple he declared openly: "God, however, raised him from the dead, and of that fact we are the witnesses; and it is the name of Jesus which, through our faith in it, has brought back the strength of this man whom you see here and who is well known to you. It is faith in that name that has restored this man to health, as you can see" (Acts 3:15–16). When he was brought before the Sanhedrin, he told them, "It was the God of our ancestors who raised up Jesus, but it was you who had him executed by hanging on a tree. By his own right hand God has now raised him up to be leader and savior, to give repentance and forgiveness of sins through him to Israel. We are witnesses to all this, we and the Holy Spirit whom God has given to those who obey him" (Acts 5:30–32).

And when he was called to give witness to the Gentiles: "Now I, and those with me, can witness to everything that Jesus did throughout the countryside of Judaea and Jerusalem itself; and also to the fact that they killed him by hanging him on a tree, yet three days afterwards God raised him to life and allowed him to be seen, not by the whole people but only by certain witnesses God had chosen beforehand" (Acts 10:39–41).

Fearlessly Peter went forth to proclaim the Resurrection of the Lord Jesus Christ, his Master. So far as we know he was never laughed to scorn, as was Paul, but he was jailed (Acts 4:3) and flogged (Acts 5:40) and eventually "led where he would not go" and crucified. Jesus had prepared Peter carefully step by step to be able fully to understand and integrate the meaning and the power of the Resurrection.

One of the first steps was that day when Jesus came into Peter's home and raised his mother-in-law from her sick bed. Peter witnessed Jesus' power of resurrection again when he was one of the chosen witnesses at the restoration of Jairus' daughter:

> While he was still speaking, someone arrived from the house of the synagogue official to say, "Your daughter has died. Do not trouble the Master any further." But Jesus

> had heard this, and he spoke to the man, "Do not be afraid, only have faith and she will be safe." When he came to the house he allowed no one to go in with him except Peter and John and James, and the child's father and mother. They were all weeping and mourning for her, but Jesus said, "Stop crying; she is not dead, but asleep." But they laughed at him, knowing she was dead. But taking her by the hand he called to her, "Child, get up." And her spirit returned and she got up at once. Then he told them to give her something to eat. [Luke 8:49–55]

The mourners outside laughed Jesus to scorn when he said she was only asleep. Perhaps later Peter himself would have wondered whether that was indeed the case. But the experience at Nain was even stronger and clearer, for here there could seem to be no doubt about the death of the young man who was already being carried to the cemetery:

> Now soon afterwards he went to a town called Nain, accompanied by his disciples and a great number of people. When he was near the gate of the town it happened that a dead man was being carried out for burial, the only son of his mother, and she was a widow. And a considerable number of the townspeople were with her. When the Lord saw her he felt sorry for her. "Do not cry," he said. Then he went up and put his hand on the bier and the bearers stood still, and he said, "Young man, I tell you to get up." And the dead man sat up and began to talk, and Jesus gave him to his mother. [Luke 7:11–15]

If any question still lurked in Peter's heart, raised by the skeptics who would have said that somehow the lad of Nain was really only in some deep coma and not truly dead, all such skepticism would have been dissipated with the experience of Lazarus:

> Jesus said in great distress, with a sigh that came straight from the heart, "Where have you put him?" They said, "Lord, come and see." Jesus wept; and the Jews said, "See how much he loved him!" But there were some who remarked, "He opened the eyes of the blind man, could he not have prevented this man's death?" Still sighing, Jesus reached the tomb: it was a cave with a stone to close the opening. Jesus said, "Take the stone away." Martha said to him, "Lord, by now he will smell; this is the fourth day." Jesus replied, "Have I not told you that if you believe you will see the glory of God?" So they took away the stone. Then Jesus lifted up his eyes and said:
>
> Father: I thank you for hearing my prayer.
> I knew indeed that you always hear me,
> but I speak
> for the sake of all these who stand round me,
> so that they may believe it was you who sent me.
>
> When he had said this, he cried in a loud voice, "Lazarus, here! Come out!" The dead man came out, his feet and hands bound with bands of stuff and a cloth round his face. Jesus said to them, "Unbind him, let him go free." [John 11:33–44]

After such experiences it was not so difficult, even though the apostles generally took the story of the women as "pure nonsense and they did not believe them," for Peter to run with hope to an empty tomb. We will never know the details, not to speak of the inner emotions experienced by Peter, in that moment when he did indeed encounter his Risen Lord.

Peter internalized the meaning and the power of the grace of the Resurrection. And when the occasion came, with the courage of a true disciple he did not hesitate to call upon the power of his Master.

> At Jaffa there was a woman disciple called Tabitha, or Dorcas in Greek, who never tired of doing good or giving in charity. But the time came when she got ill and died, and they washed her and laid her out in a room upstairs. Lydda is not far from Jaffa, so when the disciples heard that Peter was there, they sent two men with an urgent message for him: "Come and visit us as soon as possible."
>
> Peter went back with them straightaway, and on his arrival they took him to the upstairs room, where all the widows stood round him in tears, showing him tunics and the other clothes which Dorcas had made when she was with them. Peter sent them all out of the room and knelt down and prayed. Then he turned to the dead woman and said, "Tabitha, stand up." She opened her eyes, looked at Peter and sat up. Peter helped her to her feet, then called in the saints and widows and showed them she was alive. [Acts 9:36–41]

When we compare this scene with that which took place in the house of Jairus, we see very much the disciple in the shadow of his Master—just as when we look back in the Old Testament we see in Elijah the Prophet the foreshadowing of what was to come. But there is this great difference both in the case of Elijah and of Peter: the Prophet and the Disciple, before bringing the grace of the Resurrection, had to kneel in prayer and call upon the Lord; while the Master simply stretched forth his hand and called the child to life.

In his old age, Peter would write from Rome, fully conscious "that the time for taking off this tent is coming soon, as the Lord Jesus Christ had foretold" (2 Peter 1:14). After greeting the Christians who had been scattered to all parts of the Dispersion, he immediately proclaimed with gratitude the essence of the good news: "Blessed be God the Father of our Lord Jesus Christ, who in his great mercy has given us a new birth as his sons, by raising Jesus Christ from the dead, so that we have a sure hope and promise of an inheritance that can never be spoilt or soiled and never fade away, because it is being kept for you in the heavens" (1 Peter 1:3–4).

Peter himself had come to know how certain is the hope that he found in the Resurrection of Jesus Christ. That hope cannot be spoiled or soiled in spite of human frailty and weakness, stupidity and blundering. It was a power that could even raise the dead. But Peter knew, too, that he was able to live out the power of the Resurrection and proclaim it fearlessly only after he had received the Spirit. It is not enough to know, not even enough to experience. Knowledge and experience have to become in us a living, effective knowledge through the grace and empowerment of the Holy Spirit. Then we can continually rise from our failures and our weakness, and we can help others to rise from theirs; then we can live worthily as disciples of a Risen Master.

The Resurrection must be central in the life and thinking of a disciple of Christ, not only as the source of all that he is but as the primary proclamation of his life. If we do not live as men and women who believe in the Resurrection, we are not true disciples of Christ. If we do not bring to others the message of hope that is the Resurrection, we fail them and our Master. Christ is risen! Yes, he is truly risen.

Restoration

Later on, Jesus showed himself to his disciples. It was by the sea of Tiberias, and it happened like this: Simon Peter, Thomas called the Twin, Nathanael from Cana in Galilee, the sons of Zebedee and two more of his disciples were together. Simon Peter said, "I'm going fishing." They replied, "We'll come with you." They went out and got into the boat but caught nothing that night.

It was light by now and there stood Jesus on the shore, though the disciples did not realize that it was Jesus. Jesus called out, "Have you caught anything, friends?" And when they answered, "No," he said, "Throw the net out to starboard and you'll find something." So they dropped the net, and there were so many fish that they could not haul it in. The disciple Jesus loved said to Peter, "It is the Lord." At these words, "It is the Lord," Simon Peter, who had practically nothing on, wrapped his cloak around him and jumped into the water. The other disciples came on in the boat, towing the net and the fish; they were only about a hundred yards from land.

As soon as they came ashore they saw that there was some bread there, and a charcoal fire with fish cooking on it. Jesus said, "Bring some of the fish you have just caught."

Simon Peter went aboard and dragged the net to the shore, full of big fish, one hundred and fifty-three of them; and in spite of there being so many the net was not broken. Jesus said to them, "Come and have breakfast." None of the disciples was bold enough to ask, "Who are you?"; they knew quite well that it was the Lord. Jesus then stepped forward, took the bread and gave it to them, and the same with the fish. This was the third time that Jesus showed himself to the disciples after rising from the dead.

After the meal Jesus said to Simon Peter, "Simon son of John, do you love me more than these others do?" He answered, "Yes, Lord, you know that I love you." Jesus said to him, "Feed my lambs." A second time he said to him, "Simon son of John, do you love me?" He replied, "Yes, Lord, you know I love you." Jesus said to him, "Look after my sheep." Then he said to him a third time, "Simon son of John, do you love me?" Peter was upset that he asked him the third time, "Do you love me?" and said, "Lord, you know everything; you know that I love you." Jesus said to him, "Feed my sheep.

I tell you most solemnly,
when you were young
you put on your own belt
and walked where you liked;
but when you grow old
you will stretch out your hands,
and somebody else will put a belt around you
and take you where you would rather not go."

In these words he indicated the kind of death by which Peter would give glory to God. After this he said, "Follow me." [John 21:1–19]

Peter had denied Christ three times. Caught up in the swirl of the emotions of the moment, he acted out of reaction; he reacted rather than acting from his own true, deep self. The glance of Jesus, who understood all only too well, was much more a look of compassion, love, and pity than one of rebuke. It was enough to bring Peter back to his true self. He went out and wept bitterly.

We know nothing of the encounter of Peter with Jesus on Easter, but it certainly restored the very special bond of love that existed between Master and Disciple. Once again, Peter was fully a disciple of Jesus. But the wise Master would restore him to his very particular role of apostolic ministry and leadership only step by step.

At first he left Peter and the others waiting; only occasionally would he come to them. Prayer is often a matter of waiting. We go to prayer each day. But oftentimes the Lord doesn't seem to show up. Actually, of course, he is there, or we wouldn't be there. Only by his grace do we seek him in prayer. It is only by his grace that we wait for him. This waiting is important because it develops in us an ever-deeper longing for him. We come to know more and more in the depths of our being our need for him and how he is the center, the meaning of all our life. It is important that we be faithful to this daily waiting. For we do not know just when he will come.

Yet in the midst of this waiting, ordinary life must go on. So Peter decided to go back to his nets. Natural leader of the group that he was, he drew the others after him.

Oftentimes in our lives we have a sense of not really knowing what God does want of us. We know we want to serve him, and serve him perhaps in a special and wholehearted way, but it just isn't clear what he wants right now. Then the only thing to do is as Peter did, go fishing. Go about the daily duties of life. If God wants something else, it is his responsibility to come and find us there—that is where he will expect to find us —and let us know what he wants.

And so Peter and his friends went back to their boats and their nets. And it was there that Jesus found them. Or rather, it might be more correct to say that it was there that Jesus turned up, and they found him.

The second step in the restoration of Peter renews, as it were, his call to apostolic mission. And it is similar to the previous call, as it is described in Saint Luke's account.

> Jesus said to Simon, "Put out into deep water and pay out your nets for a catch." "Master," Simon replied, "we worked hard all night long and caught nothing, but if you say so, I will pay out the nets." And when they had done this they netted such a huge number of fish that their nets began to tear, so they signaled to their companions in the other boat to come and help them; when these came, they filled the two boats to the sinking point.
>
> When Simon Peter saw this he fell at the knees of Jesus saying, "Leave me, Lord; I am a sinful man." For he and all his companions were completely overcome by the catch they had made; so also were James and John, the sons of Zebedee, who were Simon's partners. But Jesus said to Simon, "Do not be afraid, from now on it is men you will catch." Then, bringing their boats back to land, they left everything and followed him. [Luke 5:4–11]

There is a directness and openness in this earlier call that is somewhat obscured in the restoration. A certain obtuseness seems to veil Peter's eyes. He does not recognize the stranger on the shore. And even in the moment of the miraculous draught of fishes he does not yet come to realization by himself. This is so true of ourselves. How often, even though we are really seeking the Lord, and seeking to do his will, yet there is a part in us that is reluctant to see him here and now. Perhaps it is because in the call and the response to it there is always necessarily a conversion, an acknowledgment that the past has not been all that it should have been. Perhaps too there is something in us that does not want to respond to the call for the further gift of self. The false self is hanging on to its established ways, the familiar ways where it is most comfortable. It took John, the pure, the innocent, with the keen eyes of love, to perceive that the "Friend" on the shore was indeed the Lord: "It is the Lord."

This is one of the reasons why we have such great need of a spiritual guide or friend in our lives. I don't particularly care for the term "spiritual director," for I believe that the only one who can direct is the one who truly knows in fullness that to which we are called. That is the Holy Spirit himself. He is the true director of our lives. The role of the spiritual guide or friend is to help us to hear what the Lord is saying, to see what he is doing in our lives. It was John who saw that it was Jesus, and that Jesus was now calling Peter to himself.

Peter had undergone a true reconversion to Christ. So there was no hesitation in his response once he clearly perceived the call. Yet there was a certain reverence for the Lord. This man, who had acted with such presumption that once it even called forth from the Lord the rebuke, "Get behind me, Satan," now would not appear before his Lord without properly clothing himself, even though it would indeed be cumbersome as he plunged into the water and went pell-mell with all his old enthusiasm to the feet of his Master. Here Peter shows again in graphic image his willingness to leave everything: friends, boat, prosperous income—he leaves it all in order to respond to Jesus.

The other disciples came following after, laboriously pulling the weighted ship up onto the shore until it was nestled securely in the sands. The one who has left everything behind to respond to Christ can with alacrity plunge ahead to be with him. However, the vocation of those disciples who have not been called to evangelical poverty is also very important. The Church needs the material wherewithal that they bring to her service.

Jesus with his usual graciousness had prepared a breakfast for his disciples. With great delicacy and sacramental significance, he invites Peter to play a part in providing this meal: "Bring some of the fish you have just caught." Simon in his enthusiasm doesn't bring just some of the fish. He grabs the net and single-handed brings the entire catch to the feet of the Lord. The uniqueness of Peter's role in the Church is again symbolized. However, equally symbolic is the fact that it was the community of disciples that had made available to Peter the means to serve the Lord and carry out his ministry in such fullness.

Peter stood there beaming. He was proud of himself and of what he had just accomplished. He had been able to display his strength and his command of the situation. Jesus knew the inherent dangers in accomplished and forceful leadership. So again, as at the Last Supper, he, the Lord and Master, gave the example. He quietly went about the humble tasks of cook and server. He turned the fish on the coals, made sure the bread was done, and then with his own hands he served each of his disciples the fresh-baked bread and the roasted fish. As the Lord served Peter, some of the same emotions that welled up at the Last Supper, when the Master knelt at his feet, again stirred in his breast. But Peter had learned. He knew he had to be served, nourished, and cared for by the Master if he himself was going to be able not only to be a disciple but also to serve the other disciples in the stead of the Master. Peter was ready to be restored to apostolic leadership. For many of us, especially those of us whose lives are about ministry, it is oftentimes very difficult to let others, and even the Lord himself, minister to us. But no one can minister well if he has not first been ministered unto. The best nurses are those who have been patients. The best superiors were good subjects. A good spiritual father always has a spiritual father.

After the meal was complete, Jesus looked Peter in the eye and said very simply and very directly, "Simon son of John, do you love me more than these others do?" It was a very testing question indeed. For Jesus didn't simply ask, "Do you love me?" but "Do you love me more than these others do?" Simon was being called to a special role, a special responsibility within the apostolic community of disciples. A wiser, humbler Peter answered, "Yes, Lord, *you know* that I love you." Peter trusted more in Jesus' knowledge of him than in his own knowledge of himself. And Jesus commissioned him, "Feed my lambs." Then he asked him a second time, "Simon son of John, do you love me?" Again Peter answered in the same humble way, "Yes, Lord, you know I love you." And Jesus commissioned him, "Look after my sheep." Tradition has understood the different responses of Jesus here to indicate the commissioning of Peter not only to watch over the lambs—the universal flock of disciples—but also the sheep—those who would be the more mature and responsible disciples, the other shepherds, those called to apostolic ministry.

But then Jesus went on to ask a third time, "Simon son of John, do you love me?" Peter was upset that Jesus asked him a third time. It could not help bringing back to him the fact that, as Jesus had foretold, he had denied Jesus three times. Moreover, the word Jesus used this third time for "love," at least in Saint John's Greek, is not the one that connotes the preferential love of charity, but rather the personal, human affection that binds together lovers. Jesus was giving Peter the opportunity for complete restoration. Peter was deeply moved. He realized the folly of his presumptuousness at the Last Supper: "Even if I have to die with you, I will never disown you." With great humility and a certain anguish of spirit, realizing his own possible lack of self-knowledge, he cries, "Lord, you know everything; you know that I love you." And again he is commissioned to feed the sheep.

The restoration is now complete. The man who, when caught up in the emotions of the moment and acting out of reaction, had denied the Lord three times, has been called to respond three times from the depths of his being, those depths that we know when we know ourselves in the knowledge of God, a knowledge that is gained only by deep prayer. The man who had been called to be a disciple, to apostolic ministry, and to apostolic leadership was now restored not only to full discipleship and apostolic mission but to his role of apostolic leadership, the responsibility to care not only for the lambs but also for the sheep—the shepherds of the flock.

When we fail the Lord and turn back to him in repentance, his forgiveness is complete and immediate. But as a loving Master and a good pedagogue, he knows that it is far better for us if in some way we have to work at the restoration. And thus his Church has determined that when we have seriously failed the Lord to the extent that our relationship with him has been ruptured and our spiritual life within has been killed, when our sin has been indeed mortal, it is not enough for complete restoration simply to return to the Lord in a personal encounter of repentance and love. We must go through a process of submitting our sinfulness to the ministry of the Church so that we can experience through Christ's minister the laying on of his healing hand and hear the words of pardon and absolution in our ears. If we have received and accepted the call to apostolic mission and then in our weakness have failed and been unfaithful and turned from it, in the time of our repentance we must receive not only the healing forgiveness of Christ but also the absolution of the Church from the censures that we have rightly deserved. These sacramental processes of the Church are not merely outward signs or formalities but graces that help us to experience fully and integrate into our being at every level the fact of our restoration. The Lord who made us knows us through and through, and he knows our need as human beings to experience restoration as fully and integrally as we have experienced our failure and our falls.

With the full restoration of Peter, the apostolic Church was prepared to face the loss of the Master as he ascended on high. It now had a worthy disciple of the Master—one who had been fully chastened by failure and strengthened by the restoring grace of the Resurrection—to accept the responsibilities of leadership in the Church. The Church was now ready for its great epiphany at Pentecost. It was now ready to receive and fulfill the command of its ascending Lord to be "witness not only in Jerusalem but throughout Judaea and Samaria and indeed to the ends of the earth" (Acts 1:8).

The Prophet

Saint Paul has brought out that prophecy is one of the more ordinary gifts that are to be found among the people of God. He lists it along with such gifts as teaching. It is not something as extraordinary as we have tended to think in our more recent history. The popular emphasis on the aspect of prediction of the future has perhaps detracted from the fundamental role of the prophet. His or her role is most properly to proclaim the Lord clearly under the powerful influence of the Holy Spirit. The prophet has had a personal experience of God and interprets this experience in its historical context, and then formulates and articulates that experience for the Christian community. The prophetic word may well address itself to the future, for the call of God in Christ is always a call to that ultimate fullness which is the Kingdom of Heaven. However, in the timelessness of God, that is all "now." "Today, if you hear his voice, harden not your hearts" (Psalm 95:7–8).

When Peter was still acting very much out of his own presumptuous human experience, he proved often enough to be a false prophet. When Jesus foretold for the first time his own passion, death, and resurrection, Peter would have none of it. Later when Jesus foretold Peter's denial, Peter was quick to come forth with his own false prophecy of fidelity even unto death. Happily, in the long run even this prophecy proved to be true.

Peter, very much a man of his times, was interested in prophecy. When Jesus foretold the destruction of the Temple of Jerusalem it was Peter, as spokesman for the others, who asked the Lord, "Tell us when is this going to happen, what sign will there be that all this is about to be fulfilled." When they gathered on Olivet for the leave-taking of the Lord it was the Spokesman of the Twelve who again gave voice to the question that was in the minds of all: "Lord, has the time come? Are you going to restore the Kingdom of Israel?" Jesus replied, "It is not for you to know the times or dates that the Father has decided by his own authority" (Acts 1:6–7). Peter heard this well and kept it in mind. Later, as pastor of the Churches, he would remind all the flock of the Lord that "with the Lord, a day can mean a thousand years, and a thousand years is like a day" (2 Peter 3:8). The time element of a prophecy is not the important thing. Peter, as the universal shepherd, would try to help correct some of the misapprehensions that came from Paul's prophecies of the end times (2 Peter 3:15–16).

If the important thing in prophecy, then, is not the time element, what is? The really important thing is the clear and powerful witness to the ultimate fulfillment of all things in Christ Jesus. When Peter comes into his own with the coming of the Holy Spirit and begins to speak out powerfully in his first discourse in the Temple, he not only gives a prophetic word, he identifies himself with the great prophets of God who went before:

> Now you must repent and turn to God, so that your sins may be wiped out, and so that the Lord may send the

time of comfort. Then he will send you the Christ that he has predestined, that is Jesus, whom heaven must keep till the universal restoration comes which God proclaimed, speaking through his holy prophets. Moses, for example, said: *The Lord God will raise up a prophet like myself for you, from among your own brothers; you must listen to whatever he tells you. The man who does not listen to that prophet is to be cut off from the people.* In fact, all the prophets that have ever spoken, from Samuel onwards, have predicted these days. [Acts 3:19–24]

As an old man writing his final word to the Churches, Peter continues in this same prophetic vein:

> You did not see him, yet you love him; and still without seeing him, you are already filled with a joy so glorious that it cannot be described, because you believe; and you are sure of the end to which your faith looks forward, that is, the salvation of your souls.
>
> It was this salvation that the prophets were looking and searching so hard for; their prophecies were about the grace which was to come to you. The Spirit of Christ which was in them foretold the sufferings of Christ and the glories that would come after them, and they tried to find out at what time and in what circumstances all this was to be expected. It was revealed to them that the news they brought of all the things which have now been announced to you, by those who preached to you the Good News through the Holy Spirit sent from heaven, was for you and not for themselves. Even the angels long to catch a glimpse of these things. [1 Peter 1:8–12]

That Spirit lodges in the heart of every disciple of Christ and proclaims powerfully to him, and invites him to proclaim to others, the coming fullness, the sure hope we have in the Lord Jesus as our Master, and in our fidelity to him.

However, Peter gives us a wise precautionary note in regard to the prophetic spirit that lies within us: "You will be right to depend on prophecy and take it as a lamp for lighting a way through the dark until the dawn comes and the morning star rises in your minds. At the same time, we must be most careful to remember that the interpretation of scriptural prophecy is never a matter for the individual. Why? Because no prophecy ever came from man's initiative. When men spoke for God it was the Holy Spirit that moved them" (2 Peter 1:19–21).

The sureness of prophecy comes from its adherence to the common teaching and expectations of the whole Christian community. Any prophetic word that is at odds with such teaching is not authentic.

We do find in the final words of Peter a prophecy that speaks with a special power to us in our times. For it seems to be a clear prophecy of that which we dread, a nuclear holocaust. "By the same word, the present sky and earth are destined for fire . . . The Day of the Lord will come like a thief, and then with a roar the sky will vanish, the elements will catch fire and fall apart, the earth and all that it contains will be burnt up. . . . the sky will dissolve in flames and the elements melt in the heat" (2 Peter 3:7–12).

But Peter goes immediately on to say, "What we are waiting for is what he promised: the new heavens and new earth, the place where righteousness will be at home" (2 Peter 3:13). As terrible as is the prophecy of such a holocaust—and we can hope and pray that it will be averted by our due conversion and repentance—yet it is the role of the true disciple of

Christ to bring hope that can go even beyond nuclear holocaust. Whether this earth is to be destroyed by fire or not, we know that in the end the transforming power of Christ will prevail, and there will be "new heavens and a new earth."

The function of the prophet may all too often be an unpopular one of speaking the truth in justice and calling to repentance. We can remember how poor Jonah, when called to such a prophetic mission, took a boat and sailed in the opposite direction. It was only by most extraordinary interventions of Providence that he was brought back to his prophetic task. We can also remember how fruitful was his prophetic word. It brought a city to repentance and salvation. By speaking out of the fullness of the truth that we have received in the experience of the risen Christ, we can bring the greatest hope our world has to escape the holocaust. It is only when we learn to put our trust in the Lord our God rather than in the false idols of arms and nuclear weapons that we can hope to come to a new fellowship among the children of God which will enable us to lay aside our arms and build together, in trust, a human community that will indeed under God create "new heavens and a new earth."

The challenge to us as disciples of Christ in our prophetic role is to discern how we can not only enter fully into this perspective but so live it that our lives are a clear prophetic witness to our fellows. Each of us under the guidance of the Spirit and the ecclesial community will be led to that witness which is appropriate to us in our particular roles among the people of God. While we seek to live out our Gospel witness for peace and the Kingdom of God, we will need to trust and support our brothers and sisters and respect their particular witness even if it is quite different from ours and perhaps difficult for us to understand. All true disciples of Christ are bonded in a common concern for peace on earth and good will among the children of the Father. In this community of concern we have a bonding far deeper and more significant than any of the differences we perceive in the way we concretely express this concern. The multiple expressions only ensure that all persons of good will can receive the common witness of the disciples of Christ, the Prince of Peace.

The Cost of Discipleship

To put it very simply and directly, the cost of discipleship is nothing less than everything, all that we are and all that we have. A disciple to be a true disciple must bring to his Master his whole self and all the potential of his life. Jesus had said very explicitly, "If anyone wants to be a follower of mine, let him renounce himself and take up his cross every day and follow me" (Luke 9:23). We don't take up that cross just to carry it, but to be with Christ crucified on it. He did say, "A man can have no greater love than to lay down his life for his friends" (John 15:13). But he gave us a new commandment—not a counsel, not a bit of advice—but a commandment: "Love one another as I have loved you." And how did he love us? He loved us to the extent of giving his very life for us. To fulfull the commandment of Christ, to be his disciples, we must give our whole selves to him, and to each other for love of him, to do always the things that please the Father.

When Peter wrote to "all those living among the foreigners in the Dispersion of Pontus, Galatia, Cappadocia, Asia and Bithynia," he told them that they would "for a short time have to bear to be plagued with all sorts of trials" (1 Peter 1:6). He knew whereof he spoke. He knew that faith has to be "tested and proved like gold" (1 Peter 1:7). He had before himself the example of Christ: "He was insulted and did not retaliate with insults; when he was tortured he made no threats" (1 Peter 2:23). "Anyone who in this life has bodily suffering has broken with sin, because for the rest of his life on earth he is not ruled by human passions but only by the will of God" (1 Peter 4:1–2).

> My dear people, you must not think it unaccountable that you should be tested by fire. There is nothing extraordinary in what has happened to you. If you can have some share in the sufferings of Christ, be glad, because you will enjoy a much greater gladness when his glory is revealed. It is a blessing for you when they insult you for bearing the name of Christ, because it means that you have the Spirit of glory, the Spirit of God resting on you. . . . If anyone of you should suffer for being a Christian, then he is not to be ashamed of it; he should thank God that he has been called one. [1 Peter 4:12–16]

This is the way of true discipleship.

Discipleship certainly cost Peter. It cost him a settled home and family. "The Son of Man has nowhere to lay his head" (Luke 9:58). When Peter accepted the invitation to follow his Master, he too no longer had whereon to lay his head.

It cost Peter his illusions and his self-pretence. How often do we hear the disciples bickering among themselves as to who is the greatest, who should have the first place, who should sit at the right and the left of the Lord. And Jesus cut through all of that by example and the affirmation that he who is the greatest should be among his brethren as the very least. When Peter was so pretentious as even to rebuff the Master, he was quickly put in his place as being one of Satan's. When he had the audacity to speak for the Master when he was not properly authorized to do so, he was simply told to "go fish." When he was so cocksure about his loyalty, he had to hear a cock chant his weakness, the signal for a loving glance that would burn into his very heart and bring forth searing tears that would burn their way down his cheeks, bringing about the cauterization of his pride and a conversion to a new life.

Discipleship cost Peter his freedom. More than once he would know the darkness of sitting in a prison cell.

> They arrested them [Peter and John], but as it was already late, they held them till the next day. [Acts 4:3]
>
> Then the high priest intervened with all his supporters from the party of the Sadducees. Prompted by jealousy, they arrested the apostles and had them put in the common jail. [Acts 5:17–18]
>
> It was about this time that King Herod started persecuting certain members of the Church. He beheaded James the brother of John, and when he saw that this pleased the Jews he decided to arrest Peter as well. This was during the days of Unleavened Bread, and he put Peter in prison, assigning four squads of four soldiers each to guard him in turns. Herod meant to try Peter in public after the end of Passover week. All the time Peter was under guard the Church prayed to God for him unremittingly.
>
> On the night before Herod was to try him, Peter was sleeping between two soldiers, fastened with double chains, while guards kept watch at the main entrance to the prison. Then suddenly the angel of the Lord stood there, and the cell was filled with light. He tapped Peter on the side and woke him. "Get up!" he said, "Hurry!"—the chains fell from his hands. The angel then said, "Put on

your belt and sandals." After he had done this, the angel next said, "Wrap your cloak round you and follow me." Peter followed him, but had no idea that what the angel did was all happening in reality; he thought he was seeing a vision. They passed through two guard posts one after the other and reached the iron gate leading to the city. This opened of its own accord; they went through it and had walked the whole length of one street when suddenly the angel left him. It was only then that Peter came to himself. "Now I know it is all true," he said. "The Lord did really send his angel and has saved me from Herod and from all that the Jewish people were so certain would happen to me."

As soon as he realized this he went straight to the house of Mary the mother of John Mark, where a number of people had assembled and were praying. He knocked at the outside door and a servant called Rhoda came to answer it. She recognized Peter's voice and was so overcome with joy that, instead of opening the door, she ran inside with the news that Peter was standing at the main entrance. They said to her, "You are out of your mind," but she insisted that it was true. Then they said, "It must be an angel!" Peter, meanwhile, was still knocking, so they opened the door and were amazed to see that it really was Peter himself. With a gesture of his hand he stopped them talking, and described to them how the Lord had led him out of prison. He added, "Tell James and the brothers." Then he left and went to another place. [Acts 12:1–17]

We can imagine how Peter was feeling at this time. James had been his companion, his fellow worker, his partner on the Sea of Galilee, and his partner in the adventures of life. Together they had gone to seek and search. They had found John the Baptizer. Then they found Christ. Now James was gone. He had been cruelly beheaded. Then Peter was seized, and there was no doubt about what the plans were in his regard. Have you ever thought how it would feel to sit hour after hour, contemplating the fact that you were shortly to have your head cut off? Peter knew the experience of death row. Disciples live there, too.

In addition, to make matters worse, it was the great Feast of Passover. Everyone outside, at least so it seemed to one peering out through prison bars, was rejoicing, celebrating the feast. Life was going on at a high point. And here was Peter left alone in his cell with no one, it seemed, caring the least about his fate. He was not quite alone. A couple of times already by miraculous intervention he had escaped from a prison cell. This time Herod was taking no chances. He had Peter chained, he had guards posted all over the place. As Peter sat there, his situation seemed desperate indeed.

Sometimes God lets us get pushed completely into a corner, into what seems to be an absolutely hopeless situation, before he steps forward to help us. He does this so that we might more fully realize our need of his help. He is the source of salvation—we can't do it ourselves. In the case of Lazarus, the sisters sent word to Jesus in good time that the brother whom they and he loved was sick (John 11:3). But Jesus tarried in coming. If he healed Lazarus before he died, people could say that his own natural resources had brought him back to good health. If Jesus raised him from dead almost immediately after he died, they could say the death was an illusion; he was only in a deep coma, and Jesus roused him. And so Jesus tarried, and the situation became completely hopeless. "Lord, by now he will smell; this is the fourth day" (John 11:39). Only then did he say to Lazarus, "Come forth!" All saw the glory of God.

If the Lord had kept Peter from getting caught and imprisoned, Peter might have thought that he had eluded his persecutors by using his own natural talents and abilities. Being in prison, reduced to a state of hopelessness, then indeed he, and everyone else, saw that liberation comes from the Lord.

The ultimate release and healing is that of eternal life. In our shortsightedness we do not always see that. We think that the Lord must always come to our rescue here on earth. God has heaven and all eternity in which to respond to the deep aspirations of our prayer. When it seems he is allowing things to deteriorate to their very worst—Peter ultimately was crucified—God is still going to right it all. He will respond to all our deepest aspirations raised to him in confident prayer in the ultimate victory in the Kingdom of Heaven.

For the moment, Peter was free. He hastened to the home of friends. Perhaps this was the same house in which they celebrated the Last Supper and where they sought to hide after the crucifixion. In any case, Peter was not mistaken, there were friends there. "A number of people had assembled and were praying." We see a very agitated Peter, eager to get off the streets, eager to be embraced by the love of the community, pounding feverishly at that door. The prayer inside was going strong and it took time for anyone to hear him. Finally someone did hear, and a servant-girl was sent to see who was there. She recognized Peter's voice, but in her excitement, instead of opening the door and letting the poor man in, she ran to tell everybody that Peter was there. And Peter continued to stand outside, pounding and pounding fruitlessly against the unyielding door, while the people inside, who held him in such love, incredulously debated the meaning of the pounding. Peter experienced here, even if only momentarily, what is often the fate of those who are called to exercise their discipleship through the service of responsibility and leadership. All too often, those who are called to leadership are left out of the warmth of the community. Leaders, carrying the heaviest burdens and most in need of support, are somehow seen to be beyond the ordinary everyday support of the community of brethren. Indeed, they often have to bear the brunt of failing to live up to exaggerated standards that the community sets for them, and they are expected to bear this and everything else with equanimity.

One day I had the privilege of sitting in on a dialogue between one of our Cistercian abbots and a Buddhist abbot from a monastery in Thailand. They were sharing their experiences of the service of abbatial responsibility and authority. The wise old Buddhist abbot, whose name was Achincha, queried the Cistercian abbot: "Do you know what is a superior? Do you know what is an abbot?" "No, what is an abbot?" said the gracious host, giving his guest the space to make the declaration he obviously wanted to set forth. "An abbot is a garbage collector. He is the one into whose lap the brethren can dump all their garbage. And he will carry it away for them."

All too often the Christian community surrounds its leaders with respect, veneration, and a caring love that is expressed in prayer—but unfortunately not expressed in human warmth, compassion, and solidarity. The one who is called to leadership must accept his role and accept this reality. He may do what he can to change it. He may have to create elsewhere the support he needs. But ultimately, in his lonely role as superior or leader, he must find his all in Christ, for whom and in whose name he serves.

At last the door did open and Peter was admitted into the warmth of the community. He could only remain momentarily; he did not want to endanger them. After sharing with them the good news of the powerful intervention of the angel of the Lord—Peter must have relished every detail of the escape—he had to slip away into hiding and exile.

In his discipleship Peter did find a new, deeper freedom that perdured even in the midst of imprisonment and exile. And even in death. But as he found this freedom he found another kind of enslavement, the most beautiful kind there is, the enslavement of love. When we truly love someone, when we truly become the disciple of the Master, our whole life can only be a "yes" to the Beloved. And thus discipleship cost Peter his life.

> I tell you most solemnly,
> when you were young
> you put on your own belt
> and walked where you liked;
> but when you grow old
> you will stretch out your hands,
> and somebody else will put a belt around you
> and take you where you would rather not go.
>
> In these words Jesus indicated the kind of death by which Peter would give glory to God. After this he said, "Follow me." [John 21:18–19]

In his younger days Peter did what he wanted, but in truth he was the slave of his own fears, his own false ego, his own defensiveness and bravado. In his old age, when he came into freedom from all these things, freedom indeed from himself, he became the slave of love. And out of love for his Master he would stretch forth his hands and be led forth from imprisonment to the cross. The man who once was so presumptuous as to rebuke his Master and try to tell him what he should do and how he should behave, in his love had grown so humble that he did not even feel worthy to die as his Master had died. Tradition tells us that in that last hour he begged his executioners to crucify him upside down. Thus Peter hung, and saw with full clarity that as disciples of Christ, our feet are planted in the heavens and everything hangs from the mercy of God.

Epilogue

There is certainly much more that can be said about Peter as a disciple and as a master of discipleship. We have only looked at those texts that specifically speak about Peter, and not even all of them. Any of the texts that speak about the disciples or the apostles as a group will ordinarily include Peter. My primary intention here has been to introduce the perception of Peter as one to whom we can turn to learn how to be good disciples of our Master. He is a model and an inspiration. But he can be more than that.

Peter can be a living teacher. For Peter certainly is not dead; he is very much alive in the Lord. In faith we can come to him and sit with him and let him speak to us through the Scriptures and through the communion of prayer. He can intercede for us in his own prayer, obtaining for us the grace we need to be true and worthy disciples of our common Master, the Lord Jesus.

A few years ago I had the privilege of walking along the shores of the Sea of Galilee. As I looked at the many fishermen there working in their boats or mending their nets or sorting their catch and loading them onto trucks, I wondered how many of them have the same potential as Peter. Any passerby on the shores of the Sea of Galilee in the year 30 would have seen Peter as just one more of the fishermen. He had certain outstanding qualities. He was in some ways an exceptional human being. And yet in the end, if he was outstanding, he was just an outstanding fisherman. He remained a fisherman of the Sea of Galilee.

For a moment, let us turn our glance back upon ourselves. How do others see us? One more worker going about the ordinary everyday task. Oh yes, we have our own particular outstanding qualities. We may be one of the best of our class—but we are still one of the class. Is that what we really want? Is that the way we want to live out our discipleship? Many of the disciples of Jesus, after accepting him as Master, go back to their everyday tasks. They do them with a new depth of understanding and vision. Others working beside them may remark a change; they may be invited to discover its deeper meaning, invited to join them in discipleship. This is the more usual, and a very valid way to follow Christ, to be his disciple. The call to discipleship does not always mean leaving one's home, family, goods, and daily concerns. Rather, it means bringing to them a Presence, a new Spirit.

However, the choice is ours. The Lord does invite all those who wish so to respond to him, to a fuller discipleship in the practice of those qualities of life that have been traditionally called the evangelical counsels. We can embrace a life of more complete obedience to the Lord, committing ourselves to a particular service. We can embrace a new freedom in following the Lord by giving up our possessions and living from the common sharing of the Christian community. We can find a special freedom to be to the Lord by forgoing a home and a family of our own so that the attachment of our life is an attachment to the Lord Jesus, in his love embracing the whole Christian community and the whole human family. We may want to live out these qualities of life as we embrace the Master in the contemplative way of life. We may want to reach out to others and share in the apostolic ministry. To the full practice of the evangelical councils many are called—the Lord gives witness—but few choose this way. Sometimes what holds back young men and women, or older men and women who are thinking of a second or third career, from stepping forward and choosing to follow the Lord in such a relationship is a sense of unworthiness or inadequacy. Our contact with Peter will help us to realize that this is no reason at all. We have such a Master that even the most inadequate, the weakest, the most stupid, the one who has failed abysmally again and again can still be not only a disciple of the Lord, but one with him in his apostolic ministry. Peter assures us of this in the witness of his life and the teaching of his epistles.

Reflection on Saint Peter might also help us to look with greater compassion on the men who have been chosen to be the successors of the apostles, and even that man who has been chosen to be the successor of Saint Peter. There is a certain rightness in our expectation that men called to such a lofty service, to such a close identity with our Master, the Lord Jesus, should be men of exceptional life and perfection. And yet the fact remains that they too, like Peter and like each one of us, are poor, sinful human beings, each with his own weaknesses, his own struggles. Realizing this, we can see their limitations in perspective, and can support them with our loving and compassionate prayer and with a great deal of understanding. We will not expect too much from them, but we will hope for all things for them. For the same Risen Lord who transformed the weak, defensive braggart from the Sea of Galilee into the compassionate father of the whole Christian Church who was ready to show that love greater than which no man can show in the laying down of his life, can transform each of these shepherds until they are true images of the Good Shepherd.

Peter is a source of hope for us precisely because of his weaknesses and his failures. Through these he can give us not only hope—the hope that we too can overcome by that same grace of the Risen Christ—but also joy, as in the realization that our weaknesses and failures can be an instrument in God's hands to create in our hearts a deeper compassion. We can come to realize how it was that the great apostle Paul could glory in his infirmities. We can come to see how for those who love God, all things work together unto good—even our failures and our sins.

In order to facilitate further experience with Peter, I am including in this book an appendix in which I have listed the texts that speak about Simon Peter, as well as those that speak about the apostles and the disciples. When we desire to walk with Peter, we do not want simply to read these texts. First of all, we need to call upon the Spirit who inspired the author of the text, the same Spirit who dwells in the depths of our hearts, asking him to bring alive in us now the message of life that he desired to convey when he inspired the writer. Then let us call upon Peter to intercede for us and be with us as we listen and seek to enter into his experience. We do not want so much to read these texts as to listen. We want to let the sacred writer, let the Spirit, let the Lord Jesus, our true Master, let Peter, our brother disciple, speak now to us with living words. At the end of such an encounter we want to be able to take a word or a phrase or a sentence and carry it with us as the epitome of the Word of Life that we have received. Then we can let our minds return to it again and again, letting it sink down into our hearts, forming them and creating in us that same attitude of discipleship that re-created Peter. This is true *lectio divina*—divine reading—in the sense it has always been understood in our Christian tradition. It is the kind of sacred reading that forms in us that mind which was in Christ Jesus, and makes us his disciples.

Through discipleship, Peter came to true freedom. He no longer needed the bravado of his younger years, the bravado that protected a false ego, for he came to know his own true dignity. He remained always a man of his own people and his own culture. In his public discourses and his epistles he again and again spoke out of the spirit and the letter of the Old Testament. Nevertheless, he came to know that in Christ Jesus we are "members of a chosen race, a royal priesthood, a people set apart" (1 Peter 2:9), that we are "slaves of no one except God" (1 Peter 2:16), that "no one can hurt us if we are determined to do only what is right. If we do have to suffer for being good we will count it a blessing. There is no need to be afraid or to worry. Simply reverence the Lord Christ in our hearts and always have an answer ready for those who ask us of the hope we all have" (1 Peter 3:13–15). In all this Peter had come clearly and joyfully to identify himself as the "servant and apostle of Jesus Christ" (2 Peter 1:1), a true disciple of the Divine Master.

Appendix

To facilitate our further walk with Peter in his discipleship, I am listing here the principal texts that speak of Peter, of the Apostles (or the Twelve), and of the Disciples.

Simon Peter—Cephas

The Call to Discipleship: Jn 1:35–51.
The Call to Ministry: Mt 4:18–22; Mk 1:16–20, 35–39; Lk 5:1–11.
The Call to Apostolic Leadership: Mt 10:1–42; Mk 3:13–19; Lk 6:12–16.
Mother-in-Law: Mt 8:14–15; Mk 1:29–31; Lk 4:38–39.
Jairus' Daughter: Mk 5:21–43; Mt 9:18–26; Lk 8:40–56.
Walking on the Waters: Mt 14:22–33; Mk 6:45–52; Jn 6:16–21.
Profession of Faith: Jn 6:67–71.
Peter Questions Jesus: Mt 15:15; 18:21–22; 19:27–30; Mk 10:28–31; 11:20–25; 13:3; Lk 12:35–48; 18:28–30.
Caesarea Philippi: Mt 16:13–23; Mk 8:27–33; Lk 9:18–22.
Transfiguration: Mt 17:1–13; Mk 9:2–8; Lk 9:28–36.
The Temple Tax: Mt 17:24–27.
Last Supper: Lk 22:7–13, 31–38; Jn 13:2–38; Mk 14:12–16.

Gethsemane: Mt 26:30–46; Mk 14:26–42; Lk 22:40–46; Jn 18:1–11.
Denial: Mt 26:57–75; Mk 14:53–72; Lk 22:54–62; Jn 18:15–27.
Resurrection: Mk 16:1–8; Mt 28:1–8; Lk 24:1–12, 33–35; Jn 20:1–10.
Restoration: Jn 21:1–23.
Election of Matthias: Acts 1:12–26.
Pentecost: Acts 2:1–41.
Cure of the Lame Man: Acts 3:1–4:22.
Ananias and Sapphira: Acts 5:1–11.
Confirmation Tour: Acts 8:14–17.
Cures: Acts 5:12–16; 9:32–35.
Cornelius: Acts 10:1–11:18.
Deliverance: Acts 12:1–19.
Council of Jerusalem: Acts 15:1–29.
Paul on Peter: Galatians 1:11–24; 2:1–14; 1 Cor 9:1–5; 15:3–8.
First and Second Epistles of Peter.

The Twelve Apostles

With Jesus: Mk 11:11; Lk 8:1.
Question Jesus: Mk 4:10–12.
Mission: Mk 6:7–13; Lk 9:1–6; Acts 2:42–43; 4:32–37; 5:12.
The Loaves and Fishes: Mk 6:30–44; Mt 14:13–21; 15:32–39; Lk 9:10–17; Jn 6:1–13.
Jealousy: Mt 20:24–28; Mk 9:33–37; Lk 9:46–48.
Increase Our Faith: Lk 17:5–6.
Prediction of the Passion: Mt 20:17–19; Mk 10:32–34; Lk 18:31–34.
Last Supper: Mk 14:17–21; Lk 22:14–18; Mt 26:17–25.
Resurrection: Lk 24:9–11.
Ascension: Acts 1:1–14.

Arrest: Acts 5:17–42.
Ordaining Deacons: Acts 6:1–6.
Courage: Acts 8:1.
Reward: Lk 22:28–30; Rev 18:20; 21:14.
Foundations of the Church: Ephesians 2:20–22.

Disciples

With Jesus: Mt 5:1; Mk 3:7–9; 4:34; 6:1; 8:14–21; 10:13–16, 46; 11:14; 12:41–44; 13:1; Lk 6:17–49; 7:11–17; 8:22–25; Jn 3:22; 4:27–38; 11:54.
Questioning Jesus: Mt 13:10–17, 36–43; 17:19–20; 18:1–4; 23:3–44; Mk 10:10; Lk 8:9–10; Jn 9:2; 16:17–19.
Conditions for Discipleship: Mt 8:18–22; 16:24–28; Mk 8:34–38; 10:23–27; Lk 12:22–32; Jn 8:31–32; 13:35; 15:1–8.
True Kinsmen: Mt 12:46–50.
A New Law: Mt 12:1–8; 15:1–14; Mk 7:1–23; Lk 6:1–5.
Prayer: Lk 11:1–13.
Fasting: Mk 2:18–22.
Mission: Lk 10:1–24.
Healing Ministry: Mk 9:14–29; Lk 9:37–43; Mt 17:14–20.
Children: Mt 19:13–15; Mk 10:17–22; Lk 18:15–17.
Sinners: Mk 2:15–17, 23–28; Mt 9:10–13; 12:1–8; Lk 5:29–32; 6:1–5.
Cana: Jn 2:1–11.
Calming the Storm: Mt 18:23–27; Mk 4:35–41; Lk 8:22–25.
Canaanite Woman: Mt 15:21–28.
Raising of Lazarus: Jn 11:1–44.
Anointing of Jesus: Mt 26:6–13; Mk 14:3–9; Jn 12:1–8.
Palm Sunday: Mt 21:1–11; Mk 11:1–11; Lk 19:28–40; Jn 12:12–19.

Eucharist: Mt 26:26–29; Mk 14:22–25; Lk 22:19–20; 1 Cor 11:23–25.
Resurrection: Jn 20:19–23.
Persecution: Acts 9:1–2.
Christians: Acts 11:26.

DATE DUE

FEB 30 1990			

AN UNKINDNESS OF RAVENS

Also by RUTH RENDELL
in Thorndike Large Print

ONE ACROSS, TWO DOWN
THE LAKE OF DARKNESS
THE TREE OF HANDS

Chief Inspector Wexford Novels

NO MORE DYING THEN
MURDER BEING ONCE DONE
SOME LIE AND SOME DIE
SPEAKER OF MANDARIN

Short stories

THE FEVER TREE

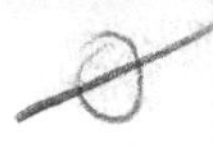

Ruth Rendell

AN UNKINDNESS OF RAVENS

A New Inspector Wexford Mystery

THORNDIKE PRESS • THORNDIKE, MAINE

Library of Congress Cataloging in Publication Data:

Rendell, Ruth, 1930–
An unkindness of ravens.

(A New Inspector Wexford mystery)
1. Large type books. I. Title. II. Series:
Rendell, Ruth, 1930– . New Inspector Wexford mystery.
[PR6068.E63U5 1986] 823'.914 85-24493
ISBN 0-89621-684-5 (alk. paper)

Large Print edition available through arrangement with Pantheon books, New York.

Cover design by Mimi Harrison.

For Sonia and Jeff with love

1

She was a neighbor. She was an acquaintance of Dora's and they spoke if they met in the street. Only this time there had been more to it than passing the time of day.

"I said I'd tell you," Dora said. "I said I'd mention it. She had that strange look she sometimes has and, to tell you the truth, I was awfully embarrassed."

"What did she say?" Wexford asked.

" 'Rod's missing' or 'Rod's disappeared' – something like that. And then she asked me if I'd tell you. Because of who you are, of course."

Detective chief inspectors have better things to do with their time than waste it listening to the complaints of women whose husbands have run off with other women. Wexford hadn't been in the house five minutes before he decided that was what had happened. But she was a neighbor. She lived in the next street to his. He ought to be glad really, he thought, that it hadn't the makings of a case for him to investigate.

His house and this one had been built at the same time, in the mid-1930s when Kingsmarkham was growing out of being a village. And structurally they were much the same house, three bedrooms, two receptions, kitchen, bathroom, and downstairs loo. But his was a home, comfortable and full of lovingly collected things, and this was – what? A shelter to keep the rain off, a place where people could eat, sleep, and watch television. Joy Williams took him into the front room that she called the lounge. There were no books. The carpet was a square surrounded by mustard yellow vinyl tiles and the furniture a three-piece suite covered in grainy, mustard-colored synthetic leather. The 1935 fireplace, which in his house had been replaced by one of York stone, accommodated an electric fire of complicated design, part Regency, part medieval, and with a portcullis effect at the front. Above it hung a mirror framed in segments of green and yellow frosted glass, a fine specimen of Art Deco if you liked that sort of thing. The only picture was a composition in colored silver paper of two cats playing with a ball of wool.

"She's rather a colorless person," Dora had said. "Doesn't seem interested in anything and always seems depressed. I don't suppose living with Rodney Williams for twenty years has done much for her."

Joy. Dora had said rather apologetically that it was a misnomer. She was a woman whose whole self had turned gray, not just her hair. Her features had once been good, were probably still good, only her awful complexion, lined, pitted, pinkish-gray, rough, and worn, masked them. Apparently she was forty-five but she looked ten years more. Up until his arrival she had been watching television and the set was still on, though with the sound turned off. It was the biggest set Wexford had ever seen, at any rate in a domestic setting. He guessed she spent a fair proportion of her time watching it and perhaps felt uneasy when the screen was blank.

There was no seat in the room that did not face it. He sat on the end of the sofa at an angle, turning his back. Joy Williams's eyes flickered over the flashing figures of skaters taking part in some contest. She sat on the extreme edge of her chair.

"Did your wife tell you what I . . . ?"

"She said something." He interrupted to save her the embarrassment he could see already mottling her nose and cheeks with dull red. "Something about your husband being missing."

Joy Williams laughed. It was a laugh he was to hear often and get to know, a harsh cackle. There was no humor in it, no gaiety, no amusement. She laughed to hide emotion or because she knew no other way of showing it. The hands in her lap stretched and clenched. She wore a very wide, heavily chased platinum or white-gold wedding ring with an even more ornate platinum or white-gold engagement ring containing amid the pits and pyramids a miniscule diamond.

"He went on a trip to Ipswich and I haven't seen him since."

"Your husband's a sales representative, I think Dora said."

"With Sevensmith Harding," she said. "The paint people."

She need not have added that. Sevensmith Harding were probably the biggest suppliers to builders' merchants and home decorating retail stores in the south of England. Sevenstar matte and silk emulsion coated a million walls, he thought, between Dover and Land's End. He and Dora had just had their second bedroom done up in it, and if he wasn't much mistaken the paintwork in Mrs. Williams's own hall was the newest shade in Sevenshine non-drip high gloss, Wholewheat.

"He covers Suffolk for them." She began pushing the rings up and down.

"It was last Thursday he went – well, yesterday week. It's the twenty-third now, that must have been the fifteenth. He said he was going to Ipswich to stop the night and start first thing in the morning."

"What time did he leave?"

"It was evening time. About six. He'd been home all afternoon."

It was at this point that Wexford had his thought about the other woman. It would be a good three-and-a-half-hour-run from Kingsmarkham to Ipswich even via the Dartford Tunnel. A salesman who was legitimately going to drive to Suffolk and could have started at four instead of six would surely have done so.

"Where did he stay in Ipswich? At a hotel presumably?"

"A motel. Outside Ipswich, I think."

She spoke listlessly, as if she knew little about her husband's work and took no interest in it. The door opened and a girl came in. She stopped on the threshold and said, "Oh, sorry."

"Sara, what time did Dad go when he left?"

"Around six."

Mrs. Williams nodded. She said, "This is my

daughter Sara," pronouncing the name so that the first syllable rhymed with "car."

"I believe you've a son too?"

"Kevin. He's twenty. He's away at university."

The girl stood with her arms over the back of the yellow plastic armchair no one was sitting in, her eyes fixed on her mother in a more or less neutral way, though one that tended towards the hostile rather than the friendly. She was very slender, fair, with the face of a Renaissance painter's model, small-featured, with a high forehead and a secretive look. Her hair was exceptionally long, reaching almost to her waist, and with the rippling appearance hair has which is usually done up in plaits. She wore jeans and a tee-shirt with a design on it of a raven and the letters ARRIA superimposed over it.

She picked up a photograph in a chrome frame off the only table in the room, a bamboo affair with a glass top almost hidden by the sofa back. Passing it to Wexford, she stuck her thumb at the head of the man sitting on a beach with a teenage boy and a girl who was herself five years before. The man was big, tall, but out of condition and running to fat around his middle. He had a huge, domed forehead. His features, perhaps because they were dominated by this bare dome, looked insignificant and crowded together, the mouth a lipless slit stretched into a smile for the camera.

Wexford handed it back to her. She replaced it on the table, let her eyes linger on her mother for a moment, a curious, faintly contemptuous look, and walked out of the room. He heard her feet going upstairs.

"When did you expect your husband to come back?"

"The Sunday night, he said. I didn't think much about it when he didn't. I thought he'd stayed another night and he'd be back Monday, but he wasn't and he never phoned."

"You didn't phone the motel yourself?"

She looked at him as if he had proposed to her some gargantuan and complex task quite beyond her capacity, writing a fifty-thousand-word thesis perhaps or devising a computer program.

"I wouldn't do that. I mean, it's a long-distance call. I haven't got the number anyway."

"Did you do anything?"

She laughed the dry humorless cackle. "What could I do? Kevin was home for the weekend but he went back to Keele on the Sunday." She spoke as if action in such a matter could be taken only by a member of the male sex. "I knew I'd have been let know if he'd had an accident. He's got his name on him, his bank card and his checkbook and ever so many things with his name on."

"You didn't phone Sevensmith Harding, for instance?"

"What good would that have done? He never went in there for weeks on end."

"And you haven't heard a word from him since? For – let's see – eight days, you've had no indication where he might be?"

"That's right. Well, five days. I expected him to be gone the first three."

He would have to ask it. After all, she had called him in. As a neighbor to confide in certainly, but primarily as a policeman. Nothing he had heard so far made him feel even a preliminary inquiry into Rodney Williams's whereabouts was called for. Looking at Mrs. Williams, the daughter, the set-up, he could only wonder with an unkindness he would never openly have expressed even to Dora why the man had stayed so long. He had run off with another woman, or run off *to* another woman, and only cowardice was holding him back from writing the requisite letter or making the obligatory phone call.

"Forgive me, but is it possible your husband could be –" he sought for a word and came out with a mealy-mouthed one he despised "– friendly with some other woman? Could he have been seeing another woman?"

She gave him a long, cold, unshocked look. Whatever she might say, Wexford could tell his suggestion had already crossed her mind and done more than cross her mind. There was something in that look which told him she was the sort of woman who made a point, a principle almost, of avoiding admitting anything unpleasant. Push it away, suppress it, get out of the habit of thinking, don't wonder or think or speculate, for that will make you unhappy. Don't think, don't wonder, turn on the telly and in mindless apathy stare at the screen until it's time for bed and the doctor's little Mogadon that comes on a permanent prescription you pick up at reception.

Of course, he might be doing her an injustice. All this was only in his imagination. "It's just a possibility," he said. "I'm sorry I had to suggest it."

"I don't know what he does when he's away days and nights on end, do I? All our married life he's been away selling as much as he's been home. I don't know what floozies he's had and I wouldn't ask."

The old-fashioned word suited the room and Mrs. Williams's gray, Crimplene-clad, scurfy respectability. For the first time he noticed the thick sprinkling of dandruff, like a fall of flour, on the shoulders of her blouse. He had given her a solution which to most women would be the least acceptable, but she, he thought, was relieved. Did she suspect her husband of having been up to something *illegal* so that something *immoral* would be seen as a happier alternative?

You suspect everyone and everything, he told himself. You policeman!

"Do you think we ought to do anything?"

"If you mean by that should you report him as a missing person and the police take steps to find him, no, certainly not. The chances are you'll have word from him in the next few days. If you don't, I think your best course will be to see a solicitor or go to your Citizen's Advice bureau. But don't do that before you've been on to Sevensmith Harding. The likelihood is you'll find him through them."

She didn't thank him for coming. He hadn't even been home yet, he had called on her on his way home, but she didn't thank him or apologize for taking up his time. He looked back and saw her still standing on the doorstep holding the door, a very thin angular woman in a fawn blouse and unfashionably cut dark green trousers with bell bottoms and a high waist. Her front garden was the only one in Alverbury Road with no spring bulbs out, not a narcissus to relieve the bit of lawn and the dark yew hedge.

It was a cloudy evening, bright as noonday still, April-cool. This little honeycomb of streets was like an orchard in springtime, puffs and clouds of pink and white blossom all over the gardens and drifts of petals already lying on the pavements. A great weeping cherry, pink as ice cream, had taken over his front lawn.

His wife was sitting in an armchair placed in much the same position at the same angle to the fireplace as the chair Joy Williams had sat in, in a room of the same size and proportions to the one he had just left. But there the resemblance ended. A log fire was burning. It had been a cold winter and the spring was cold and protracted, frosts threatening nightly to nip that blossom. Dora was making patchwork, a bedspread in blues and reds, all shades of blues and reds in a multiplicity of patterns, and the finished part covered the long red velvet skirt of the housecoat she had taken to wearing in the evenings because of the cold. Her hair was dark and plentiful. Wexford had told her she must be a gypsy to have hair still not gray at nearly sixty.

"Did you see Mike today?"

She meant Detective Inspector Burden. Wexford said no, he had been at court in Myringham.

"Jenny came in to tell me she'd had the results of the amniocentesis. The baby's all right and it's a girl."

"What's amniocentesis?"

"They stick something through the abdominal wall into the womb and take out a sample of amniotic fluid. The fluid's got cells from the fetus in it and they grow them like a sort of culture, I think. Anyway, the cells divide and they can tell if Down's syndrome is present and spina bifida too. And of course they can tell the sex by whether the chromosomes come out XY or XX."

"What a lot you know! Where did you pick up all that?"

"Jenny told me." She got up and transferred the patchwork to the seat of the chair. "They can't do an amniocentesis till the sixteenth week of pregnancy and there's always a risk of losing the baby."

He followed her out into the kitchen. He was more than usually aware this evening of the warmth and light in his own house. It occurred to him that Joy Williams had offered him nothing, not even a cup of tea. Dora had opened the oven door and was looking critically at a steak and kidney pie that was almost ready on the top shelf.

"Do you want a drink?"

"Why not?" she said. "Celebrate Jenny and Mike's healthy baby."

"I'm surprised she took any risk," he said when she had her sherry and he his Bell's and three parts water. "She's very set on having this child. They've been trying for years."

"She's forty-one, Reg. At that age there's also a much higher risk of having a mongoloid baby. Anyway, all's well."

"Don't you want to hear about your Mrs. Williams?"

"Poor Joy," said Dora. "She was rather pretty when I first knew her. Of course, that was eighteen years ago. I suppose he's gone off with some girl, has he?"

"If you knew that I don't know what you roped me in for."

Dora laughed. She had a rich throaty giggle. Immediately she said she knew she shouldn't laugh. "He's such an awful man. You never met him, did you? There's something so secretive and deceitful about him. I used to think no one could be so obviously like that if they really had something to hide."

"But now you're not so sure."

"I'll tell you something I was scared to tell

you at the time. I thought you might do something violent."

"Sure," he said. "I've always been so wild and free with my fists. What are you on about?"

"He made a pass at Sylvia."

She said it defiantly. Standing there in the long red dress, holding the sherry glass, her eyes suddenly wide and wary, she looked astonishingly young.

"So?" His elder daughter was thirty, married twelve years, and the mother of two tall sons. "She's an attractive woman. I daresay men do make passes at her and no doubt she can take care of herself."

Dora gave him a sidelong look. "I said I was scared to tell you. She was fifteen at the time."

The violent feelings she had predicted were there to hand. After all those years. His fifteen-year-old daughter! He resisted the temptation to bellow. Nor did he stamp. He took a sip of his drink and spoke coolly. "And, like a good little girl, she came to mother and told her?"

Dora said flippantly, "Sweet of her, wasn't it? I was touched. I think the truth was, Reg, she was scared stiff."

"Did you do anything?"

"Oh, yes. I went to him and told him what her father was. He didn't know. I don't think there was ever much communication between him and Joy. Anyway, it worked. He made himself very scarce and Sylvia didn't baby-sit for them again. I didn't tell Joy but I think she knew and was disillusioned. Anyway, she didn't adore him any more the way she used to."

"I was adored once," Wexford quoted.

"And still are, darling. You know we all adore you. You haven't forfeited our respect, running after little girls. Can I have some more sherry?"

"You'll have to get it yourself," said Wexford, opening the oven and taking out the pie. "All this drinking and gossiping. I want my dinner."

2

The firm of Sevensmith Harding had been founded in 1875 by Septimus Sevensmith, who called himself a color-man. He sold artists' materials in a shop in the High Street in Myringham. Paints for exterior- and interior-decorating use came along later. After the First World War in fact, when Septimus's granddaughter married a Major John Harding, who left a leg behind him at Passchendaele.

The first great house-building boom of the eighties and nineties was past and gone, the next due to begin. Major Harding got in on it. He began manufacturing in huge quantities the browns and greens dear to the hearts of builders creating the terraces and semidetacheds which were growing in branches and tentacles out of South London. And towards the end of the decade he brought out a daring shade of cream.

Already the company had been renamed Sevensmith Harding. It kept its offices in Myringham High Street, though the factory behind was soon to be moved to sites on distant industrial complexes. With the disappearance of its retail trade the shop as such also disappeared.

The world's paint industry enjoyed a steady growth during the 1960s and early 1970s. It is estimated that close on five hundred companies make paint in the United Kingdom, but the bulk of the sales volume is handled by a few large manufacturers. Four of these manufacturers dominate the British Isles and one of them is Sevensmith Harding.

Today their paints, Sevenstar vinyl silk and Sevenstar vinyl matte emulsion, Sevenshine gloss and satin finish, are manufactured at Harlow in Essex, and their wallpapers, borders, and coordinating tiles at Crawley in Sussex. The head offices in Myringham, in the center of the High Street opposite the Old Flag Hotel, have more a look of solicitors' chambers or the establishment of a very refined antique dealer than the seat of paint-makers. Indeed, there is scarcely anything to show that they are paint-makers. The bow windows with their occasional pane of distorted glass that flank the front-door contain, instead of cans of paint and display stands of delighted housewives with brushes in their hands, a *famille noire* vase of dried grasses on one side and a Hepplewhite chair on the other. But over the door, Georgian in style and of polished mahogany, are royal armorial bearings and the legend: "By appointment to Her Majesty Queen Elizabeth the Queen Mother, Colorists and Makers of Fine Pigments."

The company chairman, Jeremy Harding-Grey, divided his time between his house in Monte Carlo and his house in Nassau, and the managing director, George Delahaye, though he lived in Sussex, was seldom seen in the vicinity of Myringham. But the deputy managing director was a humbler person and altogether more on the level of ordinary men. Wexford knew him. They had met at the home of Sylvia's father-in-law, an architect, and since then the Gardners had once been guests at a drinks party at the Wexfords' and the Wexfords guests at the Gardners'. But for all that Wexford would not have considered himself on the kind of terms with Miles Gardner to warrant dropping in at Sevensmith Harding when he found himself in Myringham at lunchtime to ask Miles out for a drink and a sandwich.

A fortnight had passed since his talk with Joy Williams and he had virtually forgotten about it. He had dismissed it from his mind before he went to bed that same night. And if he had thought about it at all since then it had only been to tell himself that by now Mrs. Williams and her solicitor would be settling things to her satisfaction or that Williams had returned home, having found like many a man before him that domesticity is the better part of economics.

But even if Williams were still missing there was nothing to justify Wexford's making inquiries about him at Sevensmith Harding. Let Joy Williams do that. He wouldn't be missing as far as his employers were concerned. No matter how complex a man's love life he still has to go to work and earn his bread. Williams earned it on too humble a level though, Wexford reflected, for it to be likely Miles Gardner had ever heard of him.

He and Burden had both been at Myringham Crown Court, witnesses in two separate cases, and the court had adjourned for lunch. Burden would have to go back to watch his case – a rather ticklish matter concerning the receiving of stolen goods – through to the bitter end, but Wexford's day, at least as far as appearing in court went, was over. As they walked towards the hotel Burden was silent and morose. He had been like this since they came out of court. If it had been anyone else Wexford would have supposed his mood due to the dressing down, indeed the scathing tongue-lashing, meted out to him by the alleged receiver's counsel. But Burden was impervious to such things. He had taken that sort of stick too many times to care. This was something else, something closer to home, Wexford thought. And now he came to think of it, this, whatever it was, had been growing on Burden for days now, weeks even, a morose, surly misery that didn't seem to affect his work but militated badly against his relations with other people.

He looked the same as ever. There was no sign of anxiety or care in his appearance. He was thin but he had always been thin. Wexford didn't know if it was a new suit he was wearing or last year's cleaned and the trousers nightly pressed in the electric press his wife had given him for Christmas. ("Like those things you get in swish hotels," Burden had said proudly.) It was a happy marriage, Burden's second, as happy as his first. But almost any marriage Burden made would be happy, he had a gift for marriage. He was uxorious without making himself ridiculous. There couldn't be anything in his marriage that was bugging him. His wife was pregnant with a longed-for child – longed-for by her at any rate. Burden had a grown-up son and daughter by his first marriage. Wexford considered an idea that came to him and then dismissed it as absurd and out of character. Burden was the last man to dread the coming child just because he was now in his mid-forties. That he would take in his stride.

"What's wrong, Mike?" he asked as the silence became oppressive.

"Nothing."

The classic answer. One of the cases in which a statement means the precise opposite of what it says, as when a man in doubt says he's absolutely certain.

Wexford didn't press it. He walked along, looking about him at the old market town which had changed so much since he had first known it. A huge shopping complex had been built, and since then an arts center, incorporating theater, cinema, and concert hall. The university term was three weeks old and the place was thronged with blue-jeaned students. But up at this end of the town, where preservation orders proliferated and buildings were listed, things were much the same. Things were even rather better since the local authority had woken up to the fact that Myringham was beautiful and worth conserving and had therefore cleaned and tidied and painted and planted.

He looked into the bow windows of Sevensmith Harding, first at the Hepplewhite chair, then at the vase. Beyond the dried grasses he could see a young girl receptionist talking on the phone. Wexford and Burden crossed the road and went into the Old Flag.

Wexford had been there once or twice before. It was not a place ever to be crowded in the middle of the day. The busy lunch trade went to the cheaper brighter pubs and the wine bars. In the smaller of the lounge bars where food was being served several vacant tables remained. Wexford was making for one of them when he caught sight of Miles Gardner sitting alone.

"Won't you join me?"

"You look as if you're waiting for someone," Wexford said.

"Any congenial company that offers itself." He had a gracious warm manner of speaking that was in no way affected. Wexford recalled that this was what he had always liked about him. "They do a nice prawn salad," Miles Gardner said. "And if you can get here before one they'll send up to the butcher for a filet steak."

"What happens at one?"

"The butcher closes. He opens at two and then the pub closes. There's Myringham for you."

Wexford laughed. Burden didn't laugh but sat wearing the sort of stiff polite expression that indicates to even the most insensitive that one would be happier – or less miserable – on one's own. Wexford made up his mind to ignore him. Gardner seemed delighted with their company and, having bought a round of drinks, began to talk in the easy rather elegant way he had about the new house he had just moved into which Sylvia's father-in-law had designed. It was a valuable gift, Wexford thought, to be able to talk to people, one whom you had only just met and the other a mere acquaintance, as if they were old friends whom you conversed with regularly.

Gardner was a small, undistinguished-looking man. His style was in his voice and manner. He had a much taller wife and two or three rather noisy daughters, Wexford remembered. From the new house and the time it had taken to get itself built, Gardner had moved on to talk of work, lack of work, and unemployment, eliciting mild sparks of interest from Burden, at least to the extent of extracting monosyllables from him. Sevensmith Harding had battled against laying off workers at their Harlow factory and the battle had been won – allowing for the few redundancies which Gardner insisted had been acceptable to the men and women concerned.

"Yes," said Burden. "I daresay."

Always reactionary, he had until a few years back threatened to become unbearably right-wing and Blimpish, but Jenny had reversed the tide. Burden was far more of a moderate now. He did not, as he once would have, launch into a tirade against unemployment benefits, Social Security payments, and general idleness. Or perhaps it was only this depression of his that made him forbear.

"The whole attitude towards work and employment and keeping one's job is changing, I find," Gardner said. He began talking about what he thought gave rise to these new patterns and made it interesting enough. Or so Wexford thought. Burden, eating prawn salad rather too rapidly, kept looking at his watch. He had to be back in court by two. Wexford thought he would be glad to be rid of him for a while.

"Isn't what you're really saying," he said to Gardner, "that, in spite of the threat of unemployment and the inadequacy of unemployment benefits, men seem to have lost that craven fear of losing their jobs they had in the thirties?"

"Yes, and to a great extent, at any rate among the middle class, lost the feeling they used to have that they had to stick in a hated job or career for the rest of their lives just because it's the job or career they went into at twenty."

"Then what's brought this change about?"

"I don't know. I've thought about it but the answers I come up with don't satisfy me. But I can tell you that just as the fear has gone, and the respect for employers because they were employers, so has pride in one's job and the old loyalty to a company. My marketing manager is a case in point. Time was when you could say a man in that position would also be a responsible person, someone you could trust not to let you down. He'd have been proud – and yes, I'll say it, *grateful* – to be where he was and he'd have had a real feeling for the firm's welfare too."

"What's he done?" said Burden. "Decided to change his career in midstream?"

It was said acidulously but Gardner gave no sign of having noticed the edge to Burden's voice and replied pleasantly.

"Not so far as I know. He simply walked out on me. He's on three months' notice, or supposed to be. First we get a phone call from his wife saying he's sick, then not a word until a letter of resignation comes, very clipped and curt, and a note at the bottom –" Gardner looked apologetic and said almost apologetically, "Quite an *insolent* sort of note, saying he'd be in touch with our accounts department about his superannuation."

"Had he been with you long?"

"All his working life, I gather, and five years as marketing manager."

"At least you'll have no difficulty in finding a replacement in these hard times."

"It's going to be a case of promotion for one of our best reps. That's always been Sevensmith Harding's policy. Promote rather than take in from outside. Only usually, of course, we're given a bit more time."

Burden got up and said he must get back to court. He shook hands with Gardner and had the grace to mutter something about its having been good to meet him.

"Let me get you another beer," said Wexford when Burden had left and been described (very much to his surprise) by Gardner as a "nice chap."

"Thanks so much. I don't suppose they'll sling us out before two-thirty, will they?"

The beer came, one of the 130 varieties of "real ale" the Old Flag claimed to stock.

"It's not by any chance my neighbor Rodney Williams you'll be promoting, is it?"

Gardner looked up at him, surprised.

"Rod Williams?"

"Yes. He lives in the next street to me."

Gardner said in a patient tone, "Rod Williams is our former marketing manager, the one I was telling you resigned."

"Williams?"

"Yes, I thought I explained. Perhaps I didn't say the name."

"Somebody," said Wexford, "is getting hold of the wrong end of the stick here."

"It's you," said Gardner, smiling.

"Yes, I expect it is. Somebody has given me the wrong end of the stick. Am I to take it then that Williams wasn't one of your reps and didn't cover the Suffolk area for you?"

"He was once. He did once. Up till five years ago. We kept to our customary policy and when our former marketing manager took early retirement due to a heart condition, we promoted Rod Williams."

"As far as his wife knows he's still a rep. That is, he's still spending half his time selling up in Suffolk."

Gardner's eyebrows went up. He gave a twisted grin. "His private life is no affair of mine."

"Nor mine."

It was Gardner who changed the subject. He

began talking about his eldest daughter, who was getting married in the late summer. Wexford finally parted from him with a promise to be in touch, to "get Dora to give Pam a ring and fix something up." Driving home to Kingsmarkham, he thought for a while about Rodney Williams. There had been no room in his own marriage for alibis. He wondered what it would be like to have a marriage in which a permanent, on-going, five-year-long alibi existed as an integral part of life. Unthinkable. Unimaginable. He stopped trying to identify and thought about it with detachment.

What had happened perhaps was that five years ago Williams had met a girl with whom he wanted to spend time without ending his marriage. Keeping his promotion a secret from his wife would have been a way of achieving this. Probably the girl lived in Myringham. While Joy Williams believed her husband was staying at a motel outside Ipswich he was in reality seeing this other girl, no doubt sharing her home and doing his nine-to-five job at Sevensmith Harding in Myringham.

It was the sort of situation some men chuckle over. Wexford wasn't one of them. And there was another aspect, one that few men would find funny. If Williams hadn't told his wife about his promotion he presumably also hadn't told her about the considerable increase in salary that went with it. Still, there was no more mystery. Williams had written to the company. Joy had phoned with excuses. Back in Alverbury Road Williams was still perhaps managing to shore up a few fragments of deceit against discovery.

It was nine at night and he was still in his office, going through for the tenth time the statements he had taken for the preparation of a case of fraud against one Francis Wingrave Adams. He still doubted whether they would constitute a watertight case and so did counsel representing the police, though both knew he was guilty. On the final stroke of nine – St. Peter's clock had a dead sound too, like St. Mary Woolnoth's – he put the papers away and set off to walk homewards.

Lately he had taken to walking to and from work. Dr. Crocker recommended it, pointing out that it was less than half a mile.

"Hardly worth it then," Wexford said.

"A couple of miles' walk a day could make a difference of ten years' life to you."

"Does that mean that if I walked six miles a day I could prolong my life by thirty years?"

The doctor had refused to answer that one. Wexford, though feigning to scoff, had gone some way towards obeying him. Sometimes his walk took him down Tabard Road past Burden's bungalow, sometimes along Alverbury Road, where the Williams family lived, and there was an occasional longer route along one of the meadow footpaths. Tonight he intended to drop in and see Burden for a final assessment of the Adams business.

But now he began to feel that there was very little left to say about this man who had conned an elderly woman out of £20,000. He wouldn't talk about that. Instead he would try to get out of Burden what was happening in his life to account for his depression.

The Burdens still lived in the bungalow Burden had moved into soon after his first marriage, where the garden after twenty years and more still had an immature look and the ivy which tried to climb up the house had been ruthlessly cut back with secateurs. Only the front door was changed. It had been all colors – Burden was a relentless decorator – but Wexford had liked the rose pink best. Now it was a dark greenish blue – Sevenshine Oriental Peacock, probably. Above the door, now dusk had come, the porch light was on, a lantern of leaded lights in the shape of a star.

Jenny came to let him in. She was halfway through her pregnancy now and "showing," as the old wives say. Instead of a smock she wore a full-sleeved, square-necked dress with a high waist, like the one the woman is wearing in Vermeer's *The Letter*. She had let her golden-brown hair grow and it hung to her shoulders. But, for all that, Wexford was shocked by her appearance. She looked drawn and dispirited.

Burden, having years ago agreed to stop calling Wexford "sir," now called him nothing at all. But Jenny called him Reg. She said, "Mike's in the living room, Reg." and added in a way quite unlike her usual self, "I was just going to bed."

He felt constrained to say he was sorry for calling so late, though it was only twenty past nine. She shrugged and said it didn't matter and she said it in a way which seemed to imply that nothing much mattered. He followed her into the room where Burden was.

On the middle cushion of the three-seater settee Burden sat reading *Police Review*. Wexford would have expected Jenny to have been sitting beside him but she hadn't been. Beside a chair at the far end of the room lay her book face downwards and a piece of white knitting that had a look about it of the knitter's having no enthusiasm for her task. In a glass vase on the windowsill dying wallflowers stood in three inches of water.

"Have a drink," said Burden, laying down his magazine. "There's beer. There is beer, isn't there, Jenny?"

"I don't know. I never touch the stuff."

Burden said nothing. He left the room, went out to the kitchen, and came back with two cans on a tray. Burden's first wife would have said, and Jenny once would have said, that they must have glasses to drink the beer out of. Jenny, languidly sitting down, picking up book and knitting but looking at neither, said, "You can drink it out of the can, can't you?"

Wexford began to feel awkward. Some sort of powerful angry tension that existed between these two seemed to hang in the air like smoke, to get in his throat and give him a choky feeling. He snapped the top off his beer can. Jenny was holding the knitting needles in one clenched hand and staring at the wall. He had no intention of talking about Francis Wingrave Adams in her presence. On other occasions like this he and Burden would have gone into one of the other rooms. Burden sat on the settee, wearing his half-frown. He opened the beer can with a sharp, rough movement and a spurt of froth shot out across the carpet.

Three months before Wexford had seen Jenny soothing and practical when her husband had dropped, not a spoonful of beer, but a bowl of strawberry mousse on the paler newer carpet of the dining room. She had laughed and told him to leave the clearing-up to her. Now she gave a cry of real distress and jumped up out of her chair.

"All right," said Burden. "All right. I'll do it. It's nothing anyway. I'll get a cloth."

She burst into tears. She put one hand up to her face and ran out of the room. Burden followed her. That is, Wexford thought he had followed her but he came back almost immediately holding a floorcloth.

"Sorry about that," he said on his hands and knees. "Of course it's not the beer. It's just any little thing sets her off. Take no notice." He lifted an angry face. "I've made up my mind I'm simply not going to take any notice any more."

"But if she's not well, Mike . . ."

"She is perfectly well." Burden got up and dropped the cloth onto the tiled hearth of the fireplace. "She is having an ideal trouble-free pregnancy. Why, she wasn't even sick. When I remember what Jean went through . . ." Wexford could hardly believe his ears. For a husband – and such a husband as Burden – to make that comparison! Burden seemed to realize what he had said and a dull flush crept across his face. "No, honestly, she's perfectly fit, she says so herself. It's simply neurotic behavior."

Wexford had sometimes thought in the past that if every instance diagnosed by Burden as neurotic were taken as sound, almost the entire population would have to be tranquilized, not to say confined in mental hospitals. He said, "The amniocentesis was all right, wasn't it? They didn't tell her something to worry her?"

Burden hesitated. "Well, as a matter of fact they did." He gave an ugly, humorless laugh. "That's just what they did. They told her something to worry her. You've hit the nail bang on the head. It doesn't worry *me* and I'm the child's father. But it worries her like hell and I'm the one who has to bear the brunt of it." He sat down and said very loudly, almost shouting. "I don't want to talk about it anyway. I've said too much already and I've no intention of saying any more. I feel like learning a formula to explain my wife's conduct and repeating it to people when they first come in the door."

Wexford said quietly, "You can do it extempore for it is nothing but roaring."

He got a glare for that. "I came to talk about Adams. Or are you too preoccupied with your domestic fracas to care?"

"I told you, I'm simply not going to take

notice any more," said Burden, and they talked about Adams not very profitably for the next half-hour.

Dora was in bed when he got home, sitting up reading. While he undressed he told her about the Burdens.

"They're too old to have babies," was all she would say.

"Flying in the face of nature, would you call it?"

"You'd be surprised, my lad. I might. And by the way, Rod Williams hasn't come back. I saw Joy and she hasn't heard a word."

"But I had the distinct impression she'd phoned Sevensmith Harding," Wexford began.

"You told her to, you mean. You told her to phone them and find out if they could tell her anything and she's going to."

That wasn't what he had meant. He got into bed, sure now that he hadn't heard the last of the Williams affair.

3

For more than a couple of weeks now he had been keeping his eye on the dark blue Ford Granada parked outside his house in Arnold Road, Myringham. It had appeared there for the first time soon after Easter. Graham Gee couldn't see it from his front windows nor, because of the tall lonicera hedge, from his front garden. He saw it when he drove his own car out of the entrance to his garage each morning and when he drove it in each afternoon at 5:30.

At first (he told the police) he thought it might have something to do with the boy opposite, the teenage son of the people in the bungalow. But it was too respectable a car for that. Well, it was *then*. Dismissing that theory, he wondered if it belonged to some commuter who was using Arnold Road as a station car park. Arnold Road wasn't very near Myringham Southern Region Station, it was a good quarter of a mile away, but it was probably the nearest street to the station not clogged on both sides with commuters' cars.

Graham Gee began to see the presence of the Ford Granada outside his gate as the thin end of the wedge. Soon there would be a hundred rail travelers' cars parked in Arnold Road. He was not a commuter himself but a partner in a firm of accountants in Pomfret.

Arnold Road was known as a "nice neighborhood." The houses were detached, standing in large gardens. There weren't any rough elements, there wasn't any trouble, except perhaps for the theft of dahlias from someone's front garden the previous autumn. So Graham Gee was suprised to notice one morning that the Granada's hub caps had gone. Perhaps they had always been gone though, he couldn't remember. Still, he knew the wheels hadn't always been gone. The car hadn't always been propped up on bricks. Dirty now, streaked with rain, it sat on its brick supports, looking as if it might after all be the property of the teenager opposite.

He still did nothing about it, though he knew by now that it was there all the time. It wasn't driven there in the morning and taken away in the evening. For a week now it hadn't been drivable. It took the smashing of a rear window to get him to do something.

The rear window had been broken, the front doors opened, and the interior stripped. The radio had been removed, the headrests taken off the front seats, and something dug out of the dashboard, a clock perhaps. Though the boot was open, the thieves hadn't thought it worth their while to help themselves to the snow shovel inside. Gee phoned the police.

There was no need for the police to go through the procedure of tracing the driver through the Vehicle Licensing Department in Swansea, for the vehicle registration document was in the Granada's glove compartment along with a road map of southern England, a ballpoint pen, and a pair of sunglasses.

Vehicle registration documents have named on them the "keeper" of the vehicle, not its owner, a fact which was also of assistance to the police. This one listed the keeper as Rodney John Williams of 31 Alverbury Road, Kingsmarkham.

Why had Williams dumped the car in Arnold Road when Sevensmith Harding's own car park was less than a quarter of a mile away behind the company's High Street offices? That car park was never locked. It had no gates, only an opening in the fence and on the fence a notice requesting "unauthorized personnel" not to park there.

"I don't understand it," Miles Gardner said. "Frankly, we've been wondering what to do about recovering the car but we don't know where Williams is. He didn't mention the car in his letter of resignation. Apparently, wherever he was when he first left, he's no longer with his wife, otherwise we would have tackled her. He's disappeared into thin air. It's a bit much really, isn't it? I gather the car's in a state, not much more than a shell?"

"The engine's still there," said Wexford.

Gardner made a face. They were in his rather gloomy though luxurious office, a room not so much paneled as lined with oak, the decor dating from those between-wars days when hardwood was plentiful. None of your Sevenstar matte emulsion here, Wexford thought to himself.

There were more framed photographs than in the average elderly couple's living room. On Gardner's desk, placed to catch his eye every time he looked up, was a big one of tall Mrs. Gardner and her three girls, all affectionate nestling and entwined arms. The walls were reserved for various groups and gatherings of men at company functions or on sporting occasions. One was of a cricket match with a tall, gangling man going in to bat. Rodney Williams. The high forehead, slight concavity of features that would no doubt show more clearly in profile, the thin mouth stretched in a grin, were unmistakable.

Gardner looked at it dolefully.

"He was a lot younger then," he said. "The company had a crack team in those days." He made as if to take the photograph down, angered no doubt by the sight of the permanently grinning Williams, but seemed to change his mind. "The whole thing's extraordinary. He was very keen on cars, you know, one of those car men. You don't think anything's happened to him, do you?"

The euphemism that always signified death . . .

"If you mean some sort of accident, I don't know but I don't think so. It's more what has he been up to, isn't it?"

Gardner looked mystified.

"It looks to me as if he may have been up to something he shouldn't have been, he's been on the fiddle. Either he decided he'd made enough out of it and was going to call it a day or else something happened to make him think discovery was imminent. Now the most likely place for him to have been cooking the books is here. Do you have any thoughts on that one?"

"He wouldn't have had the opportunity. He never went near any books, so to speak. Do you want me to have our chief accountant up? I mean, as far as I can see, any fiddle he was up to would have to be an expenses fiddle and Ken Risby would be the man to tell you about that."

Gardner made a call on the internal phone. While they waited for Risby, Wexford said, "There is nothing small, portable but of considerable value he could have stolen? No check coming into his hands he could have falsified? No forgery he could have perpetrated?"

Gardner looked simply bewildered. "I don't think so. I'm sure not. I mean, I should know by now. Good God, the man's been gone over three weeks." He jumped up. "Here's Ken now. He'll tell us."

But Risby was not able to tell them much. He was a thin, fair man in his thirties, with a nervous manner, and he seemed as shocked by Wexford's suggestion as Gardner had been. You'd think the pair of them lived in a world where fraud had never been heard of, Wexford thought impatiently, and every businessman was a seagreen incorruptible.

"He was a mite heavy on his expenses sometimes but that's all, that's positively all. He never had the handling of the firm's money. What makes you think he's done something like that?"

"You think about it. Look at it for yourself. For five years the man's been lying to his wife about his position with this firm. What salary was he getting, by the way?"

"Twenty-five thousand," said Gardner rather grudgingly.

More than Wexford had expected, £5000 more. "And lying about that too. You can bet on it she thinks he was getting less than half that. One day he tells her he's going to Ipswich, a place he doubtless hasn't set foot in for five years, and off he goes, dumps his company car in the street, and disappears. Apart from getting the lady he's in cahoots with to phone here and say he's ill and apart from writing his resignation he's never heard from again. And you ask me why I think he's been up to something? Tell me about the man. If he's not a man who'd steal or forge, is there some other disgraceful thing he might have done?"

They looked at him. Having no imagination, they didn't know and couldn't hazard guesses. Wexford had plenty of imagination and very little knowledge of marketing.

"For instance, he couldn't have been selling this paint of yours at prices over the odds and pocketing the difference? Something like that?"

Gardner, who had looked as if he would never smile again, burst out laughing.

"He never actually *sold* anything, Reg. It doesn't work like that. He never handled money. He never handled money in any shape or form."

"You make him sound like royalty," said Wexford. "Anyway, will you, Mr. Risby, have a good look at your books for me, please? Do a supplementary audit or whatever."

"Really not necessary, I assure you, not necessary at all. I'd go into court at this moment and swear there's not a squeak of a discrepancy in my books."

"I hope you'll never have to go into court on this matter, but don't count on it." Risby's eyes opened wide at that one. "And do as I ask and check the books, will you? And now," Wexford said to Gardner, "I'd like to see that letter of resignation Williams wrote to you."

Gardner called his secretary in to find it. Wexford noticed he called her Susan, and, what was less expected, she called him Miles. The letter was typed and by someone not accustomed to frequent use of a typewriter.

Dear Mr. Gardner,
This is to give you notice of my resignation from Sevensmith Harding from today. I am afraid it is rather sudden but is due to circumstances beyond my control. I shall not be returning to the office and would prefer you not to attempt to get in touch with me.

Yours sincerely,
Rodney J. Williams

PS. I will contact the Accounts Dept. about my superannuation refund in due course.

Wexford said, "Everyone in this office calls each other by their Christian names, but Rodney Williams called you Mr. Gardner? Is that right?"

"No, of course not. He called me Miles."

"He doesn't in this letter."

"I took that to be because he thought the occasion demanded something more formal."

"It's a possibility. Don't you find it odd when a man on three months' notice gives you one day's? Wouldn't you have expected a more detailed explanation for common courtesy's sake than 'circumstances beyond my control'?"

"Are you suggesting someone else might have written that letter?"

Wexford didn't answer directly. "I'll take it with me if I may. Maybe have some experts look at that signature. Can you let me have a specimen of his signature? One we *know* is his?"

Nine separate sets of fingerprints had been found on and in the car. These would presumably include the prints of whoever had vandalized it. The others would be Williams's, Joy's, Sara's, Kevin's. Early days yet to ask these people to let him check their own prints against those in the car. A lot of hairs, fair and gray, had been on the upholstery. No blood, of course, nothing dramatic. There was one odd thing, though. On the floor of the boot, along with the shovel, were some crumbs of plaster the lab had identified as either Tetrion or Sevensmith Harding's Stopgap.

It took a few more days to get a verdict on the letter.

A manual portable machine, the Remington 315, had been used to type it. There was a chip out of the apex of the capital A on this machine, a similar flaw in the ascender of the lower-case t and a smudging of the head of the comma. As to the signature, it wasn't Williams's. The handwriting expert was far more categorical than such people are usually willing to be. He was almost scathing in his incredulity that anyone could for a moment have believed that the signature was made by Williams.

When Joy had told Dora of her intention to phone Sevensmith Harding she had followed this up with a request to "send" Wexford round to her house once more. This time Dora had said in quite a sharp way that her husband wasn't a private detective and Wexford, of course, hadn't gone. But Williams's disappearance had stopped being a private matter. At any rate, he thought, he wouldn't be unwelcome at 31 Alverbury Road. The answer to a prayer, in fact. He walked round there in the evening, at about eight.

This time the girl Sara let him in. She spoke not a word but closed the front door after him, opened the living-room door, left him, and went back upstairs.

Joy Williams was watching television. The program was one of those contests in which teams of people go through ridiculous or humiliating ordeals. Men in dress suits and top hats were trying to walk a tightrope over what looked like a lake of mashed potato. Just before the door was opened he had heard her laughing. She didn't turn the set off, only the sound. He thought she looked anything but pleased to see him. Her expression had very quickly become sullen.

Yes, she admitted, they had a joint bank account. Rod was away so much they had had to. Wexford asked her if he might see some recent bank statements.

She hunched herself, arms wrapping her thin body, right hand on left shoulder, left hand with the ugly showy rings on right. It was a habitual gesture with her which a psychiatrist might have said began as a way of protecting herself from assault. She had the green trousers on and a knitted jumper, its shoulders sprinkled with fallen hairs and dandruff.

"How often does your bank send you statements?"

"It's been once a month lately." Her eyes strayed to the silent but tumultuous screen. A contestant had fallen into the mashed potato. "They made a mistake over something and Rod complained, so they started sending statements once a month."

Dr. Crocker had told Wexford of a recent visit to one of his patients, a woman ill with bronchitis. The television had been on in her bedroom, all her six children sitting there watching it. When he tried to examine her she had protested angrily at his request that the set be turned off.

"I pull the plug out now without a by-your-leave," said the doctor. "If the TV's on or their video I don't ask any more, I pull out the plug."

Wexford would have liked to do that. He would have done it if he had had just a fraction more evidence for disquiet over Rodney Williams. It was curious that Joy, who had come close to pestering Dora for his attention, was now making it plain she didn't want him there.

"Will you show me the statements?"

She turned her head reluctantly. "OK, if you want." He had put his request very politely, as if she would be doing him a favor, and she responded as if she was.

It didn't take her long to find the statements. She wasn't going to miss more of her program than she had to. As he began to look at the statements she leaned across and summoned a little sound out of the television, so that shrieks, exclamations, and commentary were just audible. He wondered what could possibly distract her, what real event or shock, and then he knew. The phone bell. Somewhere, elsewhere in the house, the phone began to ring.

She jumped up. "That'll be my son. My son always phones me on Thursday nights."

Wexford returned to the monthly bank statements. Each one showed the sum of £500 paid into the account more or less at the beginning of the month. A salary check apparently. Several objections to that one. Williams's salary had been £25,000 a year and there was no way £500 a month, even after all possible deductions, could amount to as much as that. Secondly, the sum would vary, not be a set round figure. Thirdly, it would be paid in on the same day of the month, give or take a day each way, not sometimes on the first and sometimes on the eighth.

It was evident what had been going on. Williams had another account somewhere into which his salary was paid. From that account he transferred £500 a month into the account he had jointly with his wife. If this was so, and it must be, it was going to be useless asking Joy, as he had intended, if her husband had drawn on their joint account since his disappearance.

Sevensmith Harding would make no bones about telling him where this other account was. The problem would be the intransigent bank manager refusing to disclose any information about a client's account. He looked at the April statement again. Five hundred pounds had been paid in on 2 April. No May statement had yet been sent to Mrs. Williams as May was only half over.

She came back into the room, looking

brighter and younger, her face more animated than he had ever seen it. She had been talking to her son, her favorite.

"I'd like you to give your bank a ring," he said, "and ask them if the usual five hundred was paid into the account at the beginning of the month. Will you do that?"

She nodded. He asked her to tell him about the last afternoon and evening Williams had spent at home. Rod had mowed the lawn in the afternoon, she said, and then he'd taken her shopping to the Tesco discount. She couldn't drive.

"We came back and had a cup of tea. Rod had a sandwich. He didn't want more than that. He said he'd get something on his way to Ipswich. Then he went upstairs and packed his bag and left. He'd be back on Sunday, he said." She gave one of her dull laughs. "And that was the last of him. After twenty-two years."

"What did you do for the rest of the evening?"

"Me?"

"Yes, what did you do? Did you stay at home? Go out? Did anyone come here?"

"I went over to my sister's. She lives in Pomfret. I went on the bus. I had something to eat and then I went to my sister's."

"And Sara?"

"She was here. Up there." Joy Williams pointed to the ceiling. "Studying for her A-levels, I suppose." She made it sound an unworthy, even slightly disgraceful thing for her daughter to have been doing.

There was something wrong with this description of how the evening had been passed, something incongruous, only Wexford couldn't put his finger on what.

"I'd like to talk to Sara, he said.

"Do as you like."

She twisted round in her chair and looked fully at him, the television for the moment forgotten.

"She'll be in her bedroom but you can go up. She won't object." The awful laugh came. "Rather the reverse if I know her."

4

So young Sara, who looked like one of Botticelli's girls, a Quattrocento virgin, had been caught in bed with a boyfriend. Or not in bed, most probably. On the yellow plastic settee or in the back of a car. It was difficult with daughters. You knew what your enlightened principles were but things looked different when it was *your* daughter. Still, that hardly justified Joy's snide insinuation. Wexford, going upstairs, decided that as well as disliking what he knew of Williams, he didn't care for Mrs. Williams either. Not that it mattered whether he liked them or not. It made no difference. Perhaps the woman did have some justification. She was going through a bad time; she, who was surely in the process of losing her man, would feel bitter towards a daughter gaining one. And the discovery of Sara and the boy might have been made very recently.

He knew which bedroom it was because music was coming from behind the door. Rock music of some kind, soft with a monotonous drumbeat. She must have heard his feet on the stairs by now. He had taken care to make a bit of noise, not difficult on the linoleum covered with thin haircord. He knocked on the door.

She didn't say, "Come in!" She opened it herself. Wexford had often noted reactions to a knock at the door. They offered indications of character and motivation. The woman, for example, who calls out "Come in!" is more open, relaxed, and easygoing than she who opens the door herself. The latter will be cagy and reserved. In the thirty seconds or so before she opens the door, what has she put away in a drawer or hidden under a magazine?

He could see that Sara had created the room herself. What attractiveness it had had nothing to do with the furniture, carpet, and curtains provided by her parents. It was the smallest bedroom. Wexford had had an extension built on to his house when the girls were little but this house remained as it had originally been. There would be a large front bedroom for the husband and wife, a slightly smaller back bedroom – in this case for the son – and a tiny boxroom no more than nine feet by seven for the daughter. She had put posters all over the walls, one of a red horse galloping in the snow from the Yugoslav naive school of painting, another of a thin naked black man playing a guitar. Between them hung a tennis racket, a corn dolly, and a montage of Tarot cards. Perhaps the most striking poster was the one that faced the door. A harpy-like creature with the head and breasts of a woman and the body, wings, and claws of a raven clutched at an unfurling ribbon on which was painted the name – acronym? – ARRIA. Wexford remembered the tee-shirt Sara had been wearing when they first met. The raven woman had a face like Britannia or maybe Boadicea, one of those noble, handsome, courageous, fanatical faces, that made you feel like locking up the knives and reaching for the Valium.

Bookshelves that looked as if put up by Sara herself held a paperback *Life of Freud*, Phyllis Grosskurth's *Havelock Ellis*, Fromm, Laing, Freud on the *Wolf Man* and *Leonardo*, Erin Pizzey and Jeff Shapiro on incest and child abuse, but not a single work of fiction. With her tiny radio providing background music, she had been sitting at a dressing table that doubled as a desk, swotting for an exam. It was evidently chemistry. The textbook lay open at a page of formulae.

"We're trying to find your father, Sara. I wouldn't exactly say he's disappeared but he's making himself very hard to find."

She had fixed him with her grave, contained look. He noticed her skin, creamy and smooth like velvet, with a gold dusting of freckles on her small nose. When she opened the door to him she had been holding a green felt-tipped pen in her hand. On the back of the other hand she had drawn a green snake. Teenagers had always drawn on their hands, they had done so when he was in his teens and when his daughters were in their teens, but now some sort of specific fashion for it had sprung up. To have black and red and green drawings on your hands and arms and body was the "in" thing. Sara had drawn with her green pen a spotted snake, not curled round itself but stretched out and slightly undulant, its forked tongue extended.

"Have you any thoughts about where he might be?"

She shook her head. She put the cap on the pen and laid it down.

"Would you like to tell me about the last time you were with your father? Were you here when he left?"

She hesitated, then gave a nod. "It was the second day of term after the Easter holidays. I was late home because I went to the library. They'd got a book in for me, a new book I'd put my name down for, and they'd sent me a card to say it was in." She lifted two books off the stack and handed him one from underneath. She was out to impress and the book was a learned work: Stern's *Principles of Human Genetics*. He didn't take much notice of that but he did look at the date stamp in the back. "I rang the library to renew it," she said defensively. "I couldn't read it in three weeks. It's very difficult." She smiled at last and became at once a beauty. "I'm not saying it's too difficult for me but genetics is an abstruse subject. I've got my A-levels and they have to take priority."

"You're interested in this sort of thing?"

"I've been offered a place in medical school, St. Biddulph's." Crocker had trained there, Wexford recalled. "I shall get it, of course, but in theory it depends on my A-level results." Her tone was such as to show she was in no real doubt that these would meet the standard. "I have to get at least three Bs but an A and two Bs would be better."

She must be a bright girl. A year or two back statistics had been published showing an excess of medical students and that at this rate there would be a surplus of forty thousand doctors by the end of the century. Medical schools were being instructed to raise their standards and cut their intake. So if Sara Williams had been offered a place at the highly prestigious St. Biddulph's . . .

"Your mother and father must be proud of you."

The sweeping glance she gave him told him he had said something stupid or at least wide of the mark.

"I can see you don't know my parents."

"They'd prefer something else for you?"

"I could be a shorthand typist, couldn't I? I could be a nurse. I'd get paid while I was being those things, wouldn't I?" Her voice was full of scorn and anger. "I can't be stopped, though. I'll get a grant anyway. I don't know what I'd have done in olden times."

By "olden times" he supposed she meant the days of his own youth when your parents paid for your education or you borrowed the money or worked your way. Things were different now. A father couldn't put his foot down with the same effect. He could only persuade or dissuade.

"The last time you saw your father," he reminded her.

Her anger had died. She was practical again, crisply reciting facts. But there was something derisive in the way she spoke of her father, as if he were a joke to her – or an organism under a microscope.

"I came in and he was just leaving. I heard him talking to Mum about the route he was going to take. The A26 for Tonbridge, then the Dartford Tunnel on the the M25 and the M25 to the A12, which would take him to Ipswich."

"Why was he telling her the route? Would she be interested? I mean, wasn't it the route he normally took?"

"I said you didn't know my father. I'd say for a start he wouldn't be much concerned about the other person's *interest*. Dad talks a lot about cars and driving, roads, that sort of thing. I'm not interested but he talks to me about it. The car's a person to him, a woman, and she's got a Christian name. He calls her Greta. Greta, the Granada, you see."

"So your father left and your mother went to Pomfret and you stayed here on your own studying?"

Was he imagining that hesitation, that brief, wary flare in her eyes?

"That's right. I don't go out in the evenings at the moment. I haven't time." She smiled again, this time with great artificiality. "I heard they'd found his car."

"In the process of being dismembered for its wheels and its radio."

"Cannibalized," she said, and she laughed the way her mother did. "Poor old Greta."

Could he have a look round the rest of the house? Notably through Williams's papers and clothes? Joy put up no objection. The television clack-clacked through the floor and the pop music thumped and droned through the wall. In the book of rules of human behavior he kept in his head one of the first laws was the one about who got which bedroom. The British middle class mostly lived in three-bedroom houses, one big bedroom, one slightly smaller, one little. In a family of parents, son, and daughter, the daughter invariably got the second bedroom and the son the tiny one, irrespective of seniority. It was one aspect of life (the women's movement might have said if they'd noticed it) in which the female had the advantage over the male. Presumably it came about because girls from the first were conditioned into being more at home, more centered on home things and being confined within walls. In which case the women's movement wouldn't like it so much. But it was the girl in this household who had the smallest bedroom, even though her brother was now away most of the time. Of course, it might be that she had chosen this arrangement, but somehow he didn't think so.

He opened the door of the second bedroom and looked inside. There was a newish pine bedroom suite, two bright Afghan rugs, a fringed bedcover that was recognizably one of Marks and Spencer's designs. It looked as if someone with not much taste or money had done her best to make a "nice" room of it and the sole personal touch its occupant had contributed was to hang a map of the world on the wall opposite the bed.

The main bedroom was like his own in size and proportions. The walls were even painted in the same color as his own, Sevenstar emulsion Orange Blossom. There the resemblance ended. The Williamses slept in twin beds, each narrower than the standard three feet, he thought. He could tell hers was the one nearest the window by the nightdress case on it, quilted peach satin in the shape of a scallop shell. The rest of the furniture consisted of a wardrobe, dressing table, dressing-table stool, chest of drawers, and two bedside tables, all in some dark reddish wood with a matte finish and with rather bright gold chrome handles. There was also a built-in cupboard.

Wexford looked first in the drawer of the bedside cabinet between Williams's bed and the door. He found a box that had once held cufflinks but was now empty, a comb, a tube of antiseptic skin cream, an unused toothbrush, a packet of tissues, a tube of throat pastilles, two safety pins, several plastic collar stiffeners, a half-full bottle of nasal drops, and an empty pill bottle labeled "Mandaret. One to be taken twice daily. Rodney Williams."

In the cupboard part of the cabinet were two paperback novels of espionage, an unused writing pad, a current British passport in the name of Mr. R. J. Williams, a clean handkerchief initialed "R," and two electric shavers.

The wardrobe contained Joy's clothes, a collection that had an unwashed, uncleaned smell about it with a whiff of camphor and some kind of disinfectant. Rodney Williams's clothes were in the cupboard. An overcoat, a sheepskin jacket, a plastic mac, two hiplength showerproof jackets, a shabby sports jacket and a new one, four suits, two pairs of slacks. All the clothes were good, all of much better quality than Joy's. Not a large wardrobe, Wexford thought, looking into the linings of coats and feeling in pockets. In the side compartments were underwear, pajamas, on the floor three pairs of shoes and a pair of sandals. Whatever Rodney Williams had spent his surplus money on it wasn't clothes. Unless he had taken more with him than Joy or Sara knew. Maybe he had secreted a couple of bulging suitcases in Greta's boot during the course of the day.

The dining room, you could see, they hardly ever used. A light-colored polished table stood in the dead center of it with four light-colored wood chairs with moquette seats around it. A sideboard with an empty Capo da Monte bowl on it nearly filled one wall and opposite this was a mahogany roll-top desk, perhaps a hand-down from a parent and certainly the nicest piece of furniture in the house. French windows, at which hung curtains of mustard-colored rep – a favorite shade with Joy Williams – gave onto the back garden, a quarter acre of grass surrounded by close-board fencing and relieved by two small apple trees on which the blossom glimmered palely in the dusk. It didn't look as if the grass, several inches long now, had been mown since Williams did it five weeks before.

The desk wasn't locked. Wexford rolled back the top. There wasn't much inside. Writing paper, not the headed kind, envelopes, a bottle of ink in a cardboard box from which it had never been removed and never would be, a box of drawing pins, a glass jar of gum, a roll of Scotch tape. In one of the drawers was nothing but old Christmas cards, in the other a receipted elecricity bill, a pocket calculator, and a broken ballpoint pen.

If Williams had meant to go away for good wouldn't he have taken his driving license? In Britain a driver is not obliged to carry his driving license with him – though he must be prepared to produce it at his local police station within three days of a police officer's asking him to do so – but would a man drive off to begin a new life somewhere with a new job and perhaps a new woman and leave his driving license behind? Come to that, would he leave his passport behind?

He looked through the pigeonholes but found no checkbooks, used or in use. Joy probably kept hers in her handbag. He went back to her. She was still watching television, and now the program was the everlasting serial *Runway*, in which his daughter Sheila played the stewardess heroine. Had, in fact, played her for the last time the previous week. But this was a secret known to no one but her own family as yet. No newspaper had so far got hold of the story that a major air disaster would in the autumn end the career of Stewardess Charlotte Riley for ever.

Joy Williams didn't know it. If she knew Sheila was his daughter – and surely she must – she gave no sign. He had the curious experience of standing beside her while they both watched his daughter attempting to placate an ill-tempered passenger. Then he did what Crocker recommended – or nearly so. If he didn't go so far as to pull out the plug he did switch off the set. She blinked at him.

"Does your husband possess a typewriter, Mrs. Williams?"

"A typewriter? No."

"Is he still taking Mandaret?"

She nodded, looking at the blank screen as if she expected it spontaneously and without benefit of electricity to spring into cinematic life.

"It's a form of methyldopa, isn't it? A drug for high blood pressure?"

"He's had blood pressure for two or three years."

"I found an empty Mandaret container in his bedside cupboard. I suppose he took a supply with him?"

"He wouldn't forget them. He didn't like to miss a day on them. He always took one when he got up and one with his tea."

"I take it he had a bag with him? A suitcase? Something to put his clothes in?"

Again she simply nodded.

"What was he dressed in?"

"Pardon?"

"What clothes was he wearing when he left here to drive to Ipswich?"

It was plain she couldn't remember. She looked blank – and she looked bored. Wexford understood in that moment that she didn't love Rodney Williams, hadn't perhaps loved him for years. His presence or absence as a life companion were matters of indifference to her but his financial support and the status he gave her were not. Or were her feelings more subtle and diffuse than that? Of course they were. Feelings always are. There is never a simple, clear analysis of a woman's reaction to her husband or his to her.

He pressed the point he had made.

"Sort of fawn trousers," she said, screwing up her face with the effort of it. "Cavalry twill, they're called. A dark blue pullover. Is his raincoat upstairs?"

"A plastic mac?"

"No, he's got a good raincoat. It's nearly new. He must have taken that. I expect he had a jacket in his bag too. He's got a brown suede one."

"Did he like a wet or dry shave?"

"Pardon?"

"Did he use a razor with shaving cream and water?"

"Oh, yes. He couldn't get on with those electrics. He'd tried but he couldn't get on with them."

And that accounted for the Remington and the Phillips upstairs. She was staring miserably at the blank, gray, shiny screen. Wexford felt it was cruel to deprive her of her solace, like keeping a dumb, hungry dog from its plate of Kennomeat. He asked her for her sister's name and address and then he switched the television on again. She looked at him as if she thought him completely mad but she said nothing, and her eyes were compelled back to the screen and to Sheila, dressing now in a hotel bedroom for an evening out with the Boeing 747 captain in Hong Kong.

Wexford walked home, thinking about Williams and money. What had he done with all that money? Even after tax and other deductions, after the stingy allotment to his household of £500 a month, he would have been left with at least £12,000 a year. He'd had a company car. It didn't go on cars. The passport, which was seven years old, showed a single visit to Majorca. It didn't go on foreign holidays. Of course, he had to keep his son Kevin at Keele and pay for his tuition and board. He wouldn't get much of a grant on his salary . . .

And then, suddenly, Wexford understood what had been bugging him for the past hour. It had been a Thursday evening when Williams had left. Kevin Williams always phoned home on Thursday evenings. And that Thursday was certainly the first since he had returned to university after the Easter vacation. Yet his mother, who plainly adored him, who waited excitedly for his call and spoke proudly of his devotion to duty in regularly phoning at that time, had gone out on that particular Thursday evening and for no more pressing or life-enhancing appointment than a visit to her sister.

If she had visited her sister.

And how about his clothes? Was she lying when she said he had taken only a jacket and a raincoat with him? Or didn't she know? Somehow he couldn't imagine Williams leaving his car in Arnold Road and then humping huge bulging suitcases the quarter of a mile to Myringham station. Why go to Myringham anyway, when, if he wanted to catch a train to London, Kingsmarkham station was eight miles nearer?

The following week the clothes, or some of them, turned up.

5

A lonely country road links Kingsmarkham with Pomfret. Once Forest Road, Kingsmarkham, is past, the only houses to be seen are those few up on the hillsides crowned by Cheriton Forest. The forest is always rather dark and forbidding as coniferous forests are. On the horizon stands an obelisk, a needle of stone, placed there by some local magnate a hundred and fifty years ago.

Almost the last building in Kingsmarkham is the police station. On the other side of the High Street Cheriton Lane runs down to the buildings and courts of the Kingsmarkham Tennis Club, and half a dozen other narrow roads compose a small residential web. The gardens of houses in Forest Park back onto open fields, and fields traversed by a footpath lie between the club grounds and the town.

The street lamps stop two hundred yards on the Pomfret side of the police station and after that there is an isolated one to light the bus stop.

Roughly halfway between the towns, at the point of no return, is the bus stop with bus shelter. The shelter was put there because there are no trees at this point to break the wind or provide cover from the rain. And on this night it was raining as it had been for many nights. The fine rain swept across the meadows in gray sheets.

The last bus from Pomfret to Kingsmarkham was due at 10:40. It came ten minutes late, rolling along not too fast through the rain, sending up fountains of spray onto the grass verges. The stop where the bus shelter was was a compulsory one, not a request, so the bus pulled in to make a token stop and prepared to pull out again, for there was no one waiting. A shout from a woman passenger sitting in a front nearside seat alerted the driver. He had already taken off the brake but he put it on again and the bus juddered to a halt.

"There's a person crawling on the pavement!"

Here, where the shelter was, the lay-by was bordered by a few yards of pavement. The driver got down. Two or three of the passengers, disobeying the driver – who was he to tell them? – got down. There was no conductor on those single-deckers. The rain was coming down in torrents, needles of it pounding the surface of the lay-by, the curb, and the sodden bundle that crawled and whimpered with blood coming from its chest.

At first the conductor had thought it a wounded dog. But the passenger was right, it was a man. It crawled up to the conductor and rolled over at his feet.

Next day, on the other side of Kingsmarkham, the Forby side, a firm called Mid-Sussex Waterways began dragging a pond. Green Pond Hall had stood empty for years, but at the end of the previous January a buyer had been found for it and the purchase was completed by April. The grounds contained the pond and a stream, and the new owner intended to turn the estate into a trout farm.

If the proper definition of a lake is a sheet of water covering the minimum of one acre, Green Pond was just too small to fit the requirement. But as a pond it was very large. It wasn't stagnant, for the small fast stream flowed through the middle of it, disappearing into a pipe which passed under a path and gushing out through a spout on the other side to fall away down to the Kingsbrook. In spite of this the pond was shallow and coated with the thick, green slime of blanket weed. The purpose of the dragging was to clean it, increase its depth, and rid the water of the algae Mid-Sussex Waterways believed might be caused by an influx of the nitrates which had been applied as fertilizer to the nearby meadows.

In the net, after the dragging, were found a wire supermarket basket minus its handle, a quantity of glass bottles, jars and light bulbs, the silencer part of a car exhaust system, wood in the form of twigs and chopped lengths, stones among which were flints and chalk pebbles, a rubber boot, a Pyrex casserole dish, chipped and cracked, a metal door handle and lock, a pair of scissors, and a dark burgundy-colored traveling bag.

The bag was coated with green slime and thin, fine-grained black mud, but when the clasps were undone and the zip unfastened it was seen that only water had penetrated the seams of the bag, soaking but hardly discoloring the clothes inside, the topmost of which was a brown suede blouson.

It was a piece of luck, Wexford thought, that William Milvey, the boss of Mid-Sussex Waterways, had found money inside the bag, £50 in fivers rolled up and fastened with a rubber band. If it had contained nothing but clothes, and damaged clothes at that, it was probable he would have tossed it into the pit which had been dug out by a mechanical digger for the purpose of receiving the rubbish caught in the dragnet. Money, Wexford had often noticed, has this kind of electric effect on people. Many a man who thinks himself honest, on finding an object bought with money will keep the object but not the money itself. It is as if the adage "Finding's keepings" applies to things but never to money, which has its own aura of sacredness, of being absolutely the preserve of him who has earned it.

But even so, Wexford might never have heard of the existence of the bag were it not for a kidney donor card which was in the breast pocket of the blouson and which was signed R. J. Williams.

William Milvey knew who R. J. Williams was. He lived next door but one to him in Alverbury Road.

This fact it took Wexford some half-hour to find out. He questioned Milvey thoroughly about the bag. Had he seen it in the pond before he saw it in the net? Well, yes, he thought he had, now Wexford came to mention it. He fancied he had. At any rate he thought he could remember seeing a brownish-red lump of something up against the bank of the pond nearest to the path and the Kingsbrook. No, he hadn't touched it or attempted to pull it out. The dragnet had pulled it out.

Milvey was a shortish, thick-set man with the heavy build and big, spread hands of someone who has done manual work for most of his life. He looked about fifty. The discovery of the bag seemed disproportionately to have excited him – or his excitement appeared disproportionate to Wexford at first.

"Fifty quid in it," he kept saying, "and that good jacket."

"Did you see anyone about the grounds of Green Pond Hall?"

"Some fella up to no good, d'you mean?"

"I meant anyone at all."

"We didn't have sight nor sound of no one."

There might have been marks of car tires on the drive in from the Forby Road or on the track that ran round the lower bank of the pond, the constant rain had turned these surfaces to mud, but any tracks there were had been obliterated by the heavy tires of Mid-Sussex Waterways mechanical digger.

Milvey simply couldn't remember if there had been any tire marks on the track. They had the other man in and asked him, but he couldn't remember either.

"Fifty quid," said Milvey, "and that good jacket. Just chucked away."

"Let me have your address, will you, Mr. Milvey? I'll very likely want to talk to you again. Home or business."

"They're one and the same. I operate from home, don't I?" He said this as if it were a fact he would have expected Wexford to know, and, adding his address, used the same patient, mildly surprised tone. "Twenty-seven Alverbury Road, Kingsmarkham."

"Are you telling me you live next door but one to Mr. Williams?"

Milvey's expression, though bland and innocent, had become a little uncomfortable. "I reckoned you knew."

"No, I didn't know." Vaguely now Wexford recalled reading of a planning application made to the local authority for permission to erect a garage – more a hangar really – large enough to house a JCB in the garden of 27 Alverbury Road. The area being strictly residential, the application had naturally been rejected. "You must know Mr. Williams, then?"

"Pass the time of day," said Milvey. "The wife has a chat with Mrs. Williams. My girl's in the same class at school with their Sara."

"Mr. Williams is missing," said Wexford flatly. "He's been missing from home for the past month and more."

"Is that right?" Milvey didn't look surprised but he didn't say he knew either. "Fifty quid in notes," he said, "and a jacket worth three times that."

Wexford let him go.

"It has to be coincidence," Burden said.

"Does it, Mike? It would be a hell of a coincidence, wouldn't it? Williams disappears because he's done something or someone's done something to him. His overnight bag is dumped in a pond and who should find it but the guy who lives two doors down the street from him? I haven't read any John Buchan for – well, it must be forty-five years. But I can remember in one of his books the hero's car breaks down and the house he calls at for help just happens to be the home of the master anarchist. A bit later on the hit man who's sent to get him turns out to be a burglar he's recently successfully defended in court. Now that's fiction and strictly for persons below fifteen, I'd say. But this that you call coincidence is comparable to those. Have you had any coincidences of that magnitude in your life?"

"Both my grandmothers were called Mary Brown."

"Were they really?" Wexford was temporarily

distracted. "You never told me that before. And did they come from the same part of the country?"

"One from Sussex and one from Herefordshire. I bet you the odds against that happening are a lot longer than against Milvey finding Williams's bag. You look at it and you'll see it's not that much of a coincidence. If it had been buried, say, or stuck in a hollow tree and Milvey had found it, that would be something else. But it was in a pond and Milvey's in the pond-dragging business. Once it got in the pond and the pond was due to be dragged – which whoever put it there wouldn't know, of course – the chances would be that Milvey *would* find it. You want to look at it like that."

Wexford knew there was more to it than that; he couldn't dismiss it in the easy way Burden did. Milvey's behavior had been a shade odd anyway, and Wexford was sure he hadn't told all he knew.

"How long do you think the bag's been in the pond?"

It was on the floor between them, deposited on sheets of newspaper, its contents, which Wexford had already examined, now replaced.

"Since the night he went, I suppose, or the next day."

Wexford didn't go along with that either but

he let it pass for the time being. As well as the brown suede blouson there was a raincoat in the bag, a trendy version of a Burberry, the fifty pounds, a toothbrush, tube of toothpaste, and disposable razor wrapped up in a pair of underpants, a bottle of Monsieur Rochas cologne, and a pair of brand-new socks with the label still on them. The underpants were a young man's Homs, pale blue and white, the socks dark brown, an expensive brand made of silk.

It was the kind of packing a man would do for an overnight stay somewhere, not for three nights, and the pants and socks and cologne seemed to indicate a night not spent alone. Or had there been more articles in the bag which had been removed? This could surely only have been done to prevent identification of the bag's owner. In that case why leave the donor card in the blouson pocket? "I would like to help someone to live after my death," it stated somewhat naively in scarlet and white, and on the reverse side Rodney Williams had requested that in the event of his death any part of his body which might be required should be used in the treatment of others. Underneath this was his signature and the date a year past. The next of kin to contact was given, as might have been expected, as Joy Williams, with the

Alverbury Road phone number.

Men's natures were a mass of contradictions, there was no consistency, and yet Wexford marveled a little that a husband and father could deliberately and ruthlessly deceive his wife over his income and pursue a course of skinflint meanness to her and his children yet want to donate his body for transplants. It would cost him nothing though, he would be dead after all. Was he dead?

"We're going to have to start looking for him. I mean really looking. Search the grounds of Green Pond Hall for a start."

Burden had been pacing the office. He had taken to doing this lately and his restless pacing had a stressful effect on anyone he happened to be with, though he himself hardly seemed aware of what was going on. Twice he had been to the window, twice back to the door, pausing once to perch briefly on the edge of the desk. Now he had reached the window again, where he stopped, turned, and stared at Wexford in irritable incredulity.

"Search for *him*? Surely it's plain he's simply done a bunk to escape the consequences of whatever it is he's done."

"All right, Mike. Maybe. But in that case what *has* he done? Nothing at Sevensmith Harding. He's as clean as a whistle there. What else could he have done? It's just possible he could be involved in some fraud that hasn't yet come to light but there's a strong case against that one. He got out. The only reason for that would be that discovery of the fraud was imminent. In that case why hasn't that discovery been made?"

Burden shrugged. "Who knows? But it may just be a piece of luck for Williams that it hasn't been."

"Why hasn't he come back, then? If the outcome of this fraud has blown over why doesn't he come home? He hasn't left the country unless he's gone on a false passport. And why bother with a false passport when he'd got one of his own and no one started missing him till three days after he'd gone?"

"Doesn't it occur to you that leaving one's clothes on the riverbank is the oldest disappearing trick in the world?"

"On the beach, I think you mean, not on the shores of a pond where the water's so shallow that to commit suicide you'd have to lie on your face and hold your breath. Besides, that bag has been in the pond only a couple of days at most. If it had been there since Williams went it'd be rotting by now, it'd stink. We'll send it over to the lab and see what they say, but we can see what they'll say with our own eyes and smell it with our own noses.

"Williams is dead. This bag of his tells me he is. If he had put it into the pond for the purpose of making us think he was dead he'd have done so immediately after he left. And the contents would have been different. More identification, for instance, no scent and powder-blue underwear. And I don't think the money would have been in it. He would have needed that money, he would have needed all the money he could lay hands on. There's no reason to think he could easily spare fifty pounds – whatever he's done he hasn't robbed a bank.

"He's dead, and, letter and phone call notwithstanding, he was dead within an hour or two of when his family last saw him."

Next day the searching of Green Pond Hall grounds began.

The grounds comprised eight acres, part woodland, part decayed overgrown formal gardens, part stables and paddock. Sergeant Martin led the search with three men and Wexford himself went down there to have a look at the dragged pond and view the terrain. It was still raining. It had been raining yesterday and the day before and for part of every day for three weeks. The weather people were saying it would be the wettest May since records began. The track was a morass, the color and texture of melted chocolate in which a giant fork had furrowed. There were other ways of getting down to the pond but only if you went on foot.

At three he had a date at Stowerton Royal Infirmary. Colin Budd had been placed in intensive care but only for the night. By morning he was sufficiently recovered to be transferred to a side room off the men's surgical ward. The stab wounds he had received were more than superficial, one having penetrated to a depth of three inches, but by a miracle almost none of the five had endangered heart or lungs.

A thick white dressing covered his upper chest, over which a striped pajama pocket had been loosely wrapped. The pajama jacket was an extra large and Wexford estimated Budd's chest measurement at thirty-four inches. He was a very thin, bony, almost cadaverous young man, white-faced and with black, longish hair. He seemed to know exactly what Wexford would want to know about him and quickly and nervously repeated his name and age, gave his occupation as motor mechanic and his address a Kingsmarkham one where he lived with his parents.

"Tell me what happened."

"This girl stuck a knife in my chest."

"Now, Mr. Budd, you know better than that. I want a detailed account, everything you can remember, starting with what you were doing waiting for a bus in the middle of nowhere."

Budd had a querulous voice that always sounded mildly indignant. He was one of those who believes the world owes him elaborate consideration as well as a living.

"That's got nothing to do with it," he said.

"I'll be the judge of that. I don't suppose you were doing anything to be ashamed of. And if you were what you tell me will be between you and me."

"I don't know what you're getting at!"

"Just tell me where you'd been last evening, Mr. Budd."

"I was at snooker," Budd said sullenly.

What a fool! He'd made it sound at least as if he was having it away with a friend's wife in one of the isolated cottages on the hillside.

"A snooker club?"

"It's on Tuesday evenings. In Pomfret, a room at the back of the White Horse. It's over at ten and I reckoned on walking home." Budd shifted his body, wincing a bit, pulling himself up in the bed. "But the rain started coming down harder, I was getting soaked. I looked at my watch and saw the ten-forty bus'd be along in ten minutes and I was nearly at the stop by then."

"I'd have expected a motor mechanic to have his own transport."

"My car was in a crunch-up. It's in a new wing. I wasn't doing no more than twenty-five when this woman came out of a side turning . . ."

Wexford cut that one short. "So you reached the bus stop, the bus shelter. What happened?"

Budd looked at him and away. "There was this girl already there, sitting on the seat. I sat down next to her."

"The bus shelter was well known to Wexford. It was about ten feet long, the seat or bench inside two feet shorter.

"Next to her?" he asked. "Or at the other end of the seat?"

"Next to her. Does it matter?"

Wexford thought perhaps it did. In England at any rate, for good or ill, for the improving of social life or its worsening, a man of honorable intent who goes to sit on a public bench where a woman is already sitting will do so as far away from her as possible. A woman will probably do this too if a woman or man is already sitting there, and a man will do it if another man is there.

"Did you know her? Had you ever seen her before?"

Budd shook his head.

"You spoke to her?"

"Only to say it was raining."

She knew that already, Wexford thought. He looked hard at Budd. Budd said, "I said it was a pity we were having such a bad May, it made the winter longer, something like that. She pulled a knife out of her bag and lunged it at me."

"Just like that? You didn't say anything else to her?"

"I've told you what I said."

"She was mad, was she? A girl who stabs men because they tell her it's raining?"

"All I said was that normally at this time I'd have had my vehicle and I could have given her a lift."

"In other words, you were trying to pick her up?"

"All right, what if I was? I didn't touch her. I didn't do anything to frighten her. That was all I said, that I could have given her a lift home. She pulled out this knife and stabbed at me four or five times and I cried out or screamed or something and she ran off."

"Would you know her again?"

"You bet I would."

"Describe her to me."

Budd made the mess of that Wexford thought

he would. He didn't know whether she was tall or short, plump or thin, because he only saw her sitting down and he thought she had a raincoat on. A thin raincoat that was a sort of pale color. Her hair was fair, he did know that, though she had a hat on or a scarf. Bits of blond hair showed under it. Her face was just an ordinary face, not what you'd call pretty. Wexford began to wonder what had attracted Budd to her in the first place. The mere facts that she was female and young? About twenty, said Budd. Well, maybe twenty-five or six. Pressed to be more precise, he said she could have been any age between eighteen and thirty, he wasn't good on ages, she was quite young though.

"Can you think of anything else about her?"

A nurse had come in and was hovering. Wexford knew what she was about to say, he could have written the script for her – "Now I think that's quite enough. It's time for Mr. Budd to have his rest . . ." She approached the bed, unhooked Budd's chart, and began reading it with the enthusiastic concentration of a scholar who has just found the key to Linear B or some such.

"She had this sack with her. She grabbed it before she ran off."

"What sort of sack?"

"The plastic kind they give you for your dustbin. A black one. She picked it up and stuck it over her shoulder and ran off."

"I think that's quite enough for now," said the nurse, diverging slightly from Wexford's text.

He got up. It was an extraordinary picture Budd's story had created and one which appealed to his imagination. The dark wet night, the knife flashing purposefully, even frenziedly, the girl running off into the rain with a sack slung over her shoulder. It was like an illustration in a fairy book of Andrew Lang, elusive, sinister, and otherworldly.

6

What had Burden meant when he said this amniocentesis had discovered something to worry Jenny? Wexford found himself brooding on that. Once or twice he had woken in the night and the question had come into his mind. Sitting in the car, being driven to Myringham, he saw a woman on the pavement with a Down's syndrome child and the question was back, presenting itself again.

He hadn't liked to pursue it with Burden. This wasn't the sort of thing you asked a prospective father about. What small defect was there a father wouldn't mind about but a mother would? It was grotesque, ridiculous, there was nothing. Any defect would be a tragedy. His mind ranged over partial deafness, a heart murmur, palate or lip deformities – the test couldn't have shown those anyway. An extra chromosome? This was an area where he found himself floundering in ignorance. He thought of his own children, perfect, always healthy, giving him no trouble really, and his heart warmed towards his girls.

This reminded him that he had the National Theatre's program brochure for the summer season in his pocket. Sheila was with the company and this would be the first season she had top lead roles. Hence the disengagement from further work on *Runway*. He got out the program and looked at it. Dora had asked him to decide which days they should go to London and see the three productions Sheila was in. For obvious reasons it always had to be he who made those kinds of decisions.

The new Stoppard, Ibsen's *Little Eyolf*, Shelley's *The Cenci*. Wexford had heard of *Little Eyolf* but he had never seen it or read it, and as for *The Cenci*, he had to confess to himself that he hadn't known Shelley had written any plays. But there it was: "Percy Bysshe Shelley" and the piece described as a tragedy in five acts. Wexford was making tentative marks on the program for a Friday in July and two Saturdays in August when Donaldson, his driver, drew into the curb outside Sevensmith Harding.

Miles Gardner had been watching for him and came rushing out with an umbrella. It made Wexford feel like royalty. They splashed across the pavement to the mahogany doors.

Kenneth Risby, the chief accountant, told him Rodney Williams's salary had been paid into the account Williams had with the Pomfret branch of the Anglian-Victorian Bank. From that account then, it would seem, Williams had each month transferred £500 into the joint account he had with Joy. Risby had been with the company for fifteen years and said he could recall no other arrangement being made for Williams, either recently or in the days when he was a sales rep. His salary had always gone to the Pomfret bank, never to Kingsmarkham.

"We've heard nothing," Miles Gardner said. "Whatever he meant by the PS to that letter he hasn't been in touch."

"Williams didn't write that letter," Wexford reminded him.

Gardner nodded unhappily.

"The first time we talked about this business," Wexford said, "you told me someone phoned here saying she was Mrs. Williams and that her husband was ill and wouldn't be coming in. Would that have been on Friday, April the sixteenth?"

"Well, yes, I suppose it would."

"Who took the call?"

"It must have been one of our telephonists. They're part-timers. I can't remember whether it was Anna or Michelle. The phone call came before I got in, you see. That is, before nine-thirty."

"Williams had a secretary, I suppose?"

"Christine Lomond. He shared her with our assistant sales director. Would you like to talk to her?"

"Not yet. Maybe not today. It's Anna or Michelle I want. But which one do I want?"

"Michelle, I expect," said Gardner. "They tend to swap shifts a bit but it's usually Michelle on mornings."

It had been that Friday, and it was today. Michelle was a very young, very pretty girl with a vividly made-up face. The room where the switchboard was, not much more than a cupboard, she had stamped with her own personality (or perhaps Anna's) and there was a blue cineraria in a pot, a stack of magazines, a pile of knitting that had reached the bulky stage, and on the table in front of her, hurriedly placed face downwards, the latest diet paperback.

It was clear that Michelle had already discussed that phone call exhaustively. Perhaps with Anna or with Christine Lomond. Williams's disappearance would have been the talk of the office.

"I get in at nine," she said. "That's when the phone calls really start. But the funny thing was there weren't any that morning till Mrs. Williams phoned at about twenty past."

"You mean till someone phoned who *called* herself Mrs. Williams."

The girl looked at him. She shook her head quite vehemently. "It was Mrs. Williams. She said, 'This is Joy Williams.' "

Wexford let it go for the time being.

"What exactly did she say?"

" 'My husband Mr. Williams won't be coming in today.' And then she sort of hesitated and said, 'That's Mr. Rodney Williams, I mean, the marketing manager.' I said there was no one else in yet and she said that didn't matter but to give Christine the message he'd got flu and wouldn't be in."

Whoever it was, it hadn't been Joy. At that time Joy didn't know her husband was Sevensmith Harding's marketing manager. Wexford had thanked Michelle and was turning away, diverting his mind to the matter of the firm's stock of typewriters, when he stopped.

"What makes you so sure the woman you spoke to was Mrs. Joy Williams?"

"It just was. I know it was."

"No, let me correct that. You know it was a

woman who *said* she was Mrs. Joy Williams. She had never phoned here before, had she, so you couldn't have recognized her voice?"

"No, but she phoned here afterwards."

"What do you mean, afterwards?"

"About three weeks later." The girl spoke with exaggererated patience now, as if to a very confused or simpleminded person. "Mrs. Joy Williams phoned here three weeks after her husband left."

Of course. Wexford remembered that call. It was he who had advised Joy to make it.

"I put her through to Mr. Gardner," Michelle said. "I was a bit embarrassed, to be perfectly honest. But I know it was the same voice, really I do. It was the same voice as the woman who phoned that Friday morning, it was Mrs. Williams."

He picked up the girl at the roundabout where the second exit is the start of the Kingsmarkham bypass. She was standing on the grass verge at the side of the roundabout, holding up a piece of cardboard with "Myringham" printed on it. Brian Wheatley pulled in to the first exit, the Kingsmarkham town-center road, and the girl got into the passenger seat. Then, for some unclear reason, perhaps because he had already pulled out of the roundabout and it would not have been easy to get back into the traffic, Wheatley decided to continue through the town instead of on the bypass. This wasn't such a bad idea anyway, the anomaly being that the bypass which had been built to ease the passage of traffic past the town was often more crowded than the old route.

Wheatley was driving from London where he worked three days a week. It was about six in the evening and of course broad daylight. He had moved to Myringham only two weeks before and was still unfamiliar with the byways and back-doubles of the area. The girl didn't speak a word. She had no baggage with her, only a handbag with a shoulder strap. Wheatley drove through Kingsmarkham, along the High Street, and became confused by the sign-posting. Instead of keeping straight on he began to think he should have taken a left-hand turn some half a mile back. He therefore – on what he admitted was a lonely and secluded stretch of road – pulled into a lay-by and consulted his road map.

His intention to do this, he said, he announced plainly to the girl. After he had stopped and switched off the engine he was obliged to reach obliquely across her in order to open the glove compartment where the map was. He was aware of the girl giving a gasp of fright or anger, and then of a sharp pain, more like a burn than a cut, in his right hand.

He never even saw the knife. The girl jumped out of the car, slamming the door behind her, and ran not along the road but onto a footpath that separated a field of wheat from a wood. Blood was flowing from a deep cut in the base of Wheatley's thumb. He tied up his hand as best he could with his handkerchief but shock and a feeling of faintness made it impossible for him to continue his journey for some minutes. Eventually he looked at his map, found himself nearer home than he had thought, and was able to drive there in about a quarter of an hour. The general practitioner with whom he had registered the week before was still holding his surgery. Wheatley's wife drove him there and the cut in his hand was stitched, Wheatley telling the doctor he had been carving meat and had inadvertently pressed his hand against the point of the carving knife. Whether or not the doctor believed this was another matter. At any rate he had made no particular comment. Wheatley himself had wanted to tell him the truth, though this would have meant police involvement. It was his wife who had dissuaded him on the grounds that if the police were called the conclusion they would reach would be that Wheatley had first made some sort of assault on the girl.

This was the story Wheatley told Wexford three days later. His wife didn't know he had changed his mind. He had come to the police, he said, because he felt more and more indignant that this girl, whom he hadn't touched, whom he had scarcely spoken to except to say he was going to stop and look at his map, should make an unprovoked attack on him and get away with it.

"Can you describe her?"

Wexford waited resignedly for the kind of useless description furnished by Colin Budd. He was surprised. In many ways Wheatley did not seem to know his way around but he was observant and perceptive.

"She was tall for a woman, about five feet eight or nine. Young, eighteen or nineteen. Brown hair or lightish hair, shoulder-length, sunglasses though it wasn't sunny, fair skin – I noticed she had very white hands. Jeans and a blouse, I think, and a cardigan. The bag was some dark color, black or navy blue."

"Did she give you the impression she lived in Myringham? That she was going home?"

"She didn't give me any sort of impression. When she got into the car she said thanks –

just the one word 'thanks,' otherwise she didn't speak. I said to her that I thought I'd drive through the town instead of the bypass and she didn't answer. Later on I said I'd stop and look at the map and she didn't answer that either, but when I reached across her – I didn't touch her, I could swear to that – she gave a sort of gasp. Those were the only sounds she made, 'thanks' and a gasp."

The same girl as attacked Budd, one would suppose. But if Wheatley were to be believed, while there was some very slight justification for the attack on Budd, there was none for this second stabbing. Could the girl possibly have thought that the hand which reached across to open the glove compartment intended instead to take hold of her by the left shoulder? Or lower itself onto her knee? There was something ridiculous about these assaults, and yet two meant that they were not ridiculous at all but serious. Next time there could be a fatality.

Or had there been one already?

The manager of the Pomfret branch of the Anglian-Victorian Bank bore an extraordinary resemblance to Adolf Hitler. This was not only in the small square moustache and the lock of dark hair half covering Mr. Skinner's forehead. The face was the same face, rather handsome, with large chin and heavy nose and small thick-lidded eyes. But all that would have passed unnoticed without the moustache and the lock of hair, so that it was impossible to avoid the uncomfortable conclusion that Mr. Skinner was doing it on purpose. He knew whom he looked like and he enhanced the resemblance. Wexford could only attribute one motive to a bank manager who wants to look like Hitler – a desire to intimidate his clients.

His manner, however, was warm, friendly, and charming. All those, and implacable, too. He could not consider either letting Wexford look into Rodney Williams's bank accounts or disclosing any information about their contents.

"Did you say accounts plural?" said Wexford.

"Yes. Mr. Williams had two current accounts here – and now I've probably said more than I should."

"Two current accounts in the name of Rodney Williams?"

Skinner was standing up with his head slightly on one side, looking like Hitler waiting for Franco's train at Hendaye. "I said two current accounts, Chief Inspector. We'll let it go at that, shall we?"

One for his salary to be paid into, Wexford thought as he was driven away, and the other for what? His Kingsmarkham household expenses were drawn from the Kingsmarkham account, which he fed with £500 a month from Pomfret account A. Then what of account B? His wife didn't know of the existence of account A anyway. It alone was sufficient to keep his resources secret from her. Why did he need a third current bank account?

They were searching for him now on the open land, partly wooded, that lay between Kingsmarkham and Forby. But so far, since the discovery of the bag in Green Pond, nothing further had come to light. He's dead, Wexford thought, he must be.

Burden had been at Pomfret, talking to the Harmer family, Joy Williams's sister, brother-in-law, and niece. John Harmer was a pharmacist with a chemist's shop in the High Street.

"They say Joy was with them that evening," Burden said, "but I wouldn't put that much credence on what they say. Not that they're intentionally lying – they can't remember. It was seven weeks ago. Besides, Joy often goes over there in the evenings. More or less to sit in front of their television instead of her own, I gather. But I suppose she's lonely, she wants company. Mrs. Harmer says she was definitely there that evening, Harmer says it must be if his wife says so and the girl doesn't know. You can't expect a teenage girl to take much notice of when her aunt comes."

Wexford told him what he had learned from the telephonist at Sevensmith Harding. "Of course, the girl may be mistaken about the voices or she may have persuaded herself they were the same voice in order to get more drama out of the situation. But it's more than possible that the woman who phoned Sevensmith Harding the day after Williams left to say he was ill and the woman who phoned three weeks later to inquire as to his whereabouts are one and the same. As we know, the second time was Joy. Now Joy was very keen to have me look for her husband when he first disappeared, but later on much less so – indeed, she was obstructive. That first time I talked to her she said nothing about having gone out herself that evening. That was only mentioned the second time. Joy is devoted to her son Kevin. Her daughter is nothing to her, her son everything . . . What on earth's the matter?"

Burden's face had set and he had gone rather pale. He had taken a hard grip on the arms of his chair. "Nothing. Go on."

"Well, then – her son always phones on Thursday evenings and that particular Thursday was the first one he had been back at college. Wouldn't a devoted mother have wanted to know all those things mothers worry about in such circumstances? Did he have a good journey? Was his room all right? Had he settled in? But this devoted mother doesn't wait in for his call. She goes out – not to some important engagement, some function booked months ahead, but to watch television at her sister's. What does all this suggest to you?"

Having struggled successfully to overcome whatever it was that had upset him, Burden forced a laugh. "You sound like Sherlock Holmes talking to Watson." Since his second marriage he occasionally read books, a change in him Wexford couldn't get used to.

"No," he said, "more 'a man of the solid Sussex breed – a breed which covers much good sense under a heavy silent exterior.' "

"I wouldn't say 'silent.' Was that from Sherlock Holmes?"

Wexford nodded. "So what do you make of it?" he said more colloquially.

"That Joy is somehow in cahoots with her husband. There's a conspiracy going on. What for and why I wouldn't pretend to know, but it's got something to do with giving everyone the impression Williams is dead. He left that evening and she went out later to meet him away from the house. Whatever they were planning was done away from the house because it had to be concealed from the daughter Sara as much as from anyone else. Next morning Joy rang Sevensmith Harding to say her husband was ill. Of course, it's nonsense to say she didn't know that he was their marketing manager and the extent of his income. Next he or she typed that letter on a *hired* typewriter. She probably did that, not knowing what he called Gardner and making the mistake of addressing him as "Mr. Gardner." The abandoned car, the dumped bag of clothes were all part of a plan to make us think him dead. But the increased police attention frightened Joy, she wanted things to go more at her pace. Hence the obstructiveness. I said I didn't know why, but it could be an insurance fiddle, couldn't it?"

"Without a body, Mike? With no more proof of death than a dumped traveling bag? And if you wanted people to think you were dead, aren't there half a dozen simpler and more convincing ways of doing it?"

"You feel the same as me then? You don't think he's dead?"

"I know he's dead," said Wexford.

Next day he was proved right.

It looked like a grave. It was in the shape of a grave, as clearly demarcated as if a slab of stone lay upon it, though Edwin Fitzgerald did not at first see this. In spite of its shape he would have passed it by as a mere curiosity, a whim of nature. It was the dog Shep who drew his attention to it.

Edwin Fitzgerald was a retired policeman who had been a dog handler. He lived in Pomfret and had a job as a part-time security guard at a factory complex on Stowerton's industrial estate. The dog Shep was not a trained dog in the sense of being police-trained – as a "sniffer," for instance. Fitzgerald had bought him after his last dog died – a wonderful dog that one, more intelligent than any human being, a dog that understood every word he said. Shep could only follow humbly in that dog's footsteps and was often the subject of unfavorable comparisons. He didn't understand every word Fitzgerald said, or at any rate behaved as if he didn't.

On this particular morning in June, a dry one, the first really fine morning of the summer, Shep disregarded all Fitzgerald's words, ignored the repeated "Leave it, sir" and "Do as you're told," and continued his frenetic digging in the corner of what his master saw as a patch of weeds. He dug like a dog possessed. Indeed, Fitzgerald informed him that he was a devil, that he didn't know what had got into him. He shouted (which a good dog handler should never do) and he shook his fist until he saw what Shep had unearthed and then he stopped.

The dog had dug up a foot.

Fitzgerald had been a policeman, which had the double advantage of having taught him not to be sickened by such a discovery and not to disturb anything in its vicinity. He attached Shep's lead to his collar and pulled the dog away. This took some doing as Shep was a big young German shepherd intent on worrying at the protruding thing for some hours if possible.

As far as Fitzgerald could see, now he had got the dog clear, the foot was still attached to a limb and the limb probably to a trunk. It was inside a sodden, blackened, slimy shoe caked with mud, and about the ankle clung a bundling of muddy wet cloth, once the hem of a trouser leg. Shep had dug it out from one of the corners of this curious little plot of ground. All around, on this edge of the meadow, grew tall grass ready to be cut for hay, high enough to hide the dog when he plunged in among it, but the rectangle – seven feet by three? – which Shep had found in there and had dug into was covered closely and in a neat rather horticultural way with fresh green plants. Weeds they were, but weeds attractive enough to be called plants, red campion, clover, speedwell, and they covered the oblong patch as precisely as if they had been sown there in a seed bed.

The grass which surrounded it, gone to seed, bearing light feathery seed heads of brown and grayish-cream and silvery-gold, hid it from the sight of anyone who kept to the footpath. It took a dog to plunge in there and find the grave. A day or two of sunshine, Fitzgerald thought, and the farmer would have cut the hay, cut those weeds too without a thought. Shep was a good dog after all, even if he didn't understand every word Fitzgerald said.

He retraced his steps to the branch of the lane that led to Myfleet and hurried down the hill to his bungalow, where he phoned the police.

7

From the Pomfret road a narrow lane winds its way up into the hills and to the verge of the forest. All down the hedges here grows the wayfarer's tree with its flat creamy bracts of blossom, and beneath, edging the meadows like a fringe of lace, the whiter, finer, more delicate cow parsley. There are houses, Edwin Fitzgerald's among them, approached by paths, cart tracks, or even smaller narrower lanes, but the lane gives the impression of leading directly to the obelisk on the hill.

It is like downland up here, the trees ceasing until the forest of conifers begins over there to the east, chalk showing in outcroppings and heather on the chalk. And all the way the obelisk looming larger, a needle of granite with its point a tetragon. The road never reaches it. A quarter of a mile this side it swerves, turns east, and divides, one fork making for Myfleet, the other for Pomfret, and soon there are meadows again and the heath is past. It was in one of these meadows, close to the overhang of the forest, traversed by a footpath leading from the road to Myfleet, that the discovery had been made. Over to the west the obelisk stabbed the blue sky, catching a shred of cloud on its point.

The grave was in a triangle formed by the wood, the lane, and the footpath, in a slightly more than right-angled corner of the field. It was near enough to the forest for the air to smell resinous. The soil was light and sandy with an admixture of pine needles.

"Easy enough to dig," said Wexford to Burden. "Almost anyone not decrepit could dig a grave like that in half an hour. Digging it deep enough would have taken a little longer."

They were viewing the terrain, the distance of the grave from the road and the footpath, while Sir Hilary Tremlett, the pathologist, stood by with the scene-of-crimes officer to supervise the careful unearthing. Sir Hilary had happened to be at Stowerton when Fitzgerald's call came in. By a piece of luck he had just arrived at the infirmary to perform a postmortem. It was not yet ten o'clock, a morning of pearly sunshine, the blue sky dotted with innumerable puffs of tiny white cloud. But every man there, the short, portly, august pathologist included, had a raincoat on. It had rained daily for so many weeks that no one was going to take the risk of going without; no one anyway could yet believe his own eyes.

"The rain made the weeds grow like that," said Wexford. "You can see what happened. It's rather interesting. All the ground here had grass growing on it, then a patch was dug to receive *that*. It was covered up again with overturned earth, the weed seeds came and rain, seemingly endless rain, and what grew up on that fertile patch and that patch only were broad-leaved plants. If it had been a dry spring there would have been more grass and it would all have been much less green."

"And the ground harder. If the ground hadn't been soft and moist the dog might not have persisted with its digging."

"The mistake was in not digging the grave deep enough. It makes you wonder why he or she or they didn't. Laziness? Lack of time? Lack of light? The six-foot rule is a good one because things of this kind do tend to work to the surface."

"If that's so," said Dr. Crocker, coming up to them, "why is it they always have to dig so far down to find ancient cities and temples and so forth?"

"Don't ask me," said Wexford. "Ask the dog. He's the archaeologist. Mind you, we don't have any lava in Sussex."

They approached a little nearer to where Detectives Archbold and Bennett were carrying out their delicate spadework. It was apparent now that the corpse of the man that lay in the earth had been neither wrapped nor covered before it was buried. The earth didn't besmear it as a heavier, clayey soil might have done. It was emerging relatively clean, soaking wet, darkly stained, giving off the awful reek that was familiar to every man there, the sweetish, fishy, breath-catching, gaseous stench of decomposing flesh. That was what the dog had smelt and liked and wanted more of.

"I often think," said Wexford to the doctor, "that we haven't much in common with dogs."

"No, it's at times like this you know what you've always suspected, that they're not almost human at all."

The face was pale, stained, bloated, the pale parts the color of a dead fish's belly. Wexford, not squeamish at all, hardened by the years, decided not to look at the face again until he had to. The big domed forehead, bigger and more domed because the hair had fallen from it, looked like a great mottled stone or lump of fungus. It was that forehead which made him pretty sure this must be Rodney Williams. Of course, he wasn't going to commit himself at this stage, but he'd have been surprised if it wasn't Williams.

Sir Hilary, squatting down now, bent closer. Murdoch, the scene-of-crimes officer, was beginning to take measurements, make calculations. He called the photographer over, but Sir Hilary held up a delaying hand.

Wexford wondered how he could stand that stink right up against his face. He seemed rather to enjoy it, the whole thing, the corpse, the atmosphere, the horror, the squalor. Pathologists did, and just as well really. It wouldn't do if they shied away from it.

The body was subjected to a long and careful scrutiny. Sir Hilary looked at it closely from all angles. He came very close to touching but he did not quite touch. His fingers were plump, clean, the color of a slice of roast pork. He stood up, nodded to Murdoch and the photographer, smiled at Wexford.

"I could have a poke-about at that after lunch," he said. He always spoke of his autopsies as "having a poke-about." "Not much doing today. Any idea who it might be?"

"I think I have, Sir Hilary."

"I'm glad to hear it. Saves a lot of hassle. We'll smarten him up a bit before his nearest and dearest come for a private view."

Joy Williams, Wexford thought. No, she shouldn't be subjected to that. He felt the warmth of the mounting sun kind and soft on his face. He turned his back and looked across the sweep of meadows to the Pomfret road, green hay gold-brushed, dark green hedgerows stitched in like tapestry, sheep on a hillside. All he could see was that face and a wife looking at it. This horrid image doth unfix my hair and make my seated heart knock at my ribs . . .

It occurred to him that the nearest point on the main road to this place was the bus stop where Colin Budd had been attacked. Did that mean anything? The lane that passed within yards of the burial place met the road almost opposite the bus stop. But Budd had been stabbed weeks after this man's death. The brother-in-law might do the identification instead. John Something, the chemist. John Harmer.

He seemed a sensible man. Younger than Williams by five or six years, he was one of those tailored people, a neat, well-made smallish man with regular features and short, crisply wavy hair. He had closed up his dispensary and left the shop in the care of his wife.

Having taken a deep breath, he looked at the body. He looked at the face, his symmetrical features controlled in blankness. He wasn't going to show anything, not he, no shock, disgust, pity. You could almost hear his mother's voice saying to a small curly-headed boy: Be a man, John. Don't cry. Be a man.

Harmer remembered and was a man. But he might have said with Macduff that he must also feel it like a man, for his face gradually paled until it became a sickly greenish white as the corpse's. His stomach, not his will, had betrayed him. Or threatened to. He came out into the air, into the sunshine, away from charnel-house corpse rot, and smelt the summer noonday, and the bile receded. He nodded to Wexford; he nodded rather more and longer than was necessary.

"Is that your brother-in-law, Rodney Williams?"

"Yes."

"You are quite certain of that?"

"I'm certain."

Wexford had thought of asking him to be the bearer of the news to Joy but he had quickly seen Harmer wouldn't be a suitable, let alone a sympathetic, messenger. He went himself, walking to Alverbury Road, thinking as he walked. There wasn't much he personally could do until the pathologist's report came and the lab had been over Williams's clothes. With distaste he recalled the bloodied mass of cloth that had wrapped the wounds. He felt glad now he had had the lab go over that car so carefully, and at a time when it looked as if Williams might have been guilty of some misdemeanor and have done a moonlight flit.

Those crumbs of plaster in the boot could be vital evidence. At first he had supposed they derived from some routine of Williams's work. But Gardner had told him there was never a question of Williams having handled the stuff he sold. More likely the truth was that those plaster crumbs had been caught up in the folds of that bloodstained cloth and the body itself had been in the boot of the car . . .

In the front garden of 31 Alverbury Road someone had mown the bit of lawn and cut the privet hedge. It looked as if both these tasks had been performed with the same bit of blunt shears. Rodney Williams had been in one respect domestically adequate – he had kept his garden trim.

Sara opened the front door to him. He hadn't expected her to be there and he was a little taken aback. He would have preferred breaking the news to her mother alone. The school term wasn't yet over but A-levels were, and with those examinations behind her there was perhaps nothing for her to go to school for.

She had on a white tee-shirt, pure unrelieved white, short-sleeved and showing felt-tipped pen drawings on her arms and hands, the snake again in green, a butterfly with a baby face, a raven woman with aggressive breasts and erect wings, somehow obscene on those smooth golden arms, childish and rounded.

"Is your mother in, Sara?"

She nodded. Had the tone of his voice told her? She looked sideways at him, fearfully, as they went down the short passage to the kitchen door.

Joy Williams anticipated nothing. On the table at which she was sitting were the remains of lunch for two. She looked up with a mildly disagreeable inquiring glance. They had been eating fish fingers with baked beans – an infelicitous mixture, Wexford thought. He could tell the constituents of their lunch by the quantity of it Sara had left on her plate. Joy had been reading a women's magazine of the royalty–sycophantic–crocheted-tea-cozy kind which was propped against a bottle of soy sauce, pathetic import surely of Sara's. What does a daughter do for her mother in a situation such as this? Go to her and put an arm round her shoulders? At least stand behind her chair? Sara went to the sink, stood with her back to them, looking out of the window above it at the grass and the fence and the meager little apple trees.

Wexford told Joy her husband had been found. Her husband's body. More than that he couldn't tell her, he knew no more. The girl's shoulders twitched. Mrs. Williams leaned forward across the table and put her hand heavily over her mouth. She sat that way for a moment or two. The whistling tea kettle on the stove began to screech. Sara turned around, turned the gas off, looked at her mother with her mouth twisted up as if she had a toothache.

"D'you want a coffee?" Joy said to Wexford.

He shook his head. Sara made the coffee, instant in two mugs, one with a big "S" on it and the other with the head of the Princess of Wales. Joy put sugar into hers, one spoonful, then after reflection, another.

"Shall I have to see him?"

"Your brother-in-law has already made the identification."

"John?"

"Have you any other brothers-in-law, Mrs. Williams?"

"Rod's got a brother in Bath. 'Had,' I should say. I mean he's still alive as far as I know and

Rod's not, is he?"

"Oh, Mum," said Sara. "For God's sake."

"You shut your mouth, you little cow!"

Joy Williams screamed it at her. She didn't utter any more words but she went on screaming, drumming her fists on the table so that the mug bounced off and broke and coffee went all over the strip of coconut matting on the floor. Joy screamed until Sara slapped her face – the doctor already, the cool head in an emergency. Wexford knew better than to do it himself. Once he'd slapped a hysterical woman's face and later been threatened with an action for assault.

"Who can we get hold of to be with her?" he asked. Mrs. Milvey? He thought of Dora and dismissed the thought.

"She hasn't any friends. I expect my Auntie Hope will come."

Mrs. Harmer that would be. Hope and Joy. My God, he thought. Although the girl was sitting beside her mother now, holding her hand, while Joy leaned back spent, her head hanging over the back of the kitchen chair, the tears silently rolling out of her eyes, he could see that it was all Sara could do to control her repugnance. She was almost shaking with it. The need to be parted, the one from the other, was mutual. Sara, no doubt, couldn't wait for those exam results, the confirmation of St. Biddulph's acceptance of her, for October and the start of term. It couldn't come fast enough for her.

"I'll stay with Mum," she said, and there was stoicism in the way she said it. "I'll give her a pill. She's got Valium. I'll give her a couple of Valium and find something nice for her on the TV."

The ever-ready panacea.

It was too late for lunch now. He and Burden might have something in the office, get a sandwich sent down from the canteen. He had said he'd see the press at 2:30. Well, young Varney of the local paper, who was a stringer for the nationals . . .

There was a van on the police station forecourt marked "TV South" and a camera crew getting out of it.

"They've been up at the forest getting shots of the grave and Fitzgerald and the dog," Burden said, "and they want you next."

"Good. I'll be able to put out an appeal for anyone who may have seen that car parked." A less encouraging thought struck Wexford. "They won't want to make me up, will they?" He had never been on television before.

Burden looked at him morosely, lifting his

shoulders in a shrug of total indifference to any eventuality.

"It's not the end of the world if they do, is it?"

There was no time like the present, even a present that would end in ten minutes with his first ever TV appearance.

"What's happened to end your world, Mike?"

Burden immediately looked away. He mumbled something which Wexford couldn't hear and had to ask him to repeat.

"I said that I supposed I should tell you what the trouble is."

"Yes. I want to know." Looking at Burden, Wexford noticed for the first time gray hairs among the fair ones. "There's something wrong with the baby, isn't there?"

"That's right." Burden's voice sounded very dry. "In Jenny's opinion, mind you. Not in mine." He gave a bark of laughter. "It's a girl."

"What?"

Wexford's phone went. He picked up the receiver. TV South, the *Kingsmarkham Courier*, and two other reporters were downstairs waiting for him. Burden had already gone, closing the door quietly behind him.

8

She was laying the table with their wedding present glass and silver. The lace cloth had been bought in Venice where they went for the first holiday after their honeymoon. Domesticity had delighted her when, as soon as she knew she was pregnant, she gave up teaching. It was the novelty, of course, being at home all day, playing house. Since then she had grown indifferent, she had grown indifferent to everything. Except to the child, and that she hated.

Sometimes, walking about the house after Mike had gone to work, pushing the vacuum cleaner or tidying up, the tears fell out of her eyes and streamed down her face. She cried because she couldn't believe that she who had longed and longed for a baby could hate the one inside her. All this she had told to the psychiatrist at their second session. She had listened to her in almost total silence. Once she said, "Why do you say that" and once "Go on," but otherwise she simply listened with a kind, interested look on her face.

Mike had suggested the psychiatrist. She had been so surprised because Mike usually scoffed at psychiatry that she said yes without even protesting. It was somewhere to go anyway, something different to do from sitting at home brooding about the future and her marriage and the unwanted child. And inevitably crying, of course, when she remembered as she always did what life used to be – when the days seemed too short, when she was teaching history to sixth-formers at Haldon Finch, playing the violin in an orchestra, taking an advanced art appreciation course.

Jenny despised herself but that changed nothing. Her self-pity sickened her.

The sound of his key in the door – time-honored heart-stopper, test of love sustained – did nothing for her beyond bringing a little dread of the evening in front of them. He came into the room and kissed her. He still did that.

"How did you get on with the shrink?"

She resented the haste he was in. He wanted her cured, she felt, so that life could get back to normal again. "What do you expect? A miracle in two easy lessons?"

She sat down. That always made her feel a little less bad because the bulge was no longer so apparent. And, thank God, the child was still, not rolling about and kicking.

"Don't let him give you drugs."

"It's a woman."

She wanted to scream with laughter. The irony of it! She was a teacher and this other woman was a psychiatrist and Mike's daughter Pat was very nearly qualified as a dentist, yet here she was reacting like a no-account junior wife in a harem. Because the baby was a girl.

He gave her a drink, orange juice and Perrier. He had a whisky, a large one, and in a minute he would have another. Not long ago he hadn't needed to drink when he got home. She looked at him, wishing she could bring herself to touch his arm or take his hand. An apathy as strong as energy held her back.

"Mike," she said, and said for the hundredth time, "I can't help it, I wish I could. I have tried."

"So you say. I don't understand it. It's beyond my understanding."

In a low voice, looking down, she said, "It's beyond mine." The child began to move, with flutters only at first, then came a hearty kick right under her lower ribs, giving her a rush of heartburn. She cried out, "I wish to God I'd never had the thing done. I wish I'd never let them do it. They shouldn't have told me. Why did I let them? If I'd been ignorant I'd have gone on being happy, I'd have had the baby and I wouldn't have minded what it was, I'd have been pleased with any healthy baby. I didn't even specially want a son, or I didn't know I did. I didn't mind what it was, but now I know what it is I can't bear it. I can't go through all this and all through having it and the work and the pain and the trouble and a lifetime of being with it, having it with me, for a *girl!*"

He had heard it all before. It seemed to him that she said it every night. This was what he came home to. With slight variations, with modifications and changed turns of phrase, that was what she said to him on and on every evening. Until she grew exhausted or wept or slumped spent in her chair, until she went away to bed – earlier and earlier as the weeks passed. In vain he had asked why this prejudice against girls, she who was a feminist, a supporter of the women's movement, who expressed a preference for her friends' small girls over their small sons, who got on better with her stepdaughter than her stepson, who professed to prefer teaching girls to boys.

She didn't know why, only that it was so. Her pregnancy, so long desired, at first so ecstatically accepted, had driven her mad. The worst of it was that he was coming to hate the unborn child himself and to wish it had never been conceived.

The wine bar was dark and cool. The restoration of an old house in Kingsmarkham's Queen Street had revealed and then opened up its cavernous cellars. The proprietor had resisted the temptations of roof beams, medieval pastiches, flintlocks, and copper warming pans and simply painted the broad squat arches white, tiled the floor, and furnished the place with tables and chairs in dark-stained pine.

Wexford and Burden had taken to lunching at the Old Cellar a couple of times a week. It had the virtue of being warm on cold days and cool on hot ones like this. The food was quiche and salad, smoked mackerel, coleslaw, pork pie, quiche, quiche, and more quiche.

"What did they serve in these places before quiche caught on? I mean, there was a time not long ago when an Englishman could say he'd never heard of quiche."

"He's always eaten it," said Wexford. "He called it cheese and onion flan."

He had the morning papers with him. The *Kingsmarkham Courier* was a weekly and wouldn't be out till Friday. The national dailies had given no more than a paragraph to the discovery of Rodney Williams's body and had left out all the background details he was sure Varney had passed on to them. The *Daily Telegraph* merely stated that the body of a man had been found in a shallow grave and later identified as Rodney John Williams, a salesman from Kingsmarkham in Sussex. Nothing about Joy, his children, his job at Sevensmith Harding, or the fact that he had been missing for two months. True, they had put him, Wexford, on TV but only on the regional bit that came after the news and then only forty-five seconds of the half-hour-long film they'd made.

The corpses of middle-aged men weren't news as women's were or children's. Women were always news. Perhaps they would cease to be when the day came that they got their equality as well as their rights. An interesting speculation and one which reminded him . . .

"You were going to tell me but we were interrupted."

"It's not that she's anti-girls usually," Burden said. "For God's sake, she's a feminist. I mean, it's not some stupid I-must-have-an-heir thing or every-woman's-got-to-have-a-son-to-prove-herself. In fact I think she secretly thinks women are better than men – I mean cleverer and more versatile, all that. She says she doesn't understand it herself. She says she had no feelings about the child's sex one way or the other, but when they told her, when she knew, she was – well, dismayed. That was at first. It's got worse. It's not just dismay now, it's hatred."

"Why doesn't she want a girl?" Wexford remembered certain sentiments expressed by his daughter Sylvia, mother of two sons. "Is it that she feels women have a raw deal and she doesn't want to be responsible for bringing another into the world?" By way of apology for this crassness, he added, "I have heard that view put."

"She doesn't know. She says that ever since the world began sons have been preferred over daughters and now it's become part of race memory, what she calls the collective unconscious."

"What Jung called it."

Burden hesitated and then passed over that one. "She's mad, you know. Pregnancy has driven her mad. Oh, don't look at me like that. I've given up caring about being disloyal. I've given up damn well caring, if you must know. Do you know what she says? She says she can't contemplate a future with a daughter she doesn't want. She says she can't imagine living for twenty years, say, with someone she hates before it's born. What's my life going to be like with that going on?"

"At the risk of uttering an old cliché, I'd say she'll feel differently when the baby's born."

"Oh, she will? You can be sure of that? She'll love it when it's put into her arms? Shall I tell you what else she says? That she never wants to see it. We're to put it up for adoption immediately without either of us seeing it. I told you she was mad."

All this made Wexford feel like a drink. But he couldn't start drinking at lunchtime with all he'd got ahead of him. Burden wasn't going to drink either. Judging by the look of him some mornings, he saved that up for when he got home. They paid the bill and climbed up the stone steps out of the Old Cellar into a bright June sunshine that made them blink.

"She's seeing a psychiatrist. I pin my faith to that. Me of all people! I sometimes wonder what I've come to, saying things like that."

Sir Hilary Tremlett's report of the results of the postmortem had come. To decipher the obscurer bits for Wexford, Dr. Crocker came into the office as Burden was departing. They nearly passed each other in the doorway, Burden long-faced, monosyllabic. The doctor laughed.

"Mike's having a difficult pregnancy."

Wexford wasn't going to enlighten him. The other chair had been pushed under the desk. He shoved it out with his toe.

"He says here he found three hundred and twenty milligrams of cyclobarbitone in the stomach and other organs. What's cyclobarbitone?"

"It's an intermediate-acting barbiturate – that means it has about eight hours' duration of effect – a hypnotic drug, a sleeping pill if you like. The proprietary brand name would be Phanodorm, I expect. Two hundred milligrams is the dose. But three hundred and twenty wouldn't kill him. It sounds as if he took two tablets of two hundred each."

"It didn't kill him, though, did it? He died of stab wounds."

Wexford looked up to see the doctor looking at him. They were both thinking the same thing. They were both thinking about Colin Budd and Brian Wheatley.

"What actually killed him was a wound that pierced the carotid."

"Did it now? The blood must have spouted like a fountain."

"There were seven other wounds in the neck and chest and back. A lot of stuff here's about fixed and mobile underlying tissues." Wexford handed the pages across the desk, retaining one. “I’m more interested in the estimate he makes of the proportions of the knife. A large kitchen knife with a dagger point, it would seem to have been.”

“I see he suggests death occurred six to eight weeks ago. What d’you reckon? He took two sleeping pills and someone did him in while he was away in the land of nod? If it happened as you seem to think soon after he left his house at six that evening, why would he take sleeping pills at that hour?”

“He might have taken them,” said Wexford thoughtfully, “in mistake for something else. Hypertension pills, for instance. He had high blood pressure.”

While the doctor was reading Wexford picked up the phone and asked the telephonist to get him Wheatley’s number. Wheatley had said he worked in London on only three days a week so there was a chance he might be at home now. He was.

“I didn’t think you showed much interest,” he said in an injured way.

That one Wexford wasn’t going to answer. It was true anyway. They hadn’t shown all that much interest in a man getting his hand scratched by a girl hitcher. Things had taken on a different aspect since then.

“You gave me a detailed description of the

girl who attacked you, Mr. Wheatley. The fact that you're a good observer makes me think you may have observed more. Will you think about that, please, and try and remember everything that happened? Principally, give us some more information about what the girl looked like, her voice, and so on. We'd like to come and see you."

Mollified, Wheatley said he'd give it some thought and tell them everything he could remember and how about some time that evening?

The doctor said, "It couldn't have happened inside a car, you know, Reg. There'd have been too much blood."

"Perhaps in the open air?"

"And tied his neck up in a Marks and Spencer's floral-printed tea-towel?"

"It doesn't say that there!"

"I happened to notice it when the poor devil was ressurected. We've got one like it at home."

The phone rang. The telephonist said, "Mr. Wexford, there's a Mrs. Williams here wanting to talk to someone about Mr. Rodney Williams."

Joy, he thought. Well.

"Mrs. Joy Williams?"

"Mrs. Wendy Williams."

"Have someone bring her up here, will you?"

The sister-in-law? The wife of the brother in Bath? When you don't know what to do next, Raymond Chandler advised writers of his sort of fiction, have a man come in with a gun. In a real-life murder case, thought Wexford, what better surprise visitor than the mysterious Wife of Bath?

He looked up as Burden re-entered the room. Burden had been going through the clothes found on Williams's body: navy blue briefs – very different from the white underwear in the cupboard in Alverbury Road – brown socks, fawn cavalry-twill slacks, blue, brown, and cream striped shirt, dark blue St. Laurent sweater. The back pocket of the slacks had contained a checkbook for one of the accounts with the Anglian-Victoria at Pomfret (R. J. Williams, private account), and a wallet containing one fiver, three £1 notes, and two credit cards, Visa and American Express. No car keys, no house keys.

"He probably kept his house key on the same ring as his car keys," Burden said. "It's what I do."

"At any rate, we'll get at that bank account now. The doctor here says there was a tea-towel wrapped around his neck. To stanch the blood, presumably."

There came a knock at the door. Bennett

came into the room with a young woman, not anyone's idea of a Wife of Bath.

"Mrs. Wendy Williams, sir."

She looked about twenty-five. She was a pretty girl with a delicate, nervous face and fair, curly hair. Wexford asked her to sit down, the doctor having sprung to his feet. She slid into the chair, gripping the arms of it, and jumped as Crocker passed behind her on his way to the door. Burden closed the door behind them and stood there.

"What did you want to see me about, Mrs. Williams?"

She didn't answer. She had fixed him with a penetrating stare and her tongue came in and out, moistening her lips.

"I take it you're Rodney Williams's sister-in-law? Is that right?"

She moved her body back a little, hands still tight on the chair arms. "What do you mean, his sister-in-law?" She didn't wait for a reply. "Look, I . . . I don't know how to say this. I've been so . . . I've been nearly out of my mind." Mounting hysteria made her voice ragged. "I saw in the paper . . . a little bit in the paper and . . . Is that, that *person* they found . . . Is that my husband?"

9

It was seldom he could give people reassuring news. He was tempted to say no, of course not. The body has been identified. She was holding on to the arms of the chair, rubbing her fingers up and down the wood.

"What is your husband's name, Mrs. Williams?"

"Rodney John Williams. He's forty-eight." She spoke in short, jerky phrases, not waiting for the questions. "Six feet tall. He's fair going gray. He's a salesman. It said in the paper a salesman."

Burden stared, then looked down. She swallowed, made an effort against panic, an effort that concentrated on tensing her muscles.

"Could you . . . please, I have a photo here."

Her hands, unlocked from the chair, refused to obey her when first she tried to open her bag. The photograph she handed to Wexford fluttered, she was shaking so. He looked at it, unbelieving.

It was Rodney Williams all right, high domed forehead, crack of a mouth parted in a broad smile. It was a more recent picture than the one Joy had and showed Williams in swimming trunks (flabby hairless chest, spindleshanks, a bit knock-kneed) with this girl in a black bikini and another girl, also bikini'd but no more than twelve years old. Wexford's eyes returned to the unmistakable face of Williams to the head you somehow wanted to slap a fringed wig on and so transform it.

She was waiting, watching him. He nodded. She brought a fluttery hand up to her chest, to her heart perhaps, froze for a moment in this tragic pose. Then her eyelids fell and she sagged sideways in the chair.

Afterwards he was to think of it as having been beautifully done but at the time he saw it only as a genuine faint. Burden held her shoulders, bringing her face down onto her knees. Picking up the phone, Wexford asked for a policewoman to come up, Polly Davies or Marion Bayliss, anyone who was around. And someone send a pot of strong tea and don't forget the sugar basin.

Wendy Williams came out of her faint, sat

up, and pressed her face into her hands.

"You are the wife of Rodney John Williams and you live in Liskeard Avenue, Pomfret?"

She drank the tea sugarless and very hot, at first with her eyes closed. When she opened her eyes and they met his he noticed they were the very clear pale blue of flax flowers. She nodded slowly.

"How long have you been married, Mrs. Williams?"

"Sixteen years. We had our sixteenth wedding anniversary in March."

He could hardly believe it. Her skin had the clear bloom of an adolescent's, her hair was baby-soft and the curl in it looked natural. She saw his incredulity and in spite of her emotion was flattered, a little buoyed up. He could tell she was the sort of woman to whom compliments, even unspoken ones, were food and drink. They nourished her. A faint, tremulous smile appeared. He looked again at the photographs.

"My daughter Veronica," she said. "I got married very young. I was only sixteen. That picture was taken three or four years back."

A bigamist he had been, then. Not a common or garden wayward husband with a girlfriend living in the next town, not a married man with a sequence of pricey mistresses, but your good old-fashioned true-blue bigamist. There was no doubt in Wexford's mind that Wendy Williams had as good-looking a marriage certificate as Joy's, and if hers happened not to be valid she would be the last to know it.

That, then was why he had taken no change of clothes with him. He had those things in his other home. And more than that, much more. Wexford now saw the point of those bank accounts: one for his salary to be paid into and two joint accounts to be fed from it, one for each household, R. J. Williams and J. Williams; R. J. Williams and W. Williams. There had been no need to assume a different name on his second marriage – Williams was common enough to make that unnecessary. He had been like a Moslem who keeps strictly to Islamic law and maintains his wives in separate and distinct dwellings. The difference here was that the wives didn't know of each other's existence.

That Williams had had another wife, what one might call in fact a chief wife, was something this girl was going to have to be told. And Joy was going to have to be told about her.

"Can you tell me when you last saw Mr. Williams?" Not calling him "your husband" any more was the beginning of breaking the news.

"About two months ago. Just after Easter."

This wasn't the time to ask her to account for that eight-week gap. He told her he would come and see her at home that evening. Polly Davies would look after her and see she got home safely.

Something had at last happened to distract Burden temporarily from his private troubles. His expression was as curious and as alert as a little boy's.

"What did he do at Christmas?" he said. "Easter? What about holidays?"

"No doubt we shall find out. Other bigamists have handled it. He probably had a Bunbury as well."

"A *what*?"

"A nonexistent friend or relative to provide him with alibis. My guess is Williams's Bunbury was an old mother."

"Did he have an old mother?"

"God knows. Creating one from his imagination wouldn't have been beyond his capacity, I'm sure. You know what they say, a mother is the invention of necessity."

Burden winced. "That night he left Alverbury Road, d'you think he went to his other home?"

"I think he set off meaning to go there.

Whether he reached it is another matter."

Fascinated by Williams's family arrangements, Burden said, "While Joy thought he was traveling for Sevensmith Harding in Ipswich he was with Wendy, and while he was with Joy Wendy thought he was where?"

"I don't suppose she knew he worked for Sevensmith Harding. He probably told her a total lie about what he did."

"You'd think he'd have got their names muddled – I mean called Wendy Joy and Joy Wendy."

"There speaks the innocent monogamist," said Wexford, casting up his eyes. "How do you think married men with girlfriends manage? Wife and all get called 'darling.' "

Burden shook his head as if even speculating about it was too much for him. "Do you reckon it was one of them killed him?"

"Carried his body and stuck it in that grave? Williams weighed a good fifteen stone or two hundred and ten pounds or ninety something kilos or whatever we're supposed to say these days."

"It might have been Wendy made that phone call."

"You reckon her voice sounds like Joy's?"

Burden was obliged to admit that it didn't. Joy's was monotonous, accent-free, uninflected;

Wendy's girlish, rather fluting, with a faint lisp. Wexford was talking about voices, about the rather unattractive but nevertheless memorable quality of Joy's voice, when his phone rang again.

"Another lady to see me," he said to Burden, putting the receiver back.

"Bluebeard's third wife?" It was the first attempt at a joke he had made in two months.

Wexford appreciated that. "Let's say a fan, rather. Someone who saw me on the telly."

"Look, why don't I take Martin and get on over to Wheatley? Then I'll be able to come to Wendy's with you tonight."

"OK, and we'll take Polly along."

The girl walked into his room in a breeze of confidence. She was seventeen or eighteen and her name was Eve Freeborn. Apposite names of the Lady Dedlock - Ernest Pontifex - Obadiah Slope kind that Victorian novelists used are in real life less uncommon than is generally supposed. That Eve Freeborn was aptly named Wexford came quickly to understand. She might have been dressed and cast for the role of Spirit of Freedom in a pageant. Her hair was cropped short and dyed purple in parts. She wore stretch jeans, a checked shirt, and thongs.

The story she told Wexford, sitting with legs wide apart, hands linked, forearms making a bridge from the chair arms to rest her chin on, was delivered in a brisk and articulate way. Eve was still at school, had come there straight from school. President of the debating society no doubt, he thought. As she turned her hands outwards, thumbs on her jaw, he noticed the felt-tipped pen drawing on her wrist, a raven with a woman's head, and then as she moved her arm the shirtsleeve covered it.

"I realized it was my duty as a citizen to come to you. I delayed just long enough to discuss the matter with my boyfriend. He's at the same school as me – Haldon Finch. In a way he's involved, you see. We have the sort of relationship where we believe in total openness."

Wexford gave her an encouraging smile.

"My boyfriend lives in Arnold Road, Myringham. It's a single-story house, number forty-three." Opposite Graham Gee, who had reported the presence of poor old Greta, Wexford thought. "His mother and father live there too," said Eve in a tone that implied enormous condescension and generosity on the part of the boyfriend in allowing his parents to live in their own house. "The point is – and you may not believe this but it's the honest truth, I promise you – they don't like him having me to stay the night with him. I mean, not me personally, you could understand that if they didn't like me, but any girl. So what we do is I come round after he's gone to bed and get in the window."

Wexford didn't gape at her. He merely felt like doing this. He couldn't resist asking, "Why doesn't he come to you?"

"I share a room with my sister. Anyway, I was telling you. I went round to his place around ten that Thursday night. There wasn't all that much space to park and when I was reversing I went into the car behind. I just bashed the wing of it a bit, not much, it wouldn't have had to have a new wing or anything, but I did think it was my duty to take responsibility and not just leave it, so I . . ."

"Just a moment. This was the night of April the fifteenth?"

"Right. It was my boyfriend's birthday."

And a charming present he must have had, Wexford thought.

"What was this car you went into?"

"A dark blue Ford Granada. It was the car you asked about on TV. I wrote a note and put it on the windscreen, under a wiper. Just with my name and address and phone number. But it blew away or got lost or something because the car was still there a long while after that and the driver never got in touch with me."

At ten that night. Greta and Grenada had been there at ten but how long had it been there?

"Just as a matter of curiosity, whose car were you driving?"

"My own," she said, surprised.

"You have your own car?"

"My mother's technically. But it comes to the same thing."

No doubt it did. They were amazing, these young people. And the most amazing thing about them was that they had no idea previous generations had not behaved as they did. People got old, of course, became dull and staid, they knew that, but in their day surely teenage girls had slept with their boyfriends, appropriated their parents' cars, stayed out all night, dyed their hair all colors of the spectrum.

He thanked her for her help and as she got up he saw the little drawing or tattoo again. He realized that he didn't know which of the local schools Sara Williams attended. And there remained the as yet unknown quantity, Veronica Williams . . .

"Do you know of a girl of your own age called Sara Williams? Is she perhaps at school with you?"

He was positive she hadn't made the connection before, was making it now for the first time. "Do you mean Sara is the daughter of this man who was murdered?"

"Yes. You go to the same school?"

"No, we don't," she said carefully, "but I know her."

Wheatley lived on an estate of new houses on the Pomfret side of Myringham. They had been built, Burden recalled, by a company so anxious to sell their houses that 100 percent mortgages had been guaranteed for them and a promise given to buy a house back for its purchase price if after two years the occupier was dissatisfied. The place had a raw look, oddly cold in the June sunshine. Wheatley's pregnant wife came to the door. A child of about three, a girl, was behind her, holding on to her skirt. Burden registered the fact of the pregnancy and the sex of the child with his heightened sensitivity to such matters and then he thought that his wife's pregnancy might have affected Wheatley's attitude to the girl he picked up. For instance, he might be sexually frustrated. Burden knew all about that. Wheatley too might have exaggerated the purity of his attitude towards the girl because he dared not risk the possibility of his pregnant wife finding out he was capable of putting his hand on other women's knees – or, in this instance no doubt, on other woman's breasts.

The third bedroom of this very small house had been turned into a study or office for Wheatley. He was on the phone but rang off within seconds of Burden's and Martin's arrival. Yes, he had remembered some more about the girl. He was sure he could give them a more detailed description. There was no question of his remembering more of what the girl had said to him because she hadn't said any more. "Thanks" and a gasp had been the only sounds that had come from her.

"I told you she was tall for a woman, at least five feet nine. Still in her teens, I'm sure. She had dark brown shoulder-length hair with a fringe, very fair skin, and very white hands. I think I can remember a ring, not a wedding or engagement ring or anything, but one of those big silver rings they wear. I wouldn't call her pretty, not a bit." Was that a sop to the wife who had come quietly into the room, carrying the little girl? "Sunglasses, a dark leather shoulder bag. She had blue denim jeans on and a gray cardigan. She was thin – really skinny, I mean." Another matrimonial sop. "And underneath the cardigan she had a tee-shirt on. It was a white tee-shirt with a crazy picture on it – some sort of bird with a woman's head."

"You didn't mention that before, Mr. Wheatley."

"I didn't mention the ring before or what color her clothes were. You asked me to think about it and I thought about it and that's what I remember. You can take it or leave it. A white tee-shirt with a bird on it with a woman's face."

"I don't believe it!"

She stared at Wexford, her mouth open in an appalled sort of way, her eyelids moving. She brought her hands up and scrabbled at her neck.

"I don't believe it!" Now there was defiance in her tone. Then, by changing one word, she showed him she accepted, she understood that what he had told her was true. "I *won't* believe it!"

Polly Davies was with him, sitting there like a good chaperone, silent but attentive. She glanced at Wexford, got a nod from him.

"I'm afraid it's true, Mrs. Williams."

"I don't – I don't have a right to be called that, do I?"

"Of course you do. Your name doesn't depend on a marriage certificate." Wexford thought of Eve Freeborn. There was a world between her and Wendy Williams, though a mere fourteen years, less than a generation, separated them. Would Eve know such a thing as a marriage certificate existed?

"Mrs. Williams," said stalwart Polly, "why don't you and I go and make some coffee? We'd all like coffee, I'm sure. Mr. Wexford will want to ask you some questions but I know he'd like you to have time to get over the shock of this."

She nodded and got up awkwardly as if her bones were stiff. A glazed look had come across her face. She walked like a sleepwalker and no one now would have mistaken her for a twenty-five-year-old.

Burden shrugged silently as the door closed behind them and subsided into one of his typical morose reveries. Wexford had a look round the room they were sitting in. The house was newer than the Williams home in Kingsmarkham, a small "townhouse" with an integral garage, built probably in the late 1960s. Wendy was a thorough, meticulous, and perhaps fanatical housekeeper. This was a through room with a dining area and it had very recently been redecorated in gleaming white with an undertone of palest pink. One of the colors in the Sevensmith Harding "Ice Cream" range? The carpet was deep strawberry pink, some of the furniture mahogany, some white canework, cushions in various shades of pink and red. It was tasteful, it was a far cry from the stereotyped shabbiness of Joy's home, but somehow it was also uncomfortable, as if everything had been placed there – hanging baskets, little tables, red Venetian glass – for effect rather than for use.

He remembered that a young girl also lived here. There were no signs of her. But what sign did he expect or would he recognize if he saw it? She had been twelve in the picture . . .

"My daughter is sixteen now," Wendy said when the coffee was brought. A slightly defiant tone came into her voice as she added, "She was sixteen three weeks ago."

Her gaze fell. He did some calculations, remembering what she had said about her wedding anniversary taking place in March. So Williams had "married" her three months before the child was born. He had had to wait until she reached the legal age of marriage.

"Where were you married, Mrs. Williams?"

"Myringham Registry Office. My mother wanted us to have a church wedding but – well, for obvious reasons . . ."

Wexford could imagine one very obvious reason if she had been six months pregnant. The nerve of Williams, a married man, "marrying" this child, as she had been, a mere dozen miles from his home town! The wedding to Joy,

Dora had told him, had been at St. Peter's, Kingsmarkham, the bride in white slipper satin . . .

Wendy was thrusting a paper at him. He saw it was her marriage certificate.

In the Registration District of Myringham, at the Register Office. Rodney John Williams, aged thirty-two. In some respects, at any rate, he had been honest. Though he could hardly have distorted those facts. They had been on his birth certificate. A Bath address, his brother's probably, his occupation sales representative. Wendy Ann Rees, aged sixteen, Pelham Street, Myringham, shop assistant. The witnesses had been Norman Rees and Brenda Rees, parents presumably, or brother and sister-in-law.

He handed it back to her. She looked at it herself and her tongue flicked out to moisten her lips. For a moment, from the way she was holding it, he thought she was going to tear the certificate across. But she replaced it in its envelope and laid the envelope on the low white melamine table that was close up against the arm of her chair.

She pressed her knees together and folded her hands in her lap. Her legs were very good, with elongated, slim ankles. To come to the police station she had worn a gray flannel suit with a white blouse. He had a feeling she was a woman who attached importance to being suitably dressed. The suit was changed now for a cotton dress. She was the type who would "save" her clothes, not sit about in a straight skirt or risk a spot on white silk. In her sad, wistful look youth had come back into her face.

"Mrs. Williams," he began, "I'm sure you won't mind telling me how it was you weren't alarmed when your husband was away for so long."

She did mind. She was reluctant. Patience, simply waiting quietly, succeeded with her where pressing the point might not have.

"Rodney and I . . ." She paused. It was always "Rodney" with her, Wexford noted, never "Rod." "We – we quarreled. Well, we had a very serious quarrel. That must have been a few days after Easter. Rodney spent Easter with his mother in Bath. He always spent Christmas and Easter with her. He was an only child, you see, and she's been in an old people's home for years and years."

Wexford carefully avoided looking at Burden. Wendy said, reminded by her own explanation, "Has she been . . . I mean, has anyone *told* her?"

Enigmatically, Wexford said that had been taken care of. "Go on please, Mrs. Williams."

"We quarreled," she went on. "It was a very private thing we quarreled about. I'll keep that to myself if you don't mind. I said to him that – well, I said that if – if *it* didn't stop, if he didn't promise me faithfully that never – well, I said I'd take Veronica away and he'd never see us again. I – I struck him, I was so angry, so distressed, I can't tell you – well, he was angry too. He denied it, of course, and then he said I needn't trouble about leaving him because he'd leave me. He said he couldn't stand my nagging any more." She lifted her head and looked Wexford straight in the eye. "I did nag him, I'll be honest about it. I couldn't bear it, never seeing him, him always being away. We'd never had a single Christmas together. I always had to go to my parents. We hardly ever had a holiday. I used to *beg* him . . ." Her voice faltered and Wexford understood that realization was dawning. She was beginning to see what the real reason was for those absences. "Anyway," she said, making an effort at control, "he – he calmed down after a while and I suppose I did too. He was going away again and he was due back on the Thursday – the fifteenth, that is. I was still very sore and upset but I said goodbye to him and that I'd see him on Thursday and he said maybe I would and maybe he'd never come back, so you see, I – when he didn't come back I thought he'd left me."

It wasn't a completely convincing explanation. He tried to put himself in her shoes. He tried to think how he would have felt years ago when he and Dora were young if they'd had a row and she, going away to visit her sister, say, had told him maybe she wouldn't come back. Probably such a thing had actually happened. It did happen in marriages, even in excellent ones. But if she hadn't come back on the appointed day, if she'd been a couple of hours late even, he'd have started going out of his mind with worry. Of course, much depended on the seriousness of the quarrel and on the reasons for it.

"Tell me what happened that Thursday."

"In the evening, do you mean?"

"When he didn't come."

"I was at work. Thursday's our late night. I didn't tell you, did I? I'm manageress of the fashion floor at Jickie's."

He was surprised. Somehow he had taken it for granted she didn't work. "In Myringham?" he asked. "Or the Kingsmarkham branch?"

"Oh, Kingsmarkham. In the Precinct."

Jickie's was Kingsmarkham's biggest department store, and the largest area of the Kingsbrook Shopping Precinct was given over to it. Doubtless Rodney Williams had taken care never to accompany Joy when she went shopping there for a jumper or a pair of tights on a Saturday afternoon. Had he risked walking arm in arm down Kingsmarkham High Street during shopping hours? With his son or daughter in the car, had he risked parking in the precinct car park? It was a tightrope he had walked and no doubt, for such is the nature of people like him, he had enjoyed walking it, but he had fallen off at last. Because of the tightrope or for some entirely different reason?

"We stay open till eight on Thursdays, but I can never get away till nine and it takes me a quarter of an hour to get home. When I did get back Veronica was here but Rodney hadn't come. I thought there was still a chance he might come but he didn't and then I knew. Or I thought I knew. I thought he'd left me."

"And in all the weeks that followed," Burden put it, "you weren't anxious. You didn't wonder what could happen to you and your daughter if he didn't come back?"

"I'd be all right financially without him. I've always had to work and now I'm doing quite well." There was a note of self-esteem in the little soft voice now. Inside the white and pink and fair curls and underneath the lisp and diffidence, Wexford thought there might be a core of steel. "We had a ninety percent mortgage on this house and up till five years ago it was all Rodney could do to keep us. He got promotion then and things were easier but I kept on working. I needed a life of my own too, he was away so much."

"Promotion?" hazarded Wexford, feeling his way.

"It's quite a small company and they haven't been doing too well lately – bathroom fittings and furniture, that sort of thing. Rodney was made sales manager for this locality."

Polly Davies picked up the tray and took it away into the kitchen. Wexford thought how easy it was to imagine Rodney Williams – or his idea of Rodney Williams – in his other home but next to impossible to imagine him here. Seated at that glass-topped dining table, for instance, with its bowl of pink and red roses or in one of those pink chintz armchairs. He had been a big, coarse man and everything here had a daintiness like a pink shell or the inside of a rose.

"I have to know what you quarreled about, Mrs. Williams."

Her tone became prissy, very genteel. "It has nothing whatsoever to do with Rodney's death."

"How do you know?"

She looked at him as if this were unfair persecution.

"How could it be? He got killed because he picked up someone hitching a lift and they killed him. Something like that . . . It's always happening."

"That's an interesting guess but it's only a guess, isn't it? You've no evidence for it and there's plenty of evidence against it. The car being returned to Myringham, for instance. A phone call was made to your husband's employers and a letter of resignation sent to them. Do you think that phone call was made by some homicidal hitchhiker?"

She sat rigid, keeping her eyes obstinately averted. Polly came back.

"Are you all right, Mrs. Williams?"

A nod. An indrawn breath and a sigh.

"What did you quarrel about?"

"I could refuse to tell you."

"You could. But why take a stand like that when what you tell us will be treated in the strictest confidence? Ask yourself if it's so awful that we won't have heard it before. And don't you think that if you don't tell us we may come to think it something worse than it really was?"

She sat silent. She wore an expression like someone who expects at any moment to see something nasty and shocking on television. It was an anticlimax when she said almost in a whisper, "There was another girl."

"You mean your husband had a woman friend he'd been seeing?"

" 'Seeing,' " she said, "I like that expression – 'seeing.' Yes, he'd been seeing a woman friend. That's one way of putting it."

"How would you put it?"

"Oh, like that. The way you do. What else does one say? Something crude, I suppose." The repressive lid suddenly jumped and let out a dribble of resentment, of bitterness. "I thought no one else but me would ever matter to him. I look young, don't I? I'm pretty enough, I don't look my age. People say I look eighteen. What was the matter with him that he . . . ? Yes, we quarreled about that. About a girl. I wanted him to promise me it would never happen again."

"He refused?"

"Oh, he promised. I didn't believe him. I thought it would start up again when he got the chance. I couldn't stand it, I didn't want him if he was going to do that. I was glad when he didn't come back. Don't you see? I was *glad*."

"I'll have to have this girl's name."

Quick as a flash: "I don't know her name."

"Come now, Mrs. Williams."

"I don't know it. He wouldn't tell me. Just a

girl. What does it matter?"

She had said too much already, she was thinking. He could read that, plain in her face, the look in her eyes of being appalled at her own indiscretion. At that moment, before he could say any more, the door opened and a young girl came in. Just before this happened there had been a sound downstairs and footsteps on the stairs – the living room was on the middle floor – but it had all taken place very quickly, within a few seconds. And now, without warning, the girl was here among them.

What first struck Wexford was that although she was not so tall and her hair was shorter she looked exactly like Sara Williams. They might have been twins.

10

Her hair was the same pale fudge color, not curly but not quite straight either, the tips just touching her shoulders. Brown eyes, ellipse eyebrows, small straight nose, fine white skin sprinkled with freckles, Rodney Williams's high domed forehead, and his small narrow mouth. But instead of jeans she wore a summer dress with white tights and white sandals. She stood in the doorway looking surprised at the sight of them, a little more than just startled.

Wendy Williams was taken aback.

In a flustered way she said, "This is my daughter Veronica," and to the girl, "You're home early."

"Not much. It's after nine."

The voice was her mother's, soft and slightly affected, but without the lisp. It was quite unlike Sara's abrupt, uninflected tones. Recovering poise Wendy said to her, "These are police officers. They'll only be a few minutes." She lied fluently, "It's to do with trouble at the shop. You won't mind leaving us alone for a bit, will you, darling?"

"I'm going to have a bath anyway."

Closing the door with the sort of precision her mother might use, she went off up the spiral staircase that was the core of this house.

"I don't know why she's so offhand with me lately. This past year . . ."

Wexford said, "You haven't told her?"

"I haven't seen her. She always goes to her friend's straight from school on a Tuesday. Or so she says, she's so secretive . . ."

"Which school, Mrs. Williams?"

"Haldon Finch Comprehensive. I'll tell her about her father after you've gone. I suppose I shall have to tell her what he was – a bigamist, with another wife somewhere. It won't be easy. I don't know if you appreciate that."

Wexford, when interrogating, would allow any amount of digression but never total distraction. Those he questioned were obliged to come back to the point sooner or later. It was hard on them, for often they believed they had escaped. The leash had snapped and freedom was surely there for the taking, but the hand always came down and snatched up the broken end.

"We were talking about this woman friend your husband had. He may have gone to her on the night he died."

"I don't know any more about her!"

Fear had come into her voice now. It was what many would have called caution or apprehensiveness, but it was really fear.

"You called her a girl. You implied a young girl."

A panicky, jerky, rapid way of speaking – "A young, single girl, very young, that's all I know. I told you, I don't know any more!"

Wexford recalled the overtures Williams had once made to Sylvia. When Sylvia was fifteen. Was it something like that that Wendy had implied when she asked so pathetically if she didn't still look young? That she at thirty-two to his forty-eight might not be young enough for him?

"Do you mean she's young enough to live at home with her parents?"

A nod, painful and perplexed.

"What else do you know of her, Mrs. Williams?"

"Nothing. I don't know any more. Do you think I wanted him to talk to me about her?"

That was reasonable enough. At first he

thought she was lying when she said she was ignorant of the girl's name. Now he was less sure. How often had he heard people say, "If my husband (my wife) were unfaithful to me I wouldn't want to know," and when they were forced to know, "I don't want to hear anything about it"? The knives of jealousy are honed on details.

The question he sensed she would hate but which must be asked he had saved till last.

"How did you know it was happening at all? How did you know of her existence?"

He had been wrong. She didn't mind. She didn't mind because her answer was a lie that she had been rehearsing in her mind, silently and busily while they talked, waiting for the past half-hour for the question to come.

"I had an anonymous letter."

Eventually he would get at the truth. It could wait.

"Now, Mrs. Williams, your daughter . . ."

"What about her?" Very quick and defensive.

"I shall want to talk to Veronica."

"Oh no, not that. Please."

"When you have told her and she has had a day or two to get over the shock."

"But why?"

"Her father has been murdered. He was due to come here and she was here, alone here. It's possible he did come and she was the last person to see him alive."

"He didn't come here. She would have told me."

"We'll see, Mrs. Williams. We shall also want to look over this house, particularly at any of your husband's personal property."

"We keep coming back to these young girls," Burden said.

"And to ravens with women's faces."

"That too. Budd and Wheatley were both attacked by a young girl – not very seriously, either of them, but they were attacked and the assault was with a knife. Rodney Williams liked young girls – I mean, he seems especially to have liked them very young – and he had a very young girlfriend. He died as the result of a knife attack, he was stabbed to death. Now Wheatley says the girl who attacked him was wearing a white tee-shirt with a design on it of a sort of bird with a woman's head . . ."

"And Sara Williams," said Wexford, "possesses just such a tee-shirt and has a poster with a similar motif on her bedroom wall."

"Does she? You're kidding."

"No. It's true. And Eve Freeborn has a raven with a woman's head tattooed or drawn on her left wrist, and since the sun came out, Mike, and women aren't bundling themselves up in cardigans and jackets I've seen no less than five girls around Kingsmarkham and Pomfret wearing white tee-shirts with ravens with women's faces on them. How about that?"

"God, and I thought we were really getting somewhere. It's like that bit in Ali Baba and the Forty Thieves when the woman says he'll know the right oil jar because it'll have a cross on it and when he gets there someone's put crosses on all the oil jars."

"You've been reading again. Or going to pantomimes. It looks to me as if these raven-happy pictures are the motif or symbol of some sort of society or cult. Latter-day anarchists or some sort of spurious freedom fighters."

"Animal rights?" said Burden doubtfully.

"It could be, I suppose. The implication being that the animal – or in this case bird – has the feelings and rights of a human being? The poster Sara Williams has in her bedroom has some letters on it as well as the picture. An acronym, I think, a,r,r,i,a, Arria."

"Animal Rights something or other?"

"There was a woman called Arria, in Roman history, I seem to remember. I'll try and find out. If it's animal rights, Mike, you would expect its members to make their attacks on people who in their view were being cruel to animals. Factory farmers, for instance, or masters of foxhounds. I don't suppose Wheatley keeps calves chained up in boxes in his back garden, does he? We'll ask Sara. But first I want to leave her and Joy to get over the shock of Williams having another wife and another child."

"You've told them?"

"Yes. It was the money aspect that seemed to mean most to Joy. She had been deprived in order that he could maintain another household. She gave that bitter laugh of hers. If I'd had to live with that laugh it would have got horribly on my nerves."

"How's Martin getting on with his typewriter inquiries?"

Wexford threw the report across the desk. It was no Sevensmith Harding machine that had been used to type Williams's letter of resignation. All the typewriters in use in the Myringham office were of the sophisticated electronic kind. Neither of the Williams households contained a typewriter of any sort. The Harmers had a typewriter in the two-story flat over the shop where they lived, and both Hope Harmer and her daughter Paulette used it. It was a small Olivetti, an electric machine.

"His new young lady typed that letter," Burden said. "Find her and we find the typewriter."

"Find her and it won't matter whether we find the typewriter or not."

Sergeant Martin had also been to Bath.

There, it seemed, Rodney Williams had had his origins. On an estate of houses some few miles outside the city, in a house very like the one Rodney had bought for his second bride, lived his brother Howard. It was Howard's address that appeared on Wendy's marriage certificate.

His parents had also once lived in Bath but his father had died when he was a child and his mother when Rodney was twenty-seven. That dead mother Rodney in his calculating way had used to his advantage. No doubt he had told Wendy that old Mrs. Williams disapproved of his marriage to a young girl, would never wish to meet her, but the good son would be obliged to pay the occasional duty visit . . .

The brother seemed honest and straightforward. There was very little contact between him and Rodney. Years ago, fifteen or sixteen at least, some of Rodney's mail had been sent to his address by mistake. He had simply sent it on. Communications from the registrar at the time of the marriage to Wendy, Wexford thought. Howard Williams was also a salesman and on 15 April he had been in Ireland on business for his firm.

Joy hadn't told him of his brother's death. He had seen it in the papers and seemed to have reacted with calm indifference.

Wendy Williams's home was on the outskirts of Pomfret and a mile from the Harmers' shop. Had the relative nearness of his inlaws to his second and bigamous home worried Williams? Had he agreed to buy a house there only to placate Wendy or gratify some wish of hers? Or did he see this sort of risk as just part of the tightrope walk?

Between the estate and the nucleus of the town, that which not long ago *was* the town, lay the sports grounds of the Haldon Finch Comprehensive School, playing fields, tennis courts, fives courts, running track. The Haldon Finch, though new and an example of the new education with its two thousand pupils of both sexes housed in no less than six buildings, was as much "into" games as any public school of the past. You might get ten O-levels but you were nothing if you weren't good at games.

At 5:30 in the afternoon twelve girls were playing tennis on the courts adjacent to Procter Road.

"It must be a match with another school," Burden said. "They start after school's finished."

He and Wexford were in the car, on their way

to see Veronica Williams. Donaldson had taken a short cut, or at least a traffic-avoiding cut, and they had found themselves amid this complex of sports fields.

"We'll get out and watch for a minute or two."

Burden got out, though demurring.

"It makes me feel funny standing about watching girls. I mean, you ask yourself – *they* ask *themselves* – what sort of blokes would do that?"

"What would you think if you saw two middle-aged women watching young men playing squash?"

Burden looked sideways at him.

"Well, nothing, would I? I mean, I'd think they were their mothers or just women who liked watching sport."

"Exactly. Doesn't that tell you something? Two things? One is that, whatever the women's movement says, there is a fundamental difference between men and women in their attitude to sex, and the other that this is an area in which women might claim – if it's occurred to them – to be superior to us."

"It's changing though, you have to admit. Look at all those clubs up north where men do strips for women audiences."

"The attitude is still different. Men go to

strip shows and gawp in a sort of seething silence."

"Don't women?"

"Apparently women laugh," said Wexford.

One of the tennis players was Eve Freeborn. He spotted her from the purple slick in her hair. Her partner was a thin, dark girl, their opponents a big, heavily built blonde and another thin, dark girl, this one wearing glasses. This four was on the court nearest to the road. Wexford could see enough of the other two courts and the other four couples only to be sure that Sara Williams was not among them. Sara didn't attend the Haldon Finch, of course – that would have been too great a risk even for Rodney Williams – but if this was a match six of the girls must come from another school. Seated on the three umpire chairs were three young women who had the look of games mistresses.

He was aware at once that no one was playing very well. Had the standard deteriorated since the days when he had watched Sylvia and Sheila play tennis? No, it wasn't that. It was television. These days you saw tennis played on TV. Top championships week after week, it seemed, here or in Europe or in America, and it spoiled you for the real thing, the local article. A pity really. It made you irritated at how often they missed the ball. Eve Freeborn had a good hard service. She would have served aces – only they were always on the wrong side of the line. Her opponent in the glasses was the worst player of the twelve, slow on her feet, with a weak service and a way of scooping the ball up into the air, making it easy prey for Eve's slamming racket.

"Two match points," said Burden, who had been attending more closely to the progress of the set.

Eve served a double fault. One match point. She served again, weakly, and the blonde shot it back like an arrow down the tramlines. The umpire announced deuce. Eve served another double fault.

"Van out," said Wexford.

"My God, but that shows your age. That's what they said at tennis parties in the thirties."

The umpire corrected him by saying crisply that the score was "advantage Kingsmarkham." So it was Kingsmarkham High who were the visitors here, once a grammar school, now private and fee-paying, no longer state-aided.

Kingsmarkham won the game. They changed ends, the girls paused by the umpire's chair and wiped faces and arms, drank Coke out of cans. Eve was standing only a few yards from Wexford. The little flame-colored badge he had till now seen only as an orange spot near the neckline of her white tee-shirt showed itself at closer quarters to be a badge. He could make out spread wings on it and the letters ARRIA. Eve didn't or wouldn't look at him. Perhaps he wasn't recognizable out of his office, in shirt-sleeves. He peered more closely. The umpire got down from her chair and came to the wire fence. She was a stocky, muscular young woman with a cross face and flashing eyes. In a voice full of crushed ice she said, "Was there something you wanted?"

Wexford inhibited all the possible replies, improper, provocative, even mildly lecherous, that sprang to mind. He was a policeman. Anyway, Burden got in first with the flasher's classic caught-before-the-act answer.

"We were just looking."

"Well, perhaps you'd like to get on with whatever you're supposed to be doing."

"Move along, Mike," said Wexford.

They went quickly to the car. The games mistresses glared after them.

"Do they still call them games mistresses?"

Burden was silent for a moment. Then he said, screwing up his face, "I'll tell you when my new daughter's eleven. If she gets to exist. If she gets to be eleven. If she and I are together when she does."

"It's not as bad as that."

"No? Maybe not. Maybe it's she and I that'll be together and not Jenny and I."

Things must be bad with Burden for him to burst out with that in Donaldson's hearing. Not that Donaldson would say a word. But he would hear and he would think. Wexford said nothing. He watched Burden's face close up, the eyes grow dull and the mouth purse, the frown that was hardly ever absent re-establish itself in a deep double ridge. The car drew away. He looked behind him and saw Eve leaping to achieve her best volley of the match.

"Veronica was supposed to be playing in a tennis match," said Wendy Williams, "but of course she was too upset. She hasn't been to school today, and I had to take the day off. I had to tell her her father had another wife and family. It was bad enough telling her he was dead."

The second Mrs. Williams, whom Wexford had at first thought of as rather sweet and gentle, he now saw had other sides to her nature, among them a rather unpleasant habit of laying the blame for her misfortunes on whomsoever else might be present.

"I told her everything and at first she wouldn't speak and then she became very distressed." The soft little voice trickled round the phrases. The eyes opened wide and wistful, like a Pear's Soap child seeing distant angels. Wexford had the disturbing thought that perhaps she had cultivated all this because Williams had fancied little girls. "You'll be gentle with her, won't you? You'll remember she's only sixteen? And it's not just that she's lost her father, it's worse than that."

No question here of being sent up to the girl's bedroom. Veronica would come down. And Wendy would be there. He supposed Veronica must have been the missing tennis player for whom the dark girl not wearing glasses had substituted. While he was speculating Veronica came in, walking diffidently, a dead look still on her face. She had been crying but that was a long while ago now. Her eyes were dry and the lids pale, but a puffiness remained. Nevertheless she had dressed herself carefully for this encounter, as had her mother. Such things, which would have been lost on many men, never escaped Wexford. Wendy was in a black cotton dress with big sleeves that was a little too becoming to qualify as true mourning and Veronica in a pink pleated skirt, a sweatshirt with a gold V on it, and pink and white running shoes. Probably Wendy got their clothes from Jickie's at a discount.

"This is Chief Inspector Wexford and Inspector Burden, darling. They want to ask you one or two questions. Nothing difficult or complicated. They know what a bad shock you've had. And I shall be here all the time."

For God's sake, she's not ten, Wexford thought. The girl's dull, staring look disconcerted him.

"I'm sorry about your dad, Veronica," he began. "I know you're feeling unhappy and you'd probably like to be left alone. But your mother's told you what's happened. Your father isn't simply dead. He was killed. And we have to find out who killed him, don't we?" A not unfamiliar doubt assailed him. Did they? *Cui bono?* Who would be satisfied, avenged, recompensed? He was a policeman and it wasn't for him to think such thoughts. Not a hint of them was in his tone. He looked at the girl and wondered what had been going on in her mind all those weeks her father was missing. Had she believed, like her mother, that he was with another woman? Or had she accepted his absence as she must have accepted all his other absences when he was allegedly away traveling for his firm or paying filial visits in Bath? She was no longer looking at him but down at the floor, her head drooping like a tired flower on a stalk.

"Do you think we could go back to April the fifteenth?" he said. "It was a Thursday. Your mother expected your father home that evening but she had to stay on late at work. You were here though, weren't you?"

The "yes" came very quietly. He might not have understood it for what it was if she hadn't nodded as well.

"What did you do? You came home from school when – at four?" He too was talking to her as if she were ten, but something in her attitude, her bowed head, feet crossed, hands in lap, seemed to invite it. Again that nod, the head lifted a little to make it. "And then what happened? What sort of time did you expect your father to come?"

She murmured that she didn't know.

"We never knew what time to expect him," Wendy said. "We never knew. It might have been anytime."

"And did he come?" said Wexford.

"Of course he didn't! I've told you."

"Please, Mrs. Williams, let Veronica answer."

The girl was shy, nervous, perhaps also unhappy. She was certainly in shock still. But suddenly she made an effort. It was as if she saw that there was no help for it, she was going to have to talk, she might as well get it over. Sara's tortoiseshell brown eyes looked into his and Sara's Primavera lips parted with a quiver.

"I had tea. Well, a Coke and some stuff Mummy left me in the fridge." Yes, Wendy for all her own youth was the kind of woman who would be smotheringly protective, even to the extent of preparing meals in advance for a sixteen-year-old as if she were an invalid. Veronica said, "I'd asked my friend round – the one whose place I was at when you came before – but she rang up and said she couldn't come. She said I could go to her."

"But you wanted to wait in for your father?"

She was no Sara, no Eve Freeborn. She turned her head and looked to her mother for help. It came, as no doubt it always did.

"Veronica had no need to wait in for Rodney. I've told you, we never really thought he'd come at all."

" 'We' Mrs. Williams?"

"Well, I don't really know what Veronica thought. I hadn't said anything to her then about the possibility of our splitting up. I was waiting to see what would happen. But the point is Veronica had no need to wait in for him and I wouldn't have . . . well, she's got her own life to lead."

What had she been going to say when she broke off and made that extraordinary statement about this little creature's obviously nonexistent independence?

"You went out then?"

"I went to my friend's. I didn't stop there long. We played records. I wanted her to come out for a coffee but she couldn't, she was baby-sitting with her brother. She's got a brother who's only two. That was why she couldn't come over to me."

"So you went back home. What time?"

"I didn't go straight home. I had a coffee on my own at Castor's. I got home about nine and Mummy came in ten minutes after."

"You must have been disappointed your father wasn't there."

"I don't know," she said. "I didn't think about it," and surprisingly, for this wasn't really at issue, "I don't mind being alone. I like it."

"Well, my goodness," said Wendy, not letting that one pass, "you're never left alone if I can help it. You needn't talk as if you'd been neglected."

Wexford asked the name of the friend and was told it was Nicola Tennyson and given an address that was between here and the town center. No objection was put up by Wendy to their examining such of his personal property as Rodney Williams had in this house. It left Wexford with the feeling that this was because she rather wanted them to see over her house, its cleanliness, its elegant appointments, and the evidence of her skill as housekeeper.

Here, at any rate, was the rest of William's wardrobe. It was interesting to observe how he had kept his more stylish and "in" clothes for this household. Jeans hung in the gilt-decorated white built-in cupboard, Westerner shirts, a denim suit, and another in a fashionably crumpled stone-colored linen mixture. There were two pairs of half-boots and a pair of beige kid moccasins. And the underwear was designed for a younger man than the part-time occupant of 31 Alverbury Road.

"He was two different men," Wexford said.

"Perhaps three."

"We shall see. At any rate he was two, one middle-aged, set in his ways, bored maybe, taking his family for granted, the other young still, even swinging – take a look at these underpants – making the grade with a young wife, living up to this little bandbox."

Wexford looked around him at the room, thinking of Alverbury Road. There were duvets on the beds here, blinds at the windows, a white cane chair suspended from the ceiling, its seat piled with green, blue, and white silk cushions. And the bed was a six-foot-wide king-size.

"He probably called it the playpen," said

Burden pulling a face.

"Once," said Wexford.

In this house Williams had had no desk, only a drawer in the gilt-handled white melamine chest of drawers. This had been Wendy's house, no doubt about it, the sanctum where Wendy held sway. Girlish, fragile, soft-voiced though she might be, she had made this place her own, feminine and exclusive – exclusive in a way of Rodney Williams. He had been there on sufferance, Wexford sensed, his presence depending on his good behavior. And yet his behavior had not been very good even from the first. There had always been the traveling, the Bunbury of a mother, the long absences. So Wendy had made a home full of flowers and colors and silk cushions in which he was allotted small corners as if – unconsciously, he was sure it was unconsciously – she knew the day would come when it would be for herself and her daughter alone. Wexford looked inside the drawer but it told him little. It was full of the kind of papers he would have expected.

Except for Williams's driving license with the Alverbury Road address.

"He was taking a risk leaving that about," said Burden.

"Taking risks was his life. He took them all the time. He enjoyed the high wire. Anyway, suspicious wives read letters, not driving licenses."

There were bills in the drawer, the carbons from credit-card chits, an American Express monthly account. Which address had that gone to? Yes, this one. It fitted somehow. Visa and Access were the workaday cards, American Express more cosmopolitan, more for the playboy. No doubt it was Wendy who paid the services' bills from the joint account. There was none in the drawer, only a rates demand, a television rental account book, an estimate from Godwin and Sculp, builders, of Pomfret, dated 30 March, for painting the living room, and an invoice from the same firm (stamped *Paid*) for renewal of a bathroom cistern. Under this lot lay Rodney's joint account checkbook, a paying-in book for the joint account, and a small glass bottle, half full of tablets, labeled "Mandaret."

On this the top floor of the house were two more bedrooms and a bathroom. Veronica's room was neat as a pin, white with a good deal of *broderie anglaise* about it and owing much to those magazine articles prevalent in Wendy's own childhood on how to make a dream bedroom for your daughter. No doubt poor Wendy had never had a dream bedroom of her own, Wexford thought, and here, no home-made mobiles, and no books either. It was designed for a girl who would do nothing in it but sit in the window seat looking pensive and wearing white socks.

The spiral staircase, a contraption of hideous discomfort and danger to all but the most agile, went through the middle of the house like a screw in a press. Down on the ground floor was a shower room, a separate lavatory, the third door on that side opening into the integral garage, and at the end of the passage a room the width of the house that opened through French windows onto patio and garden roughly the size of a large dining table. The room, which might have been for dining in or as a study for Rodney Williams if he had been allowed one, was plainly devoted to Wendy's interests. She had a sewing machine in it and a knitting machine, an ironing board set up with two irons on it, one dry and one steam, and there were clothes everywhere, neatly hung or draped, sheathed in plastic bags.

Mother and daughter were still sitting upstairs at the glass-topped table. Wendy had taken up some sewing, a handkerchief or possibly a tray-cloth into which she was inserting tiny stitches, her little finger crooked in the way it used to be said was vulgar to hold a teacup. Veronica nibbled at dry-roasted peanuts out of a foil packet. The dry kind it would be, the other sort tending to leave grease spots. They were both as tense as compressed springs, waiting for the police to go and leave them alone.

"Have you heard of a society or club called ARRIA?" Wexford said to Veronica.

The spring didn't leap free of its bonds. There was no shock. Veronica merely nodded. She didn't screw up the empty peanut packet but flattened it and began folding it very carefully, first into halves, then quarters.

"At school?"

She looked up. "Some of the girls in the sixth and seventh years belong to it."

"But you don't?"

"You have to be over sixteen."

"Why girls?" he said. "Haldon Finch is co-ed. Don't any boys belong?"

She was a normal teenager really. Underneath the prissy looks, the shyness, the Mummy's girl air, she was one of them. The look she gave him seethed with their scorn for the cretinous incomprehension evinced by adults.

"Well, it's all women, isn't it? It's for women. They're – what d'you call it? – feminists, militant feminists."

"Then I hope you'll keep clear of it, Veronica," Wendy said very quickly and sharply for her. "I hope you'll have nothing to do with it. If there's anything I really hate it's women's lib. Liberation! I'm liberated and look where it's got me. I just hope you'll do better than I have when the time comes and find a man who'll really support you and look after you, a nice good man who'll – who'll *cherish* you." Her lips trembled with emotion. She laid down her sewing. "I wasn't enough of a woman for Rodney," she said as if the girl wasn't there. "I wasn't enough of a girl. I got too hard and independent and – and *mature*, I know I did." A heroic effort was made to keep the tears in, the break out of the voice, and a victory was won. "You just remember that, Veronica, when your turns comes."

Sergeant Martin was handling the complaint, though, as he told Wexford, he hadn't much to go on. Nor had any harm been done – yet.

"A Ms. Caroline Peters, who's a physical education instructor at the Haldon Finch Comprehensive," Martin said. "Miz not Miss. She got very stroppy, sir, when I called her Miss. I called her an instructress too and had a job getting my tongue round it but that wasn't right either. She says two men were hanging about watching the girls playing a tennis match. Acting in a suspicious manner, she says.

Came in a car which was parked for the express purpose of them getting out to watch. Voyeurs she called them. Afterwards she asked the girls if any of them knew the men but they denied all knowledge."

Thank you, Miss Freeborn, thought Wexford.

"Leave it, Martin. Forget it. We've better things to do."

"Leave it altogether, sir?"

"I'll handle it." A note to the woman or a phone call explaining all, he supposed. She had a right to that. She was a good, conscientious teacher acting in a responsible manner. He mustn't laugh – except later perhaps with Burden.

There had been much food for thought picked up on his visits to Liskeard Avenue. And there had been something to make him wonder, something that was neither a piece of information nor the germ of an idea but entirely negative.

Wasn't it extraordinary that during those visits, those long talks, and during his initial interview with her, Wendy Williams had shown not the slightest interest in Rodney's other family? She had asked not a single question about the wife she had supplanted but not replaced, nor about the children who were siblings by half-blood of her own Veronica. Because she was inhibited by intense jealousy? Or for some other reason more germane to this inquiry?

11

Kevin Williams looked more like his mother than his father. He wouldn't have been recognizable as Veronica's half-brother. The genetic hand-down which was so distinctive a feature in Sara and Veronica had missed him, and his forehead was narrow, with the hair growing low on it. His manner was laconic, casual, indifferent.

Wexford, who had Martin with him, had interrupted what seemed to be a family conclave. For once the television was off, sight and sound. Joy Williams introduced no one but her son and this introduction she made proudly and with abnormal enthusiasm. Wexford was left to deduce that the woman and the girl who sat side by side on the yellow sofa must be Hope Harmer and her daughter Paulette.

Mrs. Harmer, though plumper, fairer, and

better cared for than her sister, looked too much like her for her identity to be in doubt. She was a pretty woman and even in the present crisis she looked pleased with life. But the girl – to use an expression favored by Wexford's grandsons – was "something else again." She was beautiful with a beauty that made Sara and Veronica merely pretty young girls. She reminded Wexford of a picture he had once seen, Rossetti's portrait of Mrs. William Morris. This girl was dark and her face had the same dark glow as the face in the picture, her features the same symmetry and her large dark eyes the same other-worldly soulfulness. When he asked her if she was who he thought she was she raised those dark gray dreaming eyes and nodded, then returned to what she had been looking at, a magazine that seemed entirely devoted to hairstyles.

Kevin's term had ended the day before and he had come straight home. Not to stay, though, he made clear to Wexford when they were alone in the stark dining room. He owed it to his mother to stay a few days, but next week he intended to stick to the plan he had made months before of going down to Cornwall to stay with a friend, and later he would be camping in France. He seemed astonished when Wexford asked him for the address of the Cornish friend.

"We'd rather you didn't leave the country at present."

"You can't keep me here. My father's death has nothing to do with me."

"Tell me what you did on the evening of Thursday, April the fifteenth."

"Was that when he died?" The casual manner had grown sullen. He was his mother in truculent mood all over again.

"I'll ask the questions, Kevin."

It wasn't said roughly, but nevertheless the boy looked as if no one had spoken like that to him before. His low forehead creased and his mouth pouted.

"I only asked. He was my father."

In his tone, that of contrived, badly acted sentiment, Wexford suddenly understood that no one in this household had cared a damn for Rodney Williams. And they hadn't in the other household either. People didn't care for him for long. In this area he had, at any rate, got his deserts.

"What happened that evening? What did you do?"

"Phoned home, I suppose," he said, careless again. "I always do on Thursdays or my mother goes bananas."

"You phone from college?"

"No, the phones are always out of order or it's a hassle finding one that's free." Kevin seemed to have decided he might as well give in to Wexford's questioning, if not with a good grace. "I go out to phone. Well, two or three of us do. To a pub. I phone home and transfer the charge."

"You'll remember that Thursday if I tell you it was the first Thursday after you got back to college from the Easter vacation."

The boy thought about it, seeming to concentrate. Wexford had no doubt he had known perfectly well all along.

"Yeah, I do remember. I phoned home around eight, eight-thirty – I don't reckon you want to know to the minute, do you? My mother was out. I talked to Sara."

"That must have surprised you, your mother being out when you phoned."

"Yeah, it was unusual. She thinks the sun shines out of my arse, as you've maybe noticed." He jerked his shoulders in an exaggerated shrug. "Unusual," he said, "but not unknown."

More indignation came when Wexford asked for the names of Kevin's companions on the trip to the pub where the phone was. But it was hot air, pointless obstructiveness. The names were forthcoming after some expostulation.

"How did you get on with your father?"

"There was no communication. We didn't talk. The usual sort of situation, right?"

"And your father and Sara?"

The reply came sharply. It was incredible. It was exactly the reply a boy of Kevin's age might have made a hundred years before – or, according to literature, might have made.

"You can leave my sister out of this!"

Wexford tried not to laugh. "I will for now."

He found Joy and her sister questioning Martin in depth about Wendy Williams. The girls, the two cousins, had gone. Martin was answering in monosyllables and he looked relieved when Wexford came in. Joy broke off at once and, having seen he was alone, said, "Where's my son?" as if Wexford might have arrested him and already stowed him away in a police car.

This would be his first encounter with Miles Gardner since the discovery of Rodney William's body. He and Burden waited for him in the managing director's office. The paneled room was dim and shadowy in spite of the bright day outside. A copper pot filled with Russell lupins stood on the windowsill. Wexford picked up the desk photograph of Gardner's family and looked at it dubiously.

"I suppose I'm sensitized to adolescent girls," he said. "I see them everywhere."

"Just remember what the games mistress said."

"I don't think I'm in danger, though they're a very pretty lot we're in contact with. One can almost see Williams's point of view."

"He was just a dirty old lecher," said Burden, apparently forgetting Williams had been a mere three years his senior.

"The primrose way to the everlasting bonfire."

Gardner came in, apologizing for having kept them waiting. He began on some insincere-sounding expressions of sorrow at Williams's demise which Wexford listened to patiently and then cut short.

"If you're free for lunch we might all go over to the Old Flag."

But this was something Gardner, regretfully, couldn't manage. "I've promised to give my daughter lunch, my youngest one, Jane. She's got the day off school to go for an interview at the university here. A bit of an ordeal, she's a nervous kid, so I bribed her with the offer of a slap-up lunch."

The University of the South was situated at Myringham. Another eighteen-year-old then . . .

"She should get a place," Gardner said, and with a kind of rueful pride, "There go our holidays abroad for the next three years."

Wexford said he would like to talk to Christine Lomond, and in the room that had been Williams's if possible. Gardner took him there himself, up in the small, slow lift. There were two desks and two typewriters, a Sierra 3400 and an Olympia ES 100. But this place was "clean" as far as typewriters went. Martin had seen to that. The girl who came in was fresh-paint glossy in a suit of geranium-red linen, dark green cotton blouse, green glass rhomboid hanging on a chain, and on her left wrist a watch with a red and green strap. Her hair had been touched with what his daughter Sylvia assured him were called "low lights," though Wexford couldn't quite believe this and thought she must have been having him on. Christine Lomond's fingernails were the brilliant carmine of the latest Sevenshine front-door shade, Pillarbox ("A rich true red without a hint of blue, a robust high gloss that stands up ideally to wind and weather"). They scuttled over the filing cabinet like so many red beetles.

Wexford had asked her to see what she could find him as samples of Williams's own typing, any report, assessment, rough notes even, he might have brought to the office with him. She said she was sure anything of that sort would have been handwritten, and it was two or three handwritten sheets that she produced for him, and then several more which she told him had probably been typed on the Olympia machine but using a different daisywheel, thus altering the typeface. Wexford was particularly interested because there seemed to him to be a flaw in the apex of the capital A.

The experiment, however, showed nothing but his own ignorance of typewriters or at any rate of recent technological advances made in typewriters. The red-tipped white fingers whipped a sheet of paper into the machine, switched it on, switched it off, whipped out the daisywheel, inserted another, and rapidly produced a facsimile of the first four lines of Williams's sales forecast for the first three months of the year.

"It's getting a bit ragged," Christine Lomond said. "We need a new wheel," and she pulled the damaged one out and dropped it into the wastepaper basket.

"Where do you live, Miss Lomond?"

"Here. In Myringham. Why?" She had a rather abrupt manner, of the kind that is usually called "crisp."

"Did you like Mr. Williams?"

She was silent. She seemed affronted, having

anticipated perhaps nothing more than an investigation of papers and machines. How old was she? Twenty-six? Twenty-seven? She could be a good deal less than that. The heavy make-up and elaborate hairstyle aged her.

"Well, Miss Lomond?"

"Yes, I liked him. Well, I liked him all right. I didn't think about liking or disliking him."

"Would you think back, please, and give me some idea of what you were doing on the evening of April the fifteenth?"

"I can't possibly remember that far back!"

Her eyelids flapped. They were a gleaming laminated sea blue ("Delicate turquoise with a hint of silver, ideal for that special ceiling, alcove, or display cabinet").

"Try and pinpoint it," said Burden, "by thinking of what you were doing next day. That was the morning someone phoned to say Mr. Williams was ill and wouldn't be in. Does that help?"

"I expect I was at home on my own."

She didn't sound defensive, guilty, afraid. She sounded sullen, as if the clothes and the make-up, the "grooming," had not been effective.

"Do you live on your own or with someone?"

Surely the most innocent of questions. She pounced on it as surely as if those red nails had seized and clutched.

"I certainly do not live with someone! I was at home on my own watching the TV."

Another one. What had they done in the old days before the cathode conquest? He ought to be able to remember pre-television alibis but he couldn't. I was reading, sewing, putting up shelves, fishing, listening to the radio, out for a walk, in the pub, at the pictures? Maybe.

Unwillingly, even grudgingly, she gave them her address. She admitted to possessing a typewriter, an old Smith Corona, though not a portable, and insisted it was in her parents' house in Tonbridge and she had never had it with her in the Myringham bedsit.

Downstairs in the reception area they encountered a young girl undressing. Or so to Wexford's astonished eyes it at first appeared. She was talking to the telephonist (Anna today) and in the act of pulling a cotton dress off over her head. Long slim legs in white tights, pale blue pumps with spike heels, and yes, a skirt which dropped to its former just-above-the-knee length when the garment, evidently a middy blouse, was off. Underneath it was a white tee-shirt. Her back was to Wexford. She kicked off the blue pumps, sending one flying across the room and leaving no doubt in the mind of an observer that this was a cathartic shedding of a hateful costume after an ordeal was over.

"Jane," said Anna in a warning tone, "there are some . . ."

She spun around. On the front of the tee-shirt were the printed letters ARRIA.

The first thing that struck Wexford about the house in Down Road, Kingsmarkham, was that there was no question of any of its occupants being obliged to share a bedroom. It was a very large, castellated, turreted, balconied Edwardian pile. Most houses like it had been converted into flats, but not this one. A single family inhabited it and its (at least) eight bedrooms. Yet Eve Freeborn had given him the reason for going to her boyfriend in Myringham instead of his coming to her that she shared a bedroom with her sister. Perhaps she hadn't a sister either. He would soon see.

At first he thought the girl who opened the front door to him *was* Eve. After all, the fact that this one had green hair meant nothing. They changed their hair color these days as fast as they used to change their lipstick. A second look told him they weren't even identical twins. Twins, yes, fraternal twins with the same build of body and the same eyes. That was all. God knew what color their hair really was. They had probably forgotten themselves.

The house smelt faintly of marijuana. An unmistakable smell that was like woodsmoke blended with sweet cologne.

"Eve?" Eve's sister said with incredulity. "You want to see Eve?"

"Is that so difficult?"

"I don't know really . . ."

He had shown her his warrant card. After all, she was a young girl and it was evening. She shouldn't admit unidentified men into the house. But she was looking at it as if it were a warrant for her arrest. He felt impatient.

"Perhaps I should fill in a form or produce a sponsor."

"Oh, no, come in. I'm sorry. It's just that . . ."

She had an irritating way of leaving her sentences unfinished. He followed her into the hall, darkly paneled like the offices of Sevensmith Harding, and up a big, elegant winding staircase with a gallery at the top. The marijuana smell was fainter but it was still there. What astonished him about the house was the aura of the sixties that pervaded it. On the wall here was a poster (albeit a glazed and framed poster) of John Lennon seated at a white grand piano. A vase stood on a side table filled with dried grasses and shabby peacock's tail feathers.

And hanging up as an ornament, not because it had been left there by chance, was an antique red silk dress embroidered with gold, its red and its gold tattered and shredded by time and moths. He said, "Are your parents at home?"

"They've got a flat in London. They're there half the time."

Impossible to tell if she minded or was glad. Those parents need not be more than forty themselves, he thought, and Mother might be less. Eve's twin said, "Perhaps you'd better wait here. I'll just see if . . ."

All the bedroom doors were open. Only they weren't bedrooms, not exactly. Each one, as far as he could see, had the look rather of a bedsit, with chairs and tables and floor cushions and a couch or divan with an Indian bedspread flung artlessly over it, posters on the walls, and postcards pinned up higgledy-piggledy. He sat down to wait in a rocking chair that had its rockers painted red, black, and white and a dirty lace veil draped over its back, and wondered how to explain this mysterious house.

Then he understood. It wasn't the girls who were living in the past, who were twenty years out of date, or purposely living in an anachronism. Those parents had been young in the sixties, had reveled probably in that new, inspiring freedom, and now the spirit of the sixties, the flavor, the mores would never leave them. Not the girls but the parents were the marijuana users. He would have to do something about that . . .

How long was she going to keep him waiting?

He got up and went out into the passage. There was no one about. But from somewhere he could hear the sound of female voices – a sound that was not in the least like a twittering of birds, strong earnest talk rather than a murmuration. A staircase led to the attic floor but it wasn't from up there that the voices came.

There was a burst of laughter, some sporadic clapping. He walked down the passage toward the sound, came out into another smaller, squarer landing, a map of the heavens painted on its ceiling by a trained but unsure hand. An amateur astrologer who had been to art school, he thought, which brought the sixties once more to mind. As he stood there, doubtful of the wisdom of bursting into a room full of women, the door opened and two girls came out. They stopped in the doorway, looking at him in astonishment. One was unknown to him, the other was Caroline Peters, physical training instructor.

Before anyone spoke Eve Freeborn came out of the room, shouldering her way past the two who blocked the doorway. She was once more in the pelvis-crusher jeans but this time with a purple satin blouse to match her hair. Caroline Peters, on the other hand, was dressed exactly like a boy – or like boys used to dress before punk apparel came to stay: blue jeans, brown leather jacket, halfboots, no make-up, hair cropped in a crewcut.

"Sorry," Eve said. "Have you been waiting long?"

"*They* kept *us* waiting," said Caroline Peters with the maximum venom, "for four thousand years."

She had recognized him and wasn't pleased. Or had he been recognized for what he was in addition to being a policeman – a man? Wexford had never before personally encountered the kind of militant feminist who advocates total separatism. Enlightenment broke upon him.

"Have I by any chance interrupted a meeting of ARRIA?"

"It's over," said Eve. "It's just over."

"We wouldn't have permitted interruption."

Wexford looked at Caroline Peters. "Don't go yet, please. I'd like to talk to you too."

She lifted her shoulders, went back into the room. Eve waved a hand at the other girl, a pretty, sharp-faced redhead.

"This is Nicky."

Inside the room, another, larger bedsit hung with striped bedspreads on ceilings and walls like a Bedouin tent, half a dozen more girls were standing about or preparing to leave. Sara Williams was there and her cousin Paulette, the two of them talking to Jane Gardner, and all of them wearing ARRIA tee-shirts. A black girl, thin and elegant as a model, sat crosslegged on a floor cushion.

Eve said to the company, "I don't remember what he's called," as if it hardly mattered, "but he's a policeman." She pointed to one girl after another: "Jane, Sara, Paulette, Donella, Helen, Elaine, and Amy, my sister, you've met."

Caroline Peters pushed her hands into the pockets of her leather jacket.

"What is it you want?"

"I'd like to know more about ARRIA for a start."

"For a *start* it was *started* by me and a like-minded woman, a classical scholar now at Oxford." She paused. "Arria Paeta," she said, "was a Roman matron, the wife of Caecina Paetus. Of course she was obliged to take his name." Wexford could tell she was one of those fanatics who never miss a trick. "Ancient Rome was known for its gross oppression and exploitation of women." Teacher-like, she waited for his comments.

They came – perhaps to her surprise. "The Emperor Claudius," said Wexford, who had done his homework, "ordered Paetus to commit suicide but he proved too cowardly, so his wife took the sword and, plunging it into her own heart, said, 'See, Paetus, it does not hurt . . .' "

"You've been reading Graves!"

"No. *Smith's Classical Dictionary*." The girl named Nicky laughed. "But I don't know what the letters stand for," he said.

"Action for the Radical Reform of Intersexual Attitudes."

"A case of making the nym fit the acronym? Or is it a deliberate obscuration?"

"Perhaps it is."

"How many schools are involved?"

It was Eve who answered him. "Kingsmarkham High, Haldon Finch, St. Catherine's . . ." but Caroline Peters interrupted her.

"I teach at Haldon Finch. ARRIA had its inception just over a year ago at St. Catherine's. We admitted as members only those women over sixteen, those in fact in the sixth and seventh years. I'm glad to say it had an immediate appeal – how could an organization designed expressly for women, designed to give men no quarter – be otherwise?" She turned on him a glacial look of distaste and it gave him a most unpleasant feeling. He didn't belong to a minority, there was no way he could be categorized into a minority, yet the sensation she gave him was of doing so, and of an oppressed one at that. "Our very well-organized propaganda machine," she said, "spread the good news through the other schools in the area and we soon had considerable cells at Pomfret College of the Further Education and Kingsmarkham High." The good news, he thought, the "gospel" no less. She astonished him by saying, "We now have a membership of just over five hundred women."

He suppressed the whistle he wanted to give. What must the local population of seventeen- and eighteen-year-old girls be? All of them, including those who had left school, could surely hardly amount to more than a couple of thousand and that meant 25 percent in ARRIA. Why, they could almost start a revolution!

"All right, you've got badges, you've had tee-shirts printed, you hold meetings, but what do you *do*?"

Caroline Peters answered readily. "Basically, have as little contact with men as possible. Defy men by intellectual and also by physical means."

He pricked up his ear at that. She wasn't carrying a bag but she had pockets. Most of the other girls had bags. He hadn't got a warrant, and almost more to the point, hadn't a woman with him to carry out a search.

"We have a constitution and manifesto," she said. "I expect there's a copy about and I see no objection to your having one. Would you women agree to that?" There was a murmur of assent, some of it amused. "But I must point out that our aim isn't to meet men on equal terms. It isn't to come to a truce or compromise with them nor to reach that uneasy détente which in past revolutions had sometimes come into being between a proletariat and a bourgeoisie. As Marx said in another context: Philosophers have tried to explain the world. The point surely is to change it. Good night, everyone." She went out of the room, closing the door with a somewhat sinister quietness behind her.

Silence. The black girl, Donella, cast up her eyes, rolling sloe-brown pupils in moon-white whites. Eve said, "By physical means, she only meant self-defense stuff. It's compulsory when you join to take a self-defense course, karate or judo or tai chi or whatever."

"Personally," said Donella, "I think that's one of the things that attracts people – the sport, you know."

"You may have noticed, there've been three times as many evening courses in martial arts started since ARRIA began. That's in response to increased demand, that's ARRIA."

Nicky had spoken with pride, not aggressively. She made a swift chopping movement with one arm. Wexford, a large man over six feet tall, felt relieved he wasn't on the receiving end of that blow. It was true about the judo and karate courses, he had remarked on it himself to Burden, pleased that women were at last taking steps to defend themselves against the muggings and rapes which in the past few years had so disproportionately increased.

"All right," he said, "that's for self-defense. How about aggression? I don't suppose anyone's going to admit to carrying an offensive weapon?"

Nobody was. They didn't look scared or guilty or even alert. He fancied he saw wariness in one or two faces.

"I'll give you a copy of the constitution," Eve said. "There's nothing private about it. Everyone's welcome to know what we do, men as well as women. Do you have daughters?"

"They're a lot older than you."

She looked at him in a not unkindly way, assessing. "Well, they would be, wouldn't they? You can't be too old for ARRIA, though."

The constitution was typed and photocopied. He noted that there were no flaws in the apex of the capital As or the ascenders of the lower-case ts. It went into his pocket to be read at leisure. Sara Williams, he observed, was watching his every movement. The big fair girl called Helen he now realized had been Eve's partner in the tennis match. He said to Eve, "If everyone is in fact going I'd like to talk to you alone for five minutes."

The brisk policeman's tone replacing the one of easy jocularity seemed to jolt her. She pushed fingers through the purple crest of hair.

"OK, if that's the way you want it. Everybody out, right?" She gave a hiccupping giggle. "Home, women!"

Amy said, "Well, I think I'll just . . ." and drifted vaguely towards the door.

They all began to take leave in ways peculiar to young girls, whether feminists or reactionaries. Helen and Donella closed in upon each other with a tight bear hug which ended in giggles and heads subsiding on each other's shoulders. Sara wrapped her arms round herself and moved across the floor with vague dancing steps. Jane humped her bag, filled with ARRIA constitution sheets, as if it weighed a ton, making agony faces. Nicky was lost in a dream that seemed to turn her into a sleepwalker so that she neither paused in her exit nor spoke but merely raised a languid flapping hand in farewell as she passed through the doorway.

Alone with Eve, Wexford said, "You've been telling me lies."

"I have not!"

"Why did you tell me your boyfriend couldn't come here because you had to share a bedroom with your sister? This is an enormous house and as far as I can see your parents mostly aren't here anyway. But you told me lack of space – and you implied lack of privacy – stopped him coming here."

"Well," she said, a sly look in her eyes, "I can explain that. You'll see the answer in our constitution actually. Rule 4."

He pulled the constitution out of his pocket. Here it was, Rule 4. "Women" – not ARRIA members, he saw, but always "women," as if the society contained the world's entire female population – "Women shall avoid the company of men wherever possible but should their presence be required for sexual, biological, business, or career purposes, it is expedient and desirable for women to go to them rather than permit them to come to us."

"But why?"

"Caroline and Edwina – she's the classical one who's at Oxford – they said it smacked of the sultan visiting his harem. You've got to think it through, you know. When you do you can see what they mean."

"So that's why you went to your boyfriend in Arnold Road? You required his presence for sexual or even biological purposes?"

"Isn't that why women usually require men?"

"There are more ways of putting it. More aesthetic ways, I'd say. Maybe more civilized."

"Oh, *civilized*. Men made civilization and it's not up to much, is it? It's no big deal."

He left it. "Did you know Sara Williams was the daughter of the murdered man whose car you saw in Arnold Road?"

"Not then I didn't. I do now. Look, I only know her through ARRIA and I didn't know her father. For all I knew, she mightn't have had a father."

He accepted that. "Miss Peters didn't tell me much about this society of yours, did she? Only that it's a wildfire movement, it's caught on in all the local schools. How about the – what shall I call it? – esoteric stuff? How do you join? Do you pay a subscription? Is there any sort of ritual – like Freemasons, say?"

"We don't need money," she said, "so there's no sub. Where would they get it from anyway? Most of our members are still at school. They'd have to get it from their fathers and that's out. See Rule 6 and dependence. The only thing that costs us is the photocopying, only it doesn't because Nicky does it on her dad's Xerox in the night, when he's asleep."

There was an irony there but Wexford didn't point it out. "Anyone can join?"

"Any woman over sixteen who's not married. Obviously a married woman has already capitulated. Anyway, it wouldn't be possible for her to keep to the rules."

"That would let my daughters out."

She ignored him. "I'm a founder member. When we started there was a lot of really way-out stuff going on. Edwina wanted initiation ceremonies, sort of baptisms of fire if you can imagine."

"What sort?"

He was deadly curious. At the same time he was afraid she would soon realize she was spending too much time unnecessarily in the society of a man. She considered his question in thoughtful silence. She was not a pretty girl. But perhaps this didn't matter in these days when beauty was no longer at a premium. She had one of those chinless faces, long-nosed, full-lipped, but with creamy delicate skin. A frown creased, or rather crumpled, her forehead. Creasing was for older people. Eve's frown was like the bunching of a piece of cream velvet.

"Some of the others went along with her ideas," she said, "I mean, she was a radical feminist. For instance, she used to say we couldn't make revolution on Marxist principles on account of Marx having been a man. She said sexuality was politics and the only way to get freedom was for all women to be lesbians. Any hetero behavior was collaborating with the enemy. Even Caroline Peters never went as far as that."

"You were going to tell me about initiation."

Eve seemed reluctant to reach the subject. "They actually formed a splinter group over it. Sara, the one whose father was murdered, she was one of them, and Nicky Anerley was another. One of the things they objected to was being educated along with the other sex. They wanted schools and colleges run by women and with women teachers. Of course, it would be best, it's the ideal if you know what I mean, but it's a bit fantastic."

"Particularly as it's only in very recent years that women have gained admission to certain men's colleges, notably at Oxford."

"That's beside the point. This would be a question of getting the men out altogether. Edwina and the rest of them who were at mixed schools wanted to go on strike until they agreed not to admit boys. But Caroline wouldn't have that. I suppose she was afraid of losing her job."

"And that's what caused the rift in the party?"

"Well, partly. This was all last summer and autumn. It more or less stopped when Edwina went up to Oxford in October and the others drifted back. I may as well tell you. It was all a sort of fantasy anyway. Edwina said in order to prove herself a true feminist a woman ought to kill a man." Eve looked at him warily. "I don't mean everyone who joined ARRIA was to have to kill a man to get to be a member. The idea was for groups of three or four to get together and . . .

"But that's not an initiation ceremony really, is it? I could tell you about some of those if you want."

12

With inscrutable face Jenny Burden sat reading ARRIA'S manifesto. She was past the stage now of prettifying disguises of her pregnancy. It was beyond disguise and her condition didn't flatter her. Younger than her years though she had always looked, she now appeared too old to be having a baby. Her face was not so much lined as lacking in its former firmness, caverns hollowed out under the eyes and chin muscles sagging. She had no lap now so she held the flimsy sheets against a book propped upon the table in front of her.

But Wexford could tell by Burden's pleased expression that he was content to see his wife making even this small effort to escape from the apathy that had settled on her as the psychotherapy she was having progressed. No longer in revolt, no longer violent in her hatred of the child, she had become resigned. She waited in hopeless passivity. When Wexford arrived she had taken his hand, put up her face for a kiss, inquired in a limbo voice after Dora and the girls. And he had thought: when the baby is born she could go completely mad, enter a schizophrenic world, and pass the rest of her life in hospital. She wouldn't be the first to whom such a thing had happened.

Still, now she was reading ARRIA's constitution, and apparently reading every word with care. Wexford wouldn't talk about the Williams case in her presence and Burden knew that. Suddenly she began reading aloud.

"Rule 6: With certain limited exceptions, no woman shall be financially dependent on a man. Then they list the exceptions. Rule 7. All women shall take a course in some martial art or self-defense technique. Rule 8: All women shall carry a permitted weapon for self-defense, i.e., ammonia spray, pin, penknife, pepper shaker, etc. Rule 9: No member shall marry, participate in the bourgeois concept of becoming "engaged," or share accommodation with a man in a cohabiting situation. Rule 10 . . . Do you want rule 10?"

"Oh, I have read it," Wexford said. "It is heresy!"

She didn't recognize the quotation. "You're

bound to think that way, aren't you? Perhaps I should have read all this before I met you, Mike."

He took the blow with a physical flinch.

"ARRIA didn't exist then. It was around earlier this year before I gave up work, though. I always wanted to get hold of their manifesto but no one would even talk to me about it. I was a married woman, you see."

"I suppose I was lucky to get it," Wexford conceded.

Burden was making an effort to recover from the pain she had given him. "I want to hear Rule 10."

"All right. Rule 10: Women wishing to reproduce should select the potential father for his physique, health, height, etc., and ensure impregnation in a rape or near-rape construct."

"In a *what?* What the hell does it mean?"

Wexford said, "Margaret Mead says men of the Arapesh fear rape by women just as women in other cultures fear rape by men."

"The mind boggles." By this, Wexford knew, Burden meant he would dearly have loved to inquire further into the mechanics and techniques but was hampered by inhibition. "The trouble is surely that most of this was written by lesbians like Edwina Klein and Caroline Peters. It doesn't seem to cater for women who actually *love* men – and those are surely in the vast majority."

Jenny looked coldly at her husband. "In the sort of explanation bit that comes after the rules it says the authors realize women may feel affection for men and even – I quote – 'what is termed sexual love' but it is necessary that something must be given up for the cause. Other women in the past have denied themselves this indulgence and been amply compensated. It goes on: 'After all, what does this so-called "love" amount to when a woman sets it against its concomitants: gross exploitation, pornography degradation, career prohibition or curtailment, rape, father-daughter incest, and the still-persisting double standard.' "

"It doesn't seem to bear much relation to our own home lives, does it?" said Burden.

Jenny had tears in her eyes, Wexford saw. They shone there, unshed. "Revolutionaries are always extreme," she said. "Look at the Terror of 1793, look at Stalinism. If they're not, if they compromise with liberalism, all their principles fizzle out and you're back with the status quo. Isn't that what's happened to the broader women's liberation movement?"

The men looked at her with varying expressions of doubt and dismay. Burden had gone rather pale.

"If these girls," said Jenny, "can accomplish just a fraction of what they're setting out to do, if they can begin to make people see what 'inequitable arbitration' really amounts to, perhaps – perhaps I shan't so much mind my daughter being born."

This time she didn't break down into tears. "I know you want to talk. I'll leave you." She turned to her husband, kissed his forehead, carried herself clumsily to the door. There was no dignity there and no beauty because the child that made her heavy was unwanted . . . Burden put out one finger to touch the ARRIA manifesto like someone steeling himself to make contact with something he has a phobia about.

"I feel it threatens me, all this. I'm frightened of it."

"It's good that you're honest enough to admit it."

"Do you really think there's anything in this killing a man stuff?"

He had done so at first. It had seemed the obvious answer and for a moment or two the only possible answer. At that point his whole tone towards Eve had changed. He had been dancing lightly with her and then, suddenly, the music stopped and he seized hold of her. That was what it was like. Of course, he had frightened her with his quick rough questions . . .

"But nobody ever did it! It was a fantasy – like group sex or something. Like an orgy. You think about what it would be like, you fantasize, but you don't *do* it."

"Many do."

"Well, OK, that wasn't a very good comparison. The point is fantasy doesn't become reality, the two don't mix."

"Don't they? Isn't that what a psychopath is? Someone who confuses fantasy with reality?"

She had insisted, with the panic of someone who realizes she had said too much, that Edwina Klein's idea had been hers alone, even the splinter group had opposed it. Knives next. He had gone on to ask her what was meant by "permitted weapons." Did this category include knives? Not *real* knives, she said, and she had looked at him as a child might, round-eyed, afraid of something it doesn't understand.

"It's tempting," he said to Burden, "to think of a group of those ARRIA girls grabbing hold of poor old Williams like the Maenads with Orpheus and doing him in on the Lesbian shore."

Burden looked at him, mystified. "Shall we

have a beer?" he said.

"Good idea.

> "Malt does more than Milton can
> To justify God's ways to man."

"You're right there," Burden said feelingly.

He came back with two cans and two tankards on a tray. Poor chap, Wexford thought, he's had enough. And how curious it was that all these dramatic things happened to Burden, who was such an ordinary, unimaginative, salt-of-the-earth person. The prototype surely of Kafka's man to whom, though he shut himself up in his room, hid himself, lay low, life nevertheless came in and rolled in ecstasy at his feet. Whereas for him, Wexford, nothing much came along to disturb his private peace. Thank God for it!

"Just the same," he said, "we're going to have our work cut out checking out every one of ARRIA'S members. There are said to be five hundred of them, remember."

"The girl who stabbed Budd may not be the same girl who stabbed Wheatley who may not be the same girl as the one that killed Williams, but on the other hand they may be one and the same."

"Right," said Wexford. "But don't let's talk of

the 'one' that killed Williams. No girl on her own could have carried his body into that car and then carried it out again and buried him.

"The way I see it, we have to think of it along these lines. On the one hand we have the radical feminists, of whom we know (a) that the notion of killing a man was at any rate considered by them and (b) that they are required by their own rules to carry offensive weapons. We also know that Wheatley certainly and Budd probably were stabbed by ARRIA members. We've been told too that Williams, pursuing his well-known tastes, had a very young girlfriend. Now is this girlfriend a member of ARRIA?

"Whatever the ARRIA rules may say," said Wexford, "we know members do have to do with the opposite sex. Look at Eve climbing in through her boyfriend's window. She hasn't made the supreme sacrifice of giving up men. And if you want to kill a man what better way of doing it than in what ARRIA would probably call a libido-emotional construct – in other words a love affair?"

Burden finished the last of his beer. In the next room Jenny had put a record on, Ravel's *Pavane for a Dead Infanta*. "Who said that about malt and Milton?"

"Houseman. His life was ruined by an unrequited love."

"Blimey. Why ravens?"

"In ARRIA'S logo, d'you mean? They're predatory birds, aren't they? No, I suppose not. Harsh-tongued? I really don't know, Mike. At any rate, they're not soft and submissive. The collective noun for them is an 'unkindness.' An unkindness of ravens. Appropriate, wouldn't you say? In their attitude to the opposite sex anyway. They stab at us with knives rather than beaks."

"Not without provocation, of course."

"That's true. Budd on his own admission tried to get fresh with the girl who attacked him. He may have got fresher than he says. Wheatley says he didn't get fresh at all but I'm not inclined to believe him. They made passes and got themselves stabbed. Makes you wonder what Williams did, doesn't it?"

As Wexford walked home he thought about what he had had to do as a result of his visit to the Freeborns' house. Sergeant Martin and Detective Bennett had paid a follow-up call and this morning Charles Freeborn, the girls' father, had appeared at Kingsmarkham Magistrates' Court charged with possessing cannabis and with permitting cannabis to be smoked upon his premises. Bennett, who detected the stuff in a positively cat-and-mouse way – or cat-and-catmint way – had begun a methodical search of the big overgrown garden, starting at the conservatory, following the crazy-paving path through a copse of unpruned dusty shrubs. This path curved all round the perimeter of the garden, winding its way between ghosts of flowerbeds where a few attenuated cultivated plants thrust their heads through a matting of bindweed, ground elder, and thistles. A gate in the fence at the garden's foot afforded a shortcut into a path to the High Street. Bennett had been wondering if he was getting obsessional imagining *Cannabis sativa*, which requires sunlight and space, might ever flourish here when he suddenly came upon the only tended flowerbed in the whole half-acre.

He was nearly back at the house again, the stifling, shadow-spreading trees behind him. A neat rectangular clearing had been made in the shaggy grass here, the soil well watered, weeded, and the bed bordered with bricks. Martin had declared the vigorous young plants to be seedling tomatoes but Bennett knew better. Infra-red light is essential to the Indian hemp if its effect when ingested is to be the characteristically hallucinogenic one, and these plants were basking in it, for their bed was in the only part of the garden to enjoy day-long uninterrupted sunshine.

Wexford pondered, not for the first time, on the ethics of going into someone's house for a check and a chat, while there detecting a forbidden drug, and immediately, scarcely with a qualm, taking steps to prosecute the offender. One's host in absentia, so to speak. Of course he was right, *it* was right. He was a policeman and that came first. That must always come first or chaos would come instead . . .

By the time the schools broke up towards the end of July Wexford's men had vetted and cleared something like 50 percent of the ARRIA membership. Tracking them down was the difficulty, for Caroline Peters denied the existence of a list of members. Why should a list be needed when there was no subscription, and dates and venues of meetings were passed on by grassroots?

Paulette Harmer, Williams's niece, a sixth-form-college student, was cleared. She had been out with her boyfriend, to whom she would become engaged at Christmas – thereby abrogating ARRIA membership? – on the evenings Budd and Wheatley were stabbed, and at home with her parents and her aunt Joy on 15 April. Eve Freeborn, before going to her boyfriend in Arnold Road, had spent the evening at home with her parents and her sister. This alibi also accounted for Amy. Neither could be charged with the Budd and Wheatley stabbings. Nor could Caroline Peters, who, however, had been at a meeting in London on the evening of the 15th. The redheaded Nicky turned out to be Nicola Anerley and not the Nicola Tennyson who was Veronica Williams's friend. She had been at a party on 15 April, Helen Blake's eighteenth birthday party, which had also been attended by another twelve members of ARRIA, all of whom Wexford was able to discount as far as the murder of Williams was concerned.

Jane Gardner he questioned himself. She was the right age, pretty and lively, an active member of ARRIA. He owed it to the cordial relationship he had had with her father to go himself and not send Bennett, say, or Archbold.

Miles was at home, had made a point evidently of being at home. He was affronted and preparing to be bitterly offended. He and his tall wife were in the drawing room (walls of Sevenstar Chinese yellow, black carpet, *famille jaune* porcelain) and Wexford was shown in by the cleaning lady masquerading as a maid. They spoke to him, he thought, in the aghast tones of parents asking a headmaster why he intends to expel their daughter from his school. Pamela Gardner called him "Mr. Wexford" though it had been "Reg" in the past. Since she had no means of summoning the cleaning lady except by shouting, she went to fetch Jane herself.

"This is so entirely unnecessary," Gardner said in a hard voice.

Wexford said it was routine and felt like a cop in an ancient Cyril Hare detective story.

The girl came in smiling and perfectly at ease. Then he had to ask the parents to go. They did but with a very ill grace. At first Pamela Gardner pretended she didn't understand what he meant. Light dawned, then came incredulity, lastly disgusted acceptance. She took her husband's arm as if the very cornerstones of their home life had been threatened.

"Did you get a university place?" Wexford asked Jane as soon as they were alone.

"Oh yes, thanks. We met before, didn't we? At Dad's office? I never thought I would actually. I'd even enrolled at secretarial college in London just in case. My school doesn't have a commercial department."

There came back to him a recollection of this girl changing her clothes in full view of the street. In "Dad's office." And when she had turned round to see him looking at her she hadn't turned a hair.

"Did you know Rodney Williams, Jane?"

"I'd met him. At the office. Dad introduced us. He had a lot of charm, you know." She smiled, reminiscently, a bit sadly. "He could make you feel you were the only person there worth talking to."

It struck Wexford that this was the first person he had spoken to with a good word to say for Rodney Williams. She spoiled it a little.

"I expect he was like that with all girls of my age."

Was she an enthusiastic member of ARRIA? Had she been in the splinter group? Did she carry a weapon? Where had she been when Budd was stabbed, when Wheatley was stabbed, when Williams was killed? Yes to the first and second questions, an indignant no, wide-eyed and law-abiding, to the third. A baby-sitting alibi for 15 April, a visit to her newly married sister for a Budd alibi, no memory of what she had been doing on the evening of the Wheatley stabbing. Apropos of none of this, surprising her with what seemed inconsequential, he said, "Which schools do have commercial departments?"

"Haldon Finch, Sewingbury Sixth-Form." She gave him an earnest look. "Dad's really upset that you suspect me."

"There's no question of that. This is routine."

"Well . . ." Suddenly she was the good daughter, dutiful, compliant, obedient. "He and Mummy are dead against you taking my fingerprints."

"You" presumably implied the Mid-Sussex Constabulary, or did she think he had come armed with pads and gadgets? The cleaning lady showed him out, her apron changed for rather smart dungarees. There was no sign of Miles or Pamela. Donaldson drove him back to Kingsmarkham and dropped him outside his own house. Dora, dressed up, was on the phone to Sylvia.

He passed close by her and touched her cheek with his lips. She responded to the kiss, mouthed something about getting a move on, went on talking to Sylvia. He went upstairs, changed into what he called his best suit, gray like the others but the latest and least shabby. When he retired he would never wear a suit again – not even to the theater.

In the train he told Dora about the Gardners and said he had a feeling they wouldn't be asked to any more garden parties. She said that didn't matter, did it? She didn't care. And he shouldn't care either, he should relax, especially tonight.

"I wish I'd read the play."

"You haven't had time."

"You can always make time for things you

want to do," he said.

As it was he didn't even know what *The Cenci* was about, and of its history only that it had for a long time been banned from the English stage. He and Dora, on holiday in Italy, had seen Guido Reni's portrait of Beatrice Cenci in the Galleria Nazionale in Rome, though he wouldn't have connected that with the play but for Sheila's saying it would be reproduced in the program. It would have been a good idea to have read the play – or to have read Moravia's *Beatrice Cenci*, a novel that might be more entertaining.

The play threatened at first not to entertain at all. Shelley, Wexford thought to himself while aware he was no informed critic, wasn't Shakespeare. And wasn't he, in writing this sort of five-act tragedy in blank verse, some two hundred years out of date? Then Sheila came on, not looking like the portrait but with a small cap on her golden hair and dressed in white and gray, and he forgot everything, even the play, in his consuming pride in her. She had a peculiar quality in her acting, which critics as well as he had remarked on, of bringing clarity to obscure or periphrastic lines, so that her entrances always seemed to let light in upon the arcane. It was so now, it continued to be so . . . He saw and understood.

The plot and purpose of the play began to unfold themselves for him and Shelley's style ceased to be an anachronism.

The effect on Dora was less happy.

She whispered to Wexford while they were having a glass of wine during the interval, "There's more to it than I can see, I know that. It's not just that they can't stand the old man's harshness any longer, is it? I mean, why did Sheila come tearing in screaming about her eyes being full of blood?"

"Her father raped her." Wexford realized what he had said and corrected himself. "Count Cenci raped his daughter Beatrice."

"I see. Oh yes, I do see. It's not made very clear, is it?"

"I imagine Shelley couldn't afford to spell it out. As it was, it must have been the incest theme that got the play banned."

While waiting for the curtain to go up on Act Four he read the essay on the historical facts on which the play was based, which had been written for the program by an eminent historian. Beatrice, her stepmother, and her brother had been put to death for the murder of Count Cenci. They really had. It had all happened. Guido had painted the portrait while Beatrice was in prison. Later they had tortured her to extract a confession.

It wasn't the kind of piece, he decided, that one would ever want to see again or read or remember a line from. When it was over they went backstage. They always did. Sheila, though in jeans and sweater now, still had a mask of gleaming white paint on her face and her hair topknotted for execution as when she had cried:

"... Here, Mother, tie
My girdle for me ... My Lord,
We are quite ready. Well, 'tis very well."

Going home, Dora fell asleep in the train. Wexford found his mind occupied with the prosaic subject of typewriters.

It was the caretaker of the Haldon Finch Comprehensive School, primed by a phone call from the County Education Department, who showed them round. Wexford had been inside the school before, years ago when the nucleus of these buildings had been the old county high school. Incorporated into it now were the buildings next door, a former clinic and health center, as well as a vast new assembly hall and the glass, concrete, and blue-slate complex of classrooms, music room, and concert hall, with the sports center a gilt-roofed rotunda that the sun set ablaze.

"It reminds me," Wexford said to Burden, "of a picture I once saw of the Golden Temple at Amritsar."

But the commercial department had no new buildings to house it. It was pushed away into three rear classrooms at the top of the old high school, as if the education authority had half-heartedly accepted the recent remark of a government minister that shorthand and typing were no part of education and should not be taught in schools. Wexford followed Burden and the caretaker up a remarkable (and remarkably battered) Art Deco marble staircase and along a wide vaulted passage. The caretaker unlocked and opened the double doors into the commercial department. These too were Art Deco, with parabolas and leaves in green iron-work on their frosted glass. The old high school had been built in 1930 and the class-rooms inside looked as if they had received no more than one coat of paint since then. They were shabby, typically green and cream, with a view of rooftops and a brick well full of dust-bins.

It was in the farthest room that the type-writers were. Wexford asked himself what he had expected. The latest in word processors? Obviously here the country's resources were mainly devoted to science and sport. Nor presumably would ARRIA encourage its members towards a secretarial career. There was not an electric typewriter among the machines and some of them looked older than the building itself. Burden, walking between the tables, had a piece of paper in his hand, probably with the faults of the typewriter they were looking for written on it. As if he couldn't remember without that! A break in the head of the upper-case A and the ascender of the lower-case t, a comma with a smudged head.

He felt a small flicker of excitement when he spotted the first of the Remington 315s.

"Can you type?"

"Enough to test these," said Burden and impressed Wexford by getting to work and using all his fingers.

Nothing wrong with the A, the t, and the comma on the first one. Burden slipped his paper into the roller of the second. The capital A wasn't all it might have been, but neither was the B or the D or a lot of others. The lower-case faces and the comma seemed unflawed. He tried the third machine, the caretaker watching with the fascinated awe of one who expects the litmus paper to turn not red but all the colors of the spectrum. This typewriter, however, seemed without faults. It produced the best-looking copy so far. There was only one more. Burden slipped his paper in and this time, instead of "Now is the time for All good men to come to the Aid of the party," typed "A thousand ages in Thy sight are like an evening gone." If he had been a Freudian, Wexford thought, he would have wanted to know why. Perhaps it was just done to astonish the caretaker. Anyway, whatever the reason, this wasn't the machine Rodney Williams's letter of resignation had been typed on.

"That's it then."

"Show my four samples to the experts. We could be wrong."

"We're not wrong. These are all the typewriters the school has?"

"Apart from them as has gone away to be serviced."

"Now he tells me," said Wexford.

"There's always some go away in the summer holidays. It's never the lot of them. They go in like, rotation."

"Do you know how many have gone and where?"

The caretaker didn't know the answer to either question. No more than, say, five, he thought. He had never heard the name of any firm which might be servicing the machines or seen a van arrive to take them away.

"We must be thankful," Wexford said as they came out of the school, "that at least it's an old manual portable we're looking for and not one of the modern kind with a golfball or daisy-wheel."

"A what or a *what?*"

"Let's say with a detachable typeface that our perpetrator could simply have taken out and thrown away."

School might have broken up but sport went on. Half a dozen boys in shorts and tee-shirts were running laps round the biggest playing field and on the tennis courts a doubles game and a singles were in progress. The umpire seats were empty but Caroline Peters was there in the role of coach, and as they approached the wire fencing Wexford saw that what he had supposed to be a singles match was in fact instructor and instructed, the pupil here being Veronica Williams.

The four doubles players were Eve and Amy Freeborn, Helen Blake, and another girl he had never seen before. So there were actually seventeen- and eighteen-year-olds in this corner of Sussex he had never seen before? He was beginning to think he knew them all by sight and usually by name too. He and Burden went over to the fence and watched, as they had done that previous time. Caroline Peters glared but didn't come over to admonish. She knew who they were now.

It was clear from the first that Veronica was streets ahead of the other players, though two years younger than any of them. She was the best tennis player Wexford had ever seen on a local court. This time the discrepancy between what he saw on TV and what he saw at home did not seem quite so wide. She was a strong, lithe, fast player with a hard, accurate backhand and a powerful smashing action. When Caroline Peters made her serve her service was as hard as Eve's but the balls struck the court well inside the line.

The doubles players changed ends. Eve looked in Wexford's direction and then ostentatiously away. Loyalty to the father he had had charged with possessing cannabis, he supposed. He had been getting a lot of stick of that kind lately. All part of a policeman's lot, no doubt. Veronica returned Caroline Peters's lob with a hard transverse drive which Caroline ran for but couldn't reach. It was a mystery, Wexford thought, where somebody got that kind of talent from. You couldn't imagine that finicking Wendy playing any sort of game or even walking more than half a mile, while Rodney Williams had been out of condition for years. Did the other Williams family play games?

There had been a tennis racket up on Sara's bedroom wall, he remembered. Of course, the probable answer was that any healthy young girl keen on tennis could be coached to the standard of Veronica Williams. She was already sixteen. It was already too late for her to begin competing in anything much more significant than inter-school matches.

The girl whose face and name he didn't know served a double fault. One more of those and the set would be lost. She served one more of those and threw her racket down in the kind of petulance she wouldn't have known about if she hadn't watched Wimbledon on TV. Wexford and Burden walked back to the car.

"Have we got anything on the fingerprints found in Williams's car yet?" Burden asked.

"They took about sixty prints," Wexford said, "all made by nine people. By far the greater proportion were made by one man and they've more or less established that man was Williams."

"I don't suppose his fingers were in very good shape after being in the ground for nine weeks."

"Exactly. They matched the car ones to prints in his bedroom – well, bedrooms – of course. The other prints were made by two unknown men, and may well belong to whoever began the dismantling of Greta, or by Joy,

Wendy, Sara, Veronica, and two more women or girls who might be friends of the wives and daughters – or who might not. The steering wheel had been wiped."

"Much what you would expect really," said Burden.

Nicola Tennyson, Veronica's friend, was thrilled to have her fingerprints taken. She was unable to remember much about 15 April. Certain it was that she had been baby-sitting her brother that evening and Veronica had come in, but she couldn't remember times. Veronica and she were often in each other's homes, she said.

One of the two unidentified sets of fingerprints on Greta turned out to be hers.

13

Wheatley said that the woman who stabbed him had been more than commonly tall. Budd said that because he had only seen her sitting down he couldn't tell her height. That wasn't strictly true. He had seen her running off with the sack over her shoulder. The sack was the only thing he could really remember, that and the fact she had blond hair. The girl who attacked Wheatley had brown or lightish hair. She was eighteen or nineteen. Budd thought his assailant was twenty. Or twenty-five or -six. Or any age between eighteen and thirty.

In each case their wounds had been made with the blade of a large penknife. Not necessarily the same penknife, though. Not necessarily the same woman. Wexford asked himself, what had been in the sack. He didn't think Budd had invented the sack. Budd wasn't endowed with enough imagination for that. There had been a sack all right, a black plastic dustbin liner. What had she been carrying it for and why?

It had been pouring with rain. Those plastic sacks were very good for keeping things dry. Keeping what dry? The bus stop was the nearest one to the place where they'd found Rodney Williams's body. But he had been dead six weeks by the night Budd was attacked. Wendy Williams wasn't particularly tall but she was blond and she looked much younger than she was. To Budd she might seem in her early twenties.

She had begun a fortnight of her annual holiday. Wexford thought to himself that she might be spending the major part of it at Kingsmarkham Police Station. He went with the car to fetch her.

Veronica was in the raspberry-ice-cream living room, seated at the glass-topped table, turning the pages of *Vogue*. He thought she looked like a teenage girl in a French film of the sixties. He hadn't seen many French films of the sixties but nevertheless the impression was there in Veronica's bandbox look, the beautifully cut, newly washed, pageboy hair, the clothes – primrose pinafore dress, starched white blouse, blue boot-lace tie, white ankle socks, sky-blue sandals – that were just a little too young for her, the expression on her face that was 99 percent innocence and 1 percent calculation.

"I saw you playing tennis the other day."

"Yes, I saw you too."

Why the wary look suddenly, the shade of unease across that naiveté?

"You're very good."

She knew that already, she didn't need to be told. A polite smile and then back to *Vogue*. Wendy Williams came down the spiral staircase, walking slowly, giving him a voyeur's look, if he had wanted it, of shapely legs in very fine pale tights all the way up to a glimpsed border of cream lace. He wasn't looking, but out of the corner of his eye he saw her hold her skirt down as if he had been.

She had dressed up. Women these days didn't bother with fancy dressing except for special occasions, except when it was fun. That was general, not just the ARRIA view of things. For going down the cop shop, Wexford thought, you went in the jeans and shirt you wore around the house. But this was something that hadn't yet got through to Wendy Williams and maybe never would. She probably didn't possess a pair of jeans. And Veronica's would be the designer kind with Vidal Sassoon or Gloria

Vanderbilt on the backside. Wendy had a pretty cotton dress on, the kind that needs a lot of ironing, a wide black patent belt to show she still had an adolescent waist, and red wedge-heeled shoes that pinched where they touched.

The car filled with her perfume. Estée Lauder's White Linen, decided Wexford, who was good on scent. He made up his mind to take her up to his office, not into one of the interview rooms.

"You haven't told me much about this girlfriend of your husband's, Mrs. Williams," he said when they were there.

"I've told you all I know. I've told you it was a very young girl and that's all I know."

"I don't think so," he said. "There's more if you search your memory."

A secretive look was closing up her face. Why? Why should she want to conceal this girl's identity from him?

"I wish I'd never mentioned any girl to you!" Exasperated. The tone of a mother to a child who keeps nagging her about a treat she has promised him.

"You had an anonymous letter, you said."

She hesitated. She opened her mouth to begin an explanation. He cut her short.

"You didn't keep it, though. You burned it."

"How did you know?"

"Mrs. Williams, let me tell you what I do know. First, it's only in books that people burn anonymous letters. In real life they may not care much for them, they may even recoil from them in disgust, but they don't burn them. Most people don't have fires any more, for one thing. Where would you burn something?"

She didn't say anything. A sullen, crushed look made her almost ugly.

"People who get anonymous letters may not like looking at them. Usually they put them away in a drawer in case or until we want to see them. Or there's the dustbin. You read somewhere that the requisite thing to do with an anonymous letter was burn it, didn't you? In a detective story probably. The truth is you never received one."

"All right, I didn't."

"Hasn't anyone ever told you you musn't tell lies to the police?"

He hadn't spoken harshly. His tone was almost bantering. It was mockery, even as mild as this, she couldn't stand. She flushed and her mouth set mulishly.

"I didn't tell lies. There was a girl." Perhaps she could see he wasn't going to say anything for a moment or two. "He was perverted about young girls, that's what it amounted to, and it ruined my life." Her voice rose, edgy and plaintive. "I thought he was in love with me when we first met. I thought he loved me but now I know he just fancied me because I was young. And when Veronica was coming he had to marry me. Well, *marry*. It's easy to marry, isn't it? You can do it over and over again.

"I never had any life, I never had any youth. Do you know something? I'm thirty-two and I've never so much as been taken out to dinner in a decent restaurant by a man. I've never been abroad. I've never had a thing to wear that didn't come discount from Jickie's. I never even had an engagement ring!"

He asked her how she knew of the girl's existence. Just at this point Marion came in with coffee on a tray, three unprepossessing cheese sandwiches, and three custard-cream biscuits. Wendy looked at the sandwiches and shook her head in a shuddery, genteel sort of way.

He repeated the question.

"Rodney confessed."

"Just like that? Out of the blue? You didn't suspect anything, but he confessed to you he had a young girlfriend?"

"I told you."

"Why did he confess? Was he intending to leave you for her? As in fact you thought he had done?"

That made her laugh in the way someone does who has knowledge of a secret you will never guess. He persisted and she looked exasperated, answering that she had told him already. She ate nothing, he ate a sandwich, leaving the rest for Marion, who had a hearty appetite. Afterwards, he thought, Wendy Williams would probably tell people she was kept at the police station for hours and not given a thing to eat or drink.

He asked her once more about 15 April. The evening. What time had she left Jickie's to drive home to Pomfret? All the staff at Jickie's had been questioned by Martin and Bennett and Archbold. They had forgotten. Why should they remember that particular evening? One of the girls on the fashion-floor pay desk said that if Mrs. Williams hadn't actually left the building before nine, that would have been very late for her. On Thursdays she usually left as soon after eight as possible and had been known to leave at 7:30.

Wendy insisted she had left at nine. She stuck to that. He left it. He said there was something he had to ask her. Seeing that her husband consistently neglected her and for two months she believed he had finally left her, had she formed a friendship with any other man?

"It would be a natural and normal thing to

you. You're a very young woman still. You said yourself that you felt life and youth had been denied you."

"Are you suggesting I was having a – a relationship with someone?"

"It would be very understandable."

"I think that's disgusting! That's really immoral. I've got my daughter to think of, haven't I? I've got Veronica to set an example to. Just because Rodney behaved in that horrible way, that's no reason for me to do the same. Let me tell you, I've always been absolutely faithful. I've never looked at another man, it would never have entered my head."

He was beginning to know her and her protests. He said not another word on that one but thought the more. It was afternoon now and Burden would be setting in motion their prearranged plan. It might not work, of course – and if it did what would it show or prove? He didn't even know if he expected it to work.

In the meantime he questioned her about her life, her feelings, her reactions. Still she hadn't said a word about the other Williams family. She was prepared to acknowledge Rodney Williams had married her bigamously while ignoring the existence of his first or true wife. You would have expected her natural curiosity to get the better of her. Was she rising above such human failings? That was a possible explanation.

"Mrs. Joy Williams," he said deliberately, "has a son and a daughter. Her daughter and Veronica are very much alike. Do you have any feelings about these people?" He was aware he sounded like a psychotherapist, though any interrogating policeman was one of those. But nevertheless he made a slight correction. "Aren't you interested in knowing something about them?"

"No." Once more she had flushed. She looked mulish. "Why should I be? They're nothing to me. Rodney can't have cared much for them."

"Why do you say that?"

She made a little gesture with her hands to indicate that the answer was obvious. Wexford said that was enough for today and he'd organize a car to take her home. They went down in the lift, timing it perfectly, for the lift came to a stop and the doors opened. Burden came walking across the black and white checkerboard floor towards it with Joy Williams beside him. Wexford spoke to Burden for the sake of stopping and saying something. The two women stood there, Joy staring at Wendy, Wendy contemplating the wall ahead of her as if it were the most fascinating example of interior decor since the cave paintings of Trois Frères.

They presented a contrast, pathetic and grotesque. It was almost too marked to be quite real. They were like a cartoon for an old-fashioned advertisement, the wife who doesn't use the face cream, floor polish, deodorant, stock cubes, and the wife who does. Joy had a cardigan on over a cotton dress with half its hem coming down. All her shoes had a curious way of looking like carpet slippers though they weren't. Wendy swayed a little on her high heels, craning her neck and putting on a winsome look. Wexford smelt a gush of White Linen from her, perhaps because she was sweating. The irony was that both these women had been rejected.

Burden and Joy went into the lift. The doors closed.

"Do you know who that woman was?"

"What woman?" said Wendy.

"I'm not talking about Detective Bayliss. The woman who has just gone up in the lift with Inspector Burden."

She raised her eyebrows, moved her shoulders.

"That was Mrs. Joy Williams."

"His wife?"

"Yes," said Wexford.

"She looked about sixty."

Upstairs Burden was asking Joy about the

phone call, the letter of resignation. Why had she gone out on the evening of 15 April instead of remaining at home to await her son's phone call?

"I can't be always at his beck and call," she said, her voice full of bitterness. "It's all one to him whether I'm there or not. He's his father all over again – indifferent. I've done everything for him, worshipped the ground he walked on. Might as well not have bothered. Do you know where he is now? In Cornwall. On holiday. That's all it means to him that his mother's a widow."

It could just be true. It could just be that she had at last seen the results of spoiling a son. A quarrel, Burden thought, the day before Kevin returned to university. He could hear the things that would have been said – all right, just wait till next time you want something; you phone, my lad, but don't count on me being here . . . Yet there had been no sign since then of adoration flagging.

"Do you know who that woman was with Chief Inspector Wexford?"

"I can guess." The harsh clattering laugh. "Cheap little tart. I don't admire his taste."

He asked her if Sara had a boyfriend. Incredibly, she said she didn't know. It was plain she didn't care. Hatred came into her eyes when her daughter's name was mentioned.

"And after all I've done for her," said Joy as if their discussion had been on the subject of the host of services she had performed for Sara and the girl's ingratitude. Burden had her driven home. He felt as if he had been brought up against a wall, the solid brick an inch from his face.

Carol Milvey was not a member of ARRIA but she was eighteen years old and lived next door but one to Joy Williams. And it was her father, the boss of Mid-Sussex Waterways, who had found Rodney Williams's traveling bag in Green Pond, a coincidence which had never been explained. Sergeant Martin saw her. The interview was a brief one, for Carol Milvey had been ill in bed with tonsillitis on 15 April and had taken two days off school.

A further ten members of ARRIA were cleared, both for 15 April and for the evening on which Brian Wheatley had been stabbed in the hand. It was August now and people were beginning to go away on holiday, ARRIA members surely included. The Anerley family and their daughter, the redheaded Nicola, had been in France since the end of the school term and were not expected back until 12 August. On this date too Pomfret Office Equipment Ltd. were due to reopen after two weeks' holiday closure, a southern version of North Country wakes weeks, as Wexford remarked. If the typewriters missing from Haldon Finch were serviced in the neighborhood it was with Pomfret Office Equipment they had to be. No other firm of typewriter engineers admitted to knowledge of their whereabouts.

The commerce department at Sewingbury Sixth Form College had been checked out. They had microcomputers, ACT Apricots, as well as four dedicated word processors, and their typewriters were ten highly sophisticated Brother machines. Kingsmarkham High School had only one typewriter in the building and that in the school secretary's office.

Kevin Williams came back from Cornwall and left again with six like-minded students to camp in the Channel Islands. The Harmers with Paulette's boyfriend went to North Wales for a week, leaving an Indian pharmacist and his wife, both highly qualified but jobless, in charge of shop and dispensary. Sara went nowhere. Sara stayed at home, awaiting no doubt the A-level results due the second or third week of the month, after the degree results and before the O-levels.

"I can't help wondering if there'll still be A-levels when this new baby of ours grows up," said Burden. Nowadays he talked gingerly and awkwardly about the coming child but as if its birth were a certainty and its future more or less assured. "I'll be an old man by the time she wants to go to university. Well, I'll be in my sixties. I'll be retired. Do you remember filling in those grant forms? Getting one's employer to vouch for one's earnings and all that? Still, by then they'll do it all on a computer, I suppose, a kind of twenty-first-century Apricot."

"Or an Apple," said Wexford. "Why do computer makers call their wares after fruit? There must be some unexpected Freudian explanation." A glazed look of boredom blanked Burden's face. "Talking of unexpected explanations," Wexford said quickly, "do you realize there's one aspect of this case we've given no thought to? Motive. Motive has scarcely been mentioned."

Burden looked as if he were going to say that the police need not concern themselves with motive, that perpetrators in any case often stated motives that seemed thin or incredible. But he didn't say that. He said hesitantly, "Aren't we concluding Williams was killed in what ARRIA would call self-defense?"

"Surely the difficulty there is that if we assume – which we are doing – that the woman or girl who made the phone call and wrote the letters was Williams's girlfriend, why should she need to defend herself against him? Budd and Wheatley were attacked because they made sexual advances. But this girl, being his girlfriend, presumably welcomed his sexual advances."

Burden said in his prudish way, "That might depend on their nature."

"You mean they were sadistic or he wanted to wear one of her nightdresses? We've no evidence Williams was funny in that way. And aren't you forgetting something? It looks as if this murder was somewhat premeditated. Williams was given a sleeping drug before he was stabbed. I don't see my way to accept a theory that one day Williams suggested to his girlfriend that they have sex in this new naughty way, whereupon she substitutes a sedative for his blood-pressure pill and when he's asleep stabs him eight times with a French cook's knife."

"Then what motive do you suggest?"

"I don't. I can't see a girlfriend killing him to be rid of him, because surely all she had to do was give him the out, tell him to go back to his wife or wives. And although a girl could have killed him on her own, she couldn't have disposed of his body on her own. A girl with a jealous husband or boyfriend? ARRIA members don't have husbands. ARRIA members aren't supposed to get sufficiently involved with men for a triangular jealousy situation to arise. But is she an ARRIA member? Does she exist?"

"If one could only read the book of fate," said Burden, unaware that he was quoting and no longer thinking about the Williams case anyway.

"If this were seen," said Wexford, "the happiest youth, viewing his progress through, would shut the book and sit him down and die . . ."

He went home to fetch Dora and the two of them went to see Sheila in *Little Eyolf* at the Olivier.

14

Pomfret Office Equipment Ltd. was open for business by 9:30 on the morning of 12 August. It was a shopfront with a big storage shed behind. The business was run by two men called Ovington, father and son. Edgar Ovington, the father, acknowledged at once that his firm serviced typewriters for the Haldon Finch Comprehensive School. The machines were usually attended to during the long summer holiday. His son had fetched the Haldon Finch machines the day before term ended, 26 July.

Wexford and Burden followed him into the shed at the back. It was full of typewriters, manual, electric, and electronic machines. They stretched away, rows of them ranked on slatted shelves, all labeled with tie-on luggage labels. Ovington pointed out the Haldon Finch typewriters, three on the lower shelf, two on the upper. The label on each said: H. Finch. Three portable Remington 315s, two Adler Gabrielle 5000s. Burden gave Ovington a condensed explanation of why they were looking for a particular typewriter and what made it particular. He asked for a sheet of paper. Ovington broke open a package of 70-gram white bond and peeled off two sheets from the top.

A flaw in the upper-case A, the ascender of the lower-case t and the head of the comma smudged. Burden slipped a sheet of paper into the roller of the first machine and typed a few lines from "O God Our Help in Ages Past," the only hymn he knew by heart. No flaws. No flaws in the second machine, either.

"You haven't put a new typeface on any of these machines?" Wexford asked.

"I haven't so much as touched them yet," said Ovington.

Burden tried the third Remington. It was perfect, a better face than the others had, its need of servicing apparent only in the tendency of one or two of the keys to stick.

"These were the only typewriters fetched from the Haldon Finch Comprehensive School?"

"That's right. I label everything the minute it

comes in to be on the safe side."

"Yes, I see. So there's no possibility one of these machines could accidentally have been returned to a private customer?"

"It wouldn't go to a private customer if it was labeled Haldon Finch, would it?" said Ovington truculently.

He was a dour, prickly, suspicious man, always on the lookout for slurs anyone might cast on his ability or efficiency. Burden's request to try out any other Remington 315s there might be among the two hundred or so machines in the shed started him arguing and might have held them up but for the arrival, smiling and anxious to please, of the son, James Ovington. He was a tall, big-built young man with a toothy smile and a head as bald as an egg.

"Help yourselves. Be my guest." The big white teeth glared as the lips stretched. "Would you like me to have a sample of typing done from every machine here?" He meant it too, there was no sarcasm.

"We'll do it," said Burden. "And it's only the 315s we're interested in."

Two more stood on the shelves besides the three he had tested. "Sufficient is Thine Arm alone," he typed, "And our defense is sure." Nothing wrong with that one. "The busy tribes of flesh and blood With all their cares and fears, Are carried downward by the flood, And lost in following years." No flaws.

"Thanks for your help," said Wexford.

James Ovington said it was his pleasure and smiled so widely that his dragon-seed teeth threatened to spill out. His father scowled.

"It's going to be in a ditch somewhere or a pond," said Burden.

"Not in Green Pond, anyway. Or Milvey would have found it." Wexford was reminded again of the as yet unexplained coincidence. The connecting link between Milvey and Rodney Williams wasn't Carol Milvey, for Carol Milvey had been ill with tonsillitis on the evening of Williams's death. So what was it? Connecting link there must be. Wexford refused to believe that it was by pure chance that Milvey had discovered his neighbor's overnight bag in Green Pond.

And coincidence became remarkable beyond any possible rational explanation, entering the realms of magic or fantasy, when a call came in from Milvey himself next day to say he had found not the typewriter but a long kitchen knife, a French cook's knife, in a small ornamental pond on the Green Pond Hall estate.

The three ponds in the old water garden,

now a wilderness, had been silted up with soil and fine sand washed down by springs from Cheriton Forest. Wexford's men had cleaned out these ponds during their search of the estate, but since that time a further silting-up had taken place. The prospective trout farmer had called Mid-Sussex Waterways in once more to attempt to find a solution to the problem of the clogged water course.

Had the knife been placed there since the police search? Or had it been washed down from a hiding place upstream? It was a large knife, the handle of ivory-colored plastic six inches long, the blade nine inches, a right-angled triangle with the hypotenuse the cutting edge. It had a sharp and vicious-looking point. There were traces of gray mud in the rivet sockets of the handle but not a streak or pinpoint of rust anywhere. Wexford had the knife sent to Forensics at Stowerton. The Milvey link was still a mystery to him. He confronted Milvey across the desk, at a loss for what to ask him next. The wild thought entered his head that Milvey and Joy Williams might have been lovers. It was too wild – not fat, dull Milvey and draggle-tailed Joy. And if Milvey were involved in Williams's death, why should he produce the weapon?

He found himself reduced to saying, "You do

see, don't you, Mr. Milvey, that this situation and your position in it is a very mystifying one. The man who lives next door but one to you is murdered. You find first the bag he had with him when he disappeared, then a knife that in all probability is the murder weapon."

"Somebody," said Milvey who didn't seem to see the point, "had to find them sooner or later."

"The population of Kingsmarkham is somewhere in the area of seventy-eight thousand souls."

Milvey stared at him with bull-headed stupidity. At last he said with truculence, "Next time I find something I reckon will help the police with their inquiries I'll keep quiet about it."

While Forensics were testing the knife against Williams's wound measurements, Sergeant Martin with Bennett and Archbold made inquiries as to its provenance. They listed thirty-nine shops and stores in the area where similar knives were sold. Only Jickie's, however, stocked that particular brand of French cook's knife.

"Wendy Williams may work there," Wexford said, "but everyone shops there. We do. You do. Martin's asking the staff in the hardware department if they can remember anyone recently buying a French cook's knife. You know how far that'll get us. Besides, they've stocked the things for the past five years. There's no reason to believe the knife was bought specifically to kill Williams. In fact, the chances are it wasn't."

"Yes, we're still at square one," Burden said.

"You're being faint-hearted. Come and spend an afternoon among the typewriters. I've a hunch I want to put to the test."

Ovington senior was on his own. He tried at first to fob them off with pleas of pressure of work. Wexford suggested gently that this might be construed as obstructing the police in the course of their inquiries. Ovington, grumbling under his breath, led them once more into the shed at the back of the shop.

Walking between the rows, Wexford examined the labels tied to the machines.

"You always use this method of labeling?"

"What's wrong with it?"

"I didn't say there was anything wrong with it. I don't think it's very clear, that's all. For instance, what does 'P and L' stand for?" He pointed to the labels on a pair of Smith Corona SX 440s.

"Porter and Lamb on the estate," said Ovington gruffly. He meant the industrial estate at Stowerton.

"And TML?"

"Tube Manipulators Limited."

"And you know absolutely what those initials – I might say codes – mean when you're returning machines? You know that 'P and L' stands for Porter and Lamb and not, for instance, for Payne and Lovell, the hardware people in the High Street here?"

"We don't do any work for Payne and Lovell." Ovington looked astonished.

"I think you understand me though. With this system of labeling mistakes could be made. I'll come to the point. 'H. Finch' is rather a rough and ready way of indicating the Haldon Finch Comprehensive School."

"It serves its purpose."

"Suppose you had a customer called Henry Finch. What would stop this machine getting mixed up with the Haldon Finch ones?"

"We don't have a customer called Henry Finch, that's what."

Burden said sharply, "D'you have any customers called Finch?"

"We might have."

It was the curious reply, or a version of it, Wexford had so often heard witnesses give in court when they did not want to commit themselves to a positive "yes." "I might have," "I may have done." Ovington, in his greasy old suit, open-necked shirt, his chin pulled back into his neck and his lips thrust forward, looked shifty, guilty, suspected and suspicious, truculent for the mere sake of truculence.

"I'd like you to check, please."

"Not Henry," said Ovington. "Definitely not. A lady. Not an H at all."

"You're wasting my time, Mr. Ovington."

He was enjoying it, with sly malice. "We did some repairs on a Remington for her a while back. Not a 315 though." At last, scratching his head, "I could look in the book."

"This could be it," Wexford said when he and Burden were alone for a moment. "They could have got mixed up and sent the wrong one back."

"Wouldn't she have noticed?"

"She might not be a regular typist. She might not have used the machine since its return."

He began looking at labels on all the typewriters on the lower shelf on the left-hand side. P and L, E. Ten (what could that mean?), TML, HBSS, H. Finch, J. St G, M. Br . . . Ovington came back with a ledger.

"Miss J. Finch, 22 Bodmin Road, Pomfret. She collected the machine herself on July the twenty-sixth." He slammed the book shut as if he had just proved or disproved something to his triumphant satisfaction.

July 26. The day the Haldon Finch machines were collected and brought here, Wexford thought. Did all this mean anything or nothing? Were the girlfriend and the girlfriend's typewriter after all sitting pretty somewhere in London or Brighton?

Neither he nor Burden knew where Bodmin Road was.

"You know something?" Burden said. "Wendy Williams lives in Liskeard Avenue and Liskeard's a place in Cornwall. Bodmin's the county town in Cornwall. It may be just round the corner."

"We'll look it up as soon as we get back."

It was just round the corner. Liskeard Avenue, Falmouth Road, Truro Road, with Bodmin Road running crossways to connect them all.

"She was practically a neighbor of his," Burden said, sounding almost excited. "An ARRIA member, I bet you. Here she is on the Electoral Register. Finch, Joan B."

"Wait a minute, Mike. Are we saying – are we assuming rather – that a Haldon Finch typewriter was collected by her in error or that it's her own typewriter she has, that this is the machine we're looking for, and we've stumbled upon her not by deduction but by pure luck?"

“What does that matter?” Burden said simply.

Twenty-two Bodmin Road was a small purpose-built block of four flats. According to the doorbells, J. B. Finch lived on the first floor. However, she was not at home either in the afternoon or at their two further calls at seven and eight in the evening. Wexford had been home an hour when a call came through to him to say a fourth man had been stabbed, this time in the upper arm, not a serious wound, though there had been considerable loss of blood.

The difference was that this time his cries were heard by two policemen sitting in a patrol car in a lay-by on the Kingsmarkham bypass. It was after sunset, the beginning of dusk. They had found the victim of the attack lying half across a public footpath, bleeding from a wound near his shoulder. While they were bending over him a girl came out from among the trees of the woodland on the north side of the path, announced her name as Edwina Klein, and handed them a penknife from which she had wiped most of the blood.

15

ARRIA expected a show. Its members were in Kingsmarkham Magistrates' Court in force. Wexford had never seen the small wood-walled area that passed for a public gallery so full. Caroline Peters was there and Sara Williams, redhaired Nicola Anerley, Jane Gardner and the Freeborn twins, Helen Blake and Donella the black girl, the tennis player who wore glasses and the tennis player who did not.

It was to be a test case, of course. Wexford had guessed all of it pretty well before he talked to Edwina Klein. She had not exactly been an *agent provocateur*. It was a terrible world we lived in if a woman who chose to walk alone along a field path at dusk could be called that. But the truth was that Edwina had set out to walk there, and to do so evening after evening since she came down from Oxford at the end of

June, in the expectation of being attacked. She had been frank and open with him, hiding nothing, admitting, for instance, that it was she who while home for a weekend had been Wheatley's assailant. For this reason he had decided not to oppose bail. She would talk freely to him again, she had promised, and, with a faith that would have set the Chief Constable's hair standing on end, he believed her.

With Caroline Peters a founder member of ARRIA, she was a thin, straight girl of medium height, fiercely intelligent, a pioneer and martyr. She was dressed entirely in black, black trousers, black roll-neck sweater, her hair invisible under a tightly tied black scarf. A raven of a woman, the only color about her the tiny orange ARRIA badge pinned on near her left shoulder.

What did the girls in the public gallery expect? Something like the trial of Joan of Arc, Wexford supposed. All were ignorant of magistrates' court procedure, all looked disbelieving when in five minutes it was all over and Edwina committed for trial to the crown court. The charge was unlawful wounding. She was released on bail in her own surety of a £1000 and for a similar sum in that of an elderly woman, her great-aunt, not old enough to have been a suffragette but looking as if she might regret having missed the chance.

The ARRIA contingent filed out, muttering indignantly to each other. Helen Blake and Amy Freeborn picked up the orange banner with a woman-raven on it that they had been obliged to leave outside. The others fell in behind them and what had been a group became a march. "We shall overcome," they sang, "we shall overcome some day." They marched behind the banner up to the police station forecourt and across it and out into the High Street.

Joan Finch was sixty-five years old, perhaps more. Wexford wasn't surprised. There must be few women called Joan under fifty, and even fifty years ago Joan was becoming an old-fashioned name. It was Burden who had built so much on the chance of her being the girl they were looking for.

She took them into the poky little den, designed for surely no more than luggage storage, where she worked, and showed them the typewriter, a big manual Remington at least as old as herself. Fingers today would flinch at that iron forest of keys that took so much muscle power to fell it.

As Ovington had told them, she had collected

it from Pomfret Office Equipment on 26 July. There was no doubt at all that it was hers. It had been her mother's before her and seemed as much of a family heirloom as any clock or piece of china.

Of sole significance to Wexford and Burden was the fact that it wasn't a Remington 315 portable machine. This was something Miss Finch seemed unable to grasp. She insisted on sitting down at the typewriter and producing for them a half page of men coming to the aid of the party and quick brown foxes. The Ovingtons had done a good job. There wasn't a flaw or an irregularity to be seen.

They had lunch at the little bow-fronted wine bar two doors away. Pamela Gardner was at a corner table lunching with a woman friend. She looked through Wexford with a contemptuous stare. Her daughter had bounced along that morning, singing as heartily as anyone and a good deal more loudly, waving to him as if they were old friends. Edwina Klein was coming to the police station at 2:30 to talk to him. It was no part of the conditions of her bail that she should do this but he felt sure she wouldn't fail him. Burden said, "Only three weeks to go now." He was talking of the coming baby. "They say it'll be on time. They don't really know though."

"There's more they don't know than they ever let on."

Burden picked at his quiche. "She had the heartburn at the beginning and I'm getting it now." He was pale, bilious-looking.

"We'll see if the Harmers can supply you with an indigestion remedy."

The Pre-Raphaelite head of Paulette could be seen through the window of the dispensary, where she was evidently helping her father. It was Hope Harmer who served Burden. She seemed discomfited by their visit, unable perhaps to realize that policemen too have private lives and are as liable to bodily ills as anyone else.

"Did you have a good holiday?" Wexford asked her.

"Oh yes, thank you, very nice. Very quiet," she added as people do when describing their Christmas celebrations as if to admit to liveliness and merriment were to deny respectability. "All good things come to an end though, don't they? We could have stayed away another week, only my daughter's expecting her A-level results. They're due any day."

Sara Williams must also be on tenterhooks then . . . "Another would-be doctor in the family?"

"No, no. Paulette's hoping to follow in her

Daddy's footsteps."

She was all bright placatory smiles, accompanying them to the door when they left like an old-fashioned shopkeeper. Wexford walked into the police station just before 2:30. Edwina Klein was waiting for him, shown upstairs to his room, and he felt relief at the sight of her in spite of his confidence that she would keep her word. With her, seated in the other visitor's chair, like a chaperone, was the aunt.

Wexford was surprised. He had seen Edwina as the very epitome of independence, of self-reliance.

"I happen to be a solicitor as well as an aunt."

"Very well," said Wexford, "but this won't be an interrogation, just a talk about various aspects of this case."

"That's what they all say," said the aunt, whose name was Pearl Kaufmann. In appearance she was rather like Virginia Woolf in her latter days, tallish, thin, long-faced, long-nosed, with a full mouth. She wore a navy blue silk dress, mid-calf length, and clumpy white sandals that made her feet look large.

Edwina was still in the black she had worn in court but with the roll-neck sweater changed for a sleeveless black tee-shirt that was better suited to the heat of the day. The ARRIA badge had been transferred to this. She had sunglasses on which turned her face into an expressionless mask.

"He treated me exactly as if I was a prostitute," she had said to him of Wheatley at that earlier conversation. The black glasses hadn't covered her eyes then. They had been bright with eagerness, with earnestness, with the zeal of youth. "Not that there's anything wrong with being a prostitute. That's OK, that's fine if that's where you're at. It's just the way men *assume* . . ."

"Only some men."

"A lot. He didn't even talk to me. I tried to talk to him. I asked him where he worked and where he lived. When I asked him where he lived he gave a strange sort of laugh as if I'd said something *wrong*."

"Why did you ask him for a lift? To provoke exactly the sort of situation that arose?"

"No, I didn't. Not that time. I admit I did last night but it was different with the man in the car. I'd had a lift from London to Kingsmarkham and the guy couldn't take me any farther." She seemed to consider. "It was because of what happened in the car that I decided to try walking in the forest and see."

"You'd better tell me what happened in the car, hadn't you?"

"He pulled into a lay-by. He did talk then.

He said, 'Come on, we'll go in the wood.' I didn't know what he meant, I really didn't. Do you know what he thought? He thought I wanted paying first. He said, 'Will ten pounds do?' And then he touched me." Edwina Klein laid her right hand on her left breast. "He touched me like I'm doing now. Like it was a tap or a switch. He didn't try to put his arms around me or kiss me or anything. It was just offering to pay and feeling the switch. I took out my knife and stuck it in his hand."

There had been no aunt present when she talked to him then and no black circles to take the character from her face. Her manner now was more subdued, less indignant. Her experience of the court had perhaps chastened her. She waited almost meekly for him to begin questioning her. Miss Kaufmann sat looking at Wexford's wall map with simulated interest.

"Have you stabbed any other men?" he said abruptly, knowing the remark would be objected to.

Edwina shook her head.

"We won't mind about that, Mr. Wexford." It seemed highly suitable to the aunt's manner and appearance that she should use this obsolete Victorian phrase. She elucidated with something more contemporary. "We'll forget you said that."

"As you please," said Wexford. "When the police use *agents provocateurs* – as, for example, in the case of a policewoman sitting in a cinema where a member of the audience is suspected of assaulting women – the public, particularly the public of your sort of persuasion, gets up in arms. There's an outcry when a young policeman deliberately uses a public lavatory frequented by homosexuals. In other words, it's not all right for them to do this in the interests of justice but it's all right for you to in the mere interest of a principle. There's rather a crude name for what you did and were, isn't there?"

He had been too mealy-mouthed, too gentlemanly, he quickly saw.

"A pricktease," she said flatly. The aunt didn't move an eyelid. "I didn't do that. I didn't do anything but go for a walk in a wood. I wasn't provocatively dressed." Scorn came into her voice now and she lifted up her head. "I wouldn't be! I had jeans on and a jacket. I never wear make-up, not ever. The only thing I did to provoke anyone was *be* there and be a woman."

"I think my niece is saying," said Miss Kaufmann dryly, "that it isn't possible to be a woman in certain places with impunity. She was out to prove this and she did prove it."

He let it go. He left it. He felt the force of what the two women said and he knew it was true, and that this was an instance of a policeman knowing that the opposing argument is sounder than his own but of having to stick to his own just the same. That all women who intended to go about by themselves at night should learn self-defense techniques seemed to him the best answer. The alternative was that men's natures should change, and that was something which might slowly happen over centuries but not in years or even decades. He wrote busy nothings on the sheet of paper in front of him to fill thirty seconds of time and keep them temporarily silent. At last he lifted his head and looked at Edwina Klein. For some reason, perhaps because his eyes were naked, she took off her glasses. Immediately she looked earnest again and very young.

"You know the Williams family, I think?"

She was prepared for this. Somehow she knew that this was what she was really there for. Her answer surprised him.

"Which Williams family? There are two, aren't there?"

"There may be two hundred in this neighborhood for all I know," he said sharply. "It's a common name. I'm talking about the Williams family that live in Alverbury Road, Kingsmarkham. The girl is called Sara. She was in court this morning. I think you know her."

She nodded. "We were at school together. She's a year younger than I am."

"Did you know Rodney Williams, the dead man?"

She was very quick to reply. Miss Kaufmann looked up as if warningly. "He and Mrs. Williams, yes. Sara and I used to do ballet together." She smiled. "Believe it or not." Miss Kaufmann cast up her eyes as if she could hardly believe it. "They'd come for Sara or one of them would. I remember him because he was the only father who ever came. Sometimes he'd come and sit through the whole class."

Watching pubescent girls in little tutus, thought Wexford, or more likely leotards these days.

"You asked me which family I meant," he said.

"I slightly know the other one." She lifted her shoulders. "Veronica Williams looks exactly like Sara."

He felt a tightening of nerves. She might be a link between the two families. She was the only person he had yet talked to who knew – or admitted to knowing – both sets of Williamses.

"You were aware that they were half-sisters then? You knew Williams was their father?"

"No. Oh no. I suppose I thought – well, I didn't think about it. I honestly don't know, really. Perhaps that they might be cousins."

"When did you last see Rodney Williams?"

"Years ago." She was becoming nervous, frightened. It meant nothing, it was evidence only of her realization that she had been brought here to face one sort of ordeal and, that over, was being subjected to another of an unexpected kind. "I haven't seen him for years."

"Then how do you know Veronica?"

No dramatic *crise de nerfs* and no hesitation either. "I played tennis against her. When I was at school."

"She's three years younger than you."

"OK. Sure. She was a sort of child prodigy. She was in Haldon Finch's first six when she was under fourteen."

It was all reasonable, more than plausible. She had been in Oxford the night Rodney Williams died, having gone up early, a week before her term began. She had told him so last evening and told him, in grave and careful detail, whom to check this with. Bennett was in Oxford checking now, but Wexford had little doubt Edwina hadn't lied to him.

"You knew both families," he said now, "but you didn't know, so to speak, they were one family? You didn't know Rodney Williams was the father of Veronica as well as of Sara and Kevin?"

"Kevin? I've never even heard of him before."

"Sara's older brother." He decided to be entirely frank with her. Miss Kaufmann sat watching him, an acid twist to her mouth. "They didn't know of the existence of the others," he said, "The Pomfret family didn't know of the existence of the Kingsmarkham family and the Kingsmarkham family didn't know of the existence of the Pomfret family until quite a while after Rodney Williams was dead. So if you knew, that must mean you also knew Rodney Williams was a bigamist or at least a married man maintaining two households. And if you knew that how did you know it?"

"I didn't."

The cool negative disappointed him. He had felt on the brink of a breakthrough. But she qualified it.

"I didn't know. I said they looked alike, I'd noticed that, and I remember once saying to my aunt that they must be cousins." Edwina looked at Miss Kaufmann and Miss Kaufmann nodded in a rapid, impatient way. "I didn't know either of them well," Edwina said. "You've got to remember that. I'd never spoken more than a few words to Veronica. And Mrs.

Williams, that's the real wife, I've seen her about but she's forgotten who I am or something, and as far as the other one goes I was just a customer."

He had nothing else to ask her. She had stabbed Brian Wheatley and Peter John Hyde, her assailant in the wood, but he was certain she hadn't killed Williams. If a woman had done that she would have needed a second to help her.

"That's all then, thank you, Miss Klein."

She got up and walked slowly and gracefully to the door, holding herself erect but with her head slightly bowed. They had the same figure, the same walk, this aunt and niece, though fifty years separated them. What would become of Edwina Klein now? It was inevitable she would be found guilty. Would her college have her back? Or was her whole future spoiled? Had she blown it for the sake of a lost cause? At the door, just before he opened it for her, she said, "There's one thing. You said the Pomfret Williamses and the Kingsmarkham Williamses didn't know about each other. For the sake of setting the record straight, that's not right."

The excitement was back, drying his throat. "What do you mean?"

"What I say. They did know about each other."

He took his hand from the door and leaned against it like someone barring egress. But Edwina Klein stood there willingly, looking a little puzzled, the aunt bored but patient.

"How do you know that?"

"Because I've seen them together," she said.

Relief ran over him like sweat. He felt cool and lightheaded with it. She was aware now that she had told him something revelatory, unguessed at, and her face, close to his, was full of alert inquiry.

"Whom did you see together?" he asked her.

"Those two women. I saw them in the Precinct Café in Kingsmarkham having coffee together."

"When? Can you remember when?"

If it were a week ago or even a month ago it meant nothing.

"Last Christmas, I think. It must have been Christmas or Easter for me to have been home. The only weekend I've been home was when *Wheatley* gave me that lift." Edwina put infinite scorn into the pronunciation of his name. "It wasn't then and it wasn't Easter. I know it can't have been because there was snow on the ground."

"Snow fell," said Miss Kaufmann, helpful now her niece was not directly threatened, "during the first week of January."

"It must have been then," said Edwina.

She smiled, as if pleased to have been of help at last. He knew she hadn't lied.

16

As Wexford opened the gate of 31 Alverbury Road the postman was coming down the path, a wad of mail fastened with a rubber band in his left hand. None of it apparently was for 29 and his next call was at Milvey's, two doors down. Watching him, Wexford suddenly understood how Milvey came into the case. There was no coincidence at all, it was all simple and logical, only he had been putting the cart before the horse . . .

He rang the bell. As he did so St. Peter's clock struck nine. It was Sara who opened the door, and so quickly he knew she must have been standing directly behind it. She was holding a paper.

"Two As and a B," she said, and smiled with gratification.

She had spoken as if the sole purpose of his

call had been to hear about her A-level results. Before she closed the door she must have seen the police car outside with Donaldson at the wheel and Marion Bayliss in the back.

"Congratulations," Wexford said. "Where's your mother?"

She didn't answer. She might not have heard for all the notice she took.

"St. Biddulph's told me they'd take me with three Bs or two Bs and an A, so this is rather better."

Frenetic excitement was in the girl's eyes, an excitement that was manic and all the more disconcerting for being under such tight control. He had seen her as a Botticelli girl, mild-faced, tranquil, with a spring-like innocence. Primavera should not tremble with triumph nor Venus's eyes glitter.

"I'm going to phone my cousin Paulette, find out how she did."

To crow a little? Or to be kind? Joy Williams came out from the kitchen, dressed as he had never seen her before. He hadn't told her but perhaps she had guessed she would be meeting Wendy again. Or Wendy herself had told her the evening before? He was prepared for that. He rather hoped they realized he knew of their prior acquaintance. Joy wore a clean, tidy skirt and blouse. She had washed her hair and smudged lipstick on her mouth, in the uncertain, slapdash way women do who seldom wear it and somehow feel ashamed to do so. Probably she always dresses up when she and Wendy meet, he thought. There would be rivalry there even if they were allied in a common hatred of Williams. Besides, an alliance would not mean they actually *liked* each other . . .

Sara could be heard on the phone. "Have they come? Well?"

Not much of a bedside manner. He imagined her talking in that hectoring way to a patient. A hard, neurotic little go-getter, he thought her, without an atom of concern for the mother whom the police suspected of murdering her father.

"That's not bad though, is it?" she was saying. "It's not as if you need As or even Bs."

Patronizing. Somewhat lofty. The pharmacist, of course, was the poor man's doctor, or the doctor for the fainthearted. "I'll ask the chemist to give me something for my throat." Or my head, back, cystitis, bleeding, lump in the breast . . . He took Joy out and closed the front door behind them.

Sergeant Martin and Polly Davies brought Wendy in.

The evening before she had been in tears of

vexation at missing a day's work, but that she could have refused to come – that the police were still in a position only to ask and persuade – seemed no more to have occurred to her than to Joy. They were not blessed with lawyers for aunts. The senior wife – the Sultana Valideh – was already seated in the interview room when Wendy was brought in, the expressionless face averted, the dark brown animal eyes staring past her at the window.

Wendy wore a smock dress, Kate Greenaway-like, in a Laura Ashley print, at the neck and wrists frills tied with bows. She had white tights on and white shoes. While the sergeant and Polly stood by (Polly told Wexford later) Wendy had taken her daughter Veronica in her arms and hugged her in a highly emotional way, bringing a fresh rush of tears. Veronica had looked very taken aback. But Wendy had pressed her close to her, stroking her hair, almost as if she expected never to see her again. And Polly, who was a reader of romantic period fiction, said it was like Marie Antoinette setting off in the tumbril.

"Farewell, my children, forever! I am going to your father."

Now all that remained as evidence of this scene was the swollen pinkness of Wendy's face. She gave Wexford a piteous look. She would have preferred Burden to interrogate her, she found him more sympathetic than this elderly, hard, sardonic man, but Burden wasn't there. He was in Alverbury Road in conversation with Mrs. Milvey.

Wexford said, and he seemed to be addressing either or both of them, "Which of you first found out the other existed?"

It was Wendy who answered. Her voice was even more fretful than usual. "I don't understand what you mean."

"I'll put it another way. When did you first discover Rodney Williams had a wife? And you, Mrs. Williams, when did you find out your husband had 'married' again?" He put very audible inverted commas round that past participle. "Well?" he said. "I know you haven't been truthful with me. I know you knew each other. The question is, when did you first know?"

"I never knew she existed till you told me." Joy spoke in her weary, lifeless way. "When you told me my husband was a bigamist on top of all the rest."

"All what 'rest,' Mrs. Williams?"

"Lying to me about his job for a start."

Wendy murmured something.

"I'm sorry, Mrs. Williams, I didn't catch that."

"I said 'having other women.' I meant that's what the rest was, having other women."

"He never had other women," said Joy. She was responding to Wendy's prompting but she wasn't speaking to her. It was Wexford she was addressing. "He had *her* but he never had others."

"Let her delude herself if she wants," said Wendy to no one in particular, lifting her shoulders and smiling very faintly.

"When did you first meet her, Mrs. Williams?" Wexford was finding it a shade awkward, their both sharing the name. He got up and came round the table to address the words specifically to Wendy. Joy burst out, "You've no business to call her that! She's no right to that name. She's Miss Whatever-she-used-to-be. You call her that!"

"The manners of a fishwife," said Wendy. "She's as common as dirt. No wonder he came to me."

"Nasty little bitch! Look at her, dressed up like a kid!"

They're staging it, Wexford thought, they must be. It's all set up for my benefit, rehearsed as like as not. He called the two women quietly to order.

William Milvey was at home that day. The

offices of Mid-Sussex Waterways were in his house and he was awaiting the visit of the VAT inspector. That was who he thought Burden was and for some moments they talked at cross-purposes, having one of those conversations so amusing to hearers and so frustrating to the participants.

Their hearer in this case was Mrs. Milvey, a big-built lady, very ready with her laughter. She laughed merrily at their discomfiture. But Burden's troubles were quickly over. After that all went smoothly and it turned out to be as Wexford had supposed.

"The wife's a director of our company just as much as me," Milvey said importantly. "And naturally she knows the ins and outs of the business equally to what I do."

"I have to know where he's going to be every day in case there's phone calls," said Mrs. Milvey, who was less pompous than her husband. "The fifteenth of April? I'll have a look in the book, shall I, Bill?"

At this point the VAT inspector did arrive, a man in his early twenties by the look of him, carrying a briefcase. Milvey seemed reluctant to absent himself from the more interesting (and perhaps less alarming) examination but he was obliged to go. He took the VAT man into his office and closed the door. Mrs. Milvey smiled comfortably at Burden.

"From Easter right up till the end of April they was working up Myringham way," she said, referring to the ledger she was holding. "They never started on Green Pond till a month later."

"Are you sure?"

"Positive. No doubt about it. It's down here in black and white. Green Pond, May the thirty-first. Besides, I remember it all now. Bill had a job lined up for the end of May, a big drainage job over to Sewingbury, and the chap canceled at the last minute. But as luck would have it, this trout farm chap at Green Pond had been given his name and he rung up and said could he drag the pond? Well, Bill happened to be free on account of the cancellation. Must have given the trout farm fella a bit of a surprise, him saying yes, I'll start prompt on Monday."

The office door opened again and Milvey put a hand out for his book. His wife gave it to him.

"Did you tell anyone?"

"I expect so. There was no secret about it, it was open and aboveboard. You like to have a bit of news to tell folks, don't you? Now you're wanting to know if I told my neighbor

Mrs. Williams, aren't you?"

"Did you?"

"I never knew a thing about her husband then, mind you. I met her going down to the shops. Bill was getting the van out. I said something like, Monday he'll be doing a job at Green Pond Hall. There's going to be a trout farm, did you know? Something like that."

"But you definitely told her your husband would be dragging the pond on Monday, May the thirty-first?"

"I couldn't see it would do any harm, could I?"

Had it? Wexford hadn't been entirely correct in his supposition, which was that Mrs. Milvey had told Joy the pond had already been dragged or was not to be dragged until a much later date. But this gave a different – and incomprehensible – look to things. If Joy had known Green Pond was to be dragged on the following Monday, the pond into which she had dumped her husband's traveling bag, wouldn't she have retrieved it during the weekend? The alternative possibly was that she had hidden it elsewhere and put it in Green Pond only when *she knew it was to be immediately dragged.* Why should she do such a thing, why behave so absurdly?

This was a hunch of Wexford's that had gone

awry. Burden was on his way to put the second one to the test. They seemed no nearer, as far as he could see and in spite of Edwina Klein's revelation, to breaking the case. Next week he would probably start his paternity leave . . .

Bald-headed James Ovington, the son, was alone in charge of Pomfret Office Equipment. His ingratiating smile was as broad as ever. Burden noticed a new mannerism, a nervous way he had of rubbing his hands together. At any rate, the dour and obstructive father was nowhere around.

"Now, can I help? Tell me what I can do."

"You have a method of labeling your machines here," said Burden. "Not exactly a code, a kind of speedwriting. Last time we were here we noticed one labeled 'E. Ten.' I wondered what that stood for. It wasn't a Remington 315, of course, we'd have pounced on it if it had been. This is a kind of shot in the dark and I daresay I'm not making myself too clear."

"It's clear enough you want to know what 'E. Ten' stands for and that's easy." Nevertheless, he hesitated and Burden wondered why a shade of unease seemed to cross his face.

"Eric Tennyson," Ovington said. "That's who it is, that's who 'E. Ten' stands for."

Second time lucky . . . "I don't suppose you know if he has a daughter called Nicola?"

"Well, I do know as a matter of fact. The answer's yes."

Veronica Williams's friend, her home the house to which Veronica regularly went on Tuesdays. But the typewriter labeled "E. Ten" wasn't a Remington 315. Unless . . .

"An Olivetti," said Ovington. "They're got another machine. I don't rightly remember what. She types stuff for people, I mean does it for a living." The uneasy look was back again. "I may as well tell you," he said as if about to make a confession of something that for a long while had weighed heavily on him. "They're friends of mine. I knew I ought to tell you last time you were here."

"But why shouldn't they be friends of yours, Mr. Ovington?"

"Well . . . They're friends of Mrs. Williams too. I mean the Mrs. Williams whose husband got killed, the one you're making inquiries about. I mean that's where I met her, in their house."

"Are you trying to tell me something, Mr. Ovington?"

This fresh smile, a forced straining of the muscles, turned his face into a gargoyle. He rubbed his hands briskly, then clasped them behind his back to prevent a repetition of the gesture. Light from the shallow overhead lamps in the shed shone with a yellow gleam on the hairless head. Why were the heads of bald men compared to eggs? Ovington's head more than anything resembled a polished pebble.

"What is it you're saying, Mr. Ovington?"

"I've been getting friendly with her. With Mrs. Williams. There was nothing wrong, I don't mean that. I met her at Eric's and we'd have a drink sometimes, go for a walk, that sort of thing. When it looked as if that husband of hers had finally – well, when it looked as if he'd gone for good, I – I hoped things could get more serious." He spoke jerkily, floundering, hopelessly unable to handle the situation he had got himself into. "There was nothing *wrong*. I'd like to repeat that."

Burden thought irrelevantly that Wendy Williams must be attracted by bald men, first Rodney with his exaggerated forehead, naked as an apple, then this pebble-head.

"But I thought," Ovington said earnestly, "that it would be wrong of me – disloyal, you know – to deny the relationship at this juncture, sort of deserting the sinking ship when you hear the cock crowing, if you get my meaning."

More or less Burden did get it. He thought of the joy Wexford would have in that gloriously mixed metaphor. Now for the Tennysons. Half an hour later he was in their house on the Haldon Finch side of Pomfret, being told by Mrs. Tennyson that her daughter was camping in Scotland till the end of the month but could she help him?

Her husband had fetched the repaired and serviced Olivetti from Pomfret Office Equipment three days before. Yes, she had her small portable for use when the other one was away for its annual overhaul. She showed it to him: a Remington 315.

Burden stuck the sheet of paper she gave him into the roller. "A thousand ages in Thy sight, Are like an evening gone . . ." A flaw in the apex of the capital A, the ascender of the lower-case t, the head of the comma . . .

"I'd never seen her in my life till you had us meet here."

That was Wendy. Joy said nothing.

"I put it to you that you'd known each other for a long time. I suggest it was like this: Mrs. Joy Williams came into Jickie's as a customer one day and in conversation you discovered the link between you. This happened a year ago. You've been in touch with each other ever since."

Joy gave one of her cold, rattling laughs that had something in it of the cackle of a game bird.

"If I'd known about her why should I pretend I didn't?" said Wendy.

Joy answered. She didn't exactly address Wendy, she hadn't yet done that except to abuse her, but she made her first statement not inimical to the other Mrs. Williams.

"If her and me knew each other he thinks we might have murdered Rod."

"I'm more likely to have murdered *her*," said Wendy in a lofty voice. She looked down and noticed a ladder in her pale milk-colored tights. It crept up the outside of her right leg like a millipede. Joy noticed it too. She fixed her eyes on the slowly mounting run and her mouth moved. It was nearly a smile.

Wexford said, looking at Joy, "Someone phoned Sevensmith Harding on Friday, April the sixteenth, to say Rodney Williams was ill and wouldn't be coming to work. The girl who took the call isn't in much doubt that it was your voice, Mrs. Williams."

"She doesn't know my voice. How could she, whoever she is? Aren't you forgetting, I didn't know Rod worked there?"

The door opened and Burden put his head round. Wendy was licking her finger and dabbing at the ladder with her wet fingertip, dabbing as it happened in vain, for the ladder quite suddenly crept another half-inch. It was

.this which might have occasioned Joy's rattle laugh. Wexford got up and went out of the room, leaving the two women with the two women detectives.

Burden had sent his typing sample to the forensics lab. He told Wexford the substance of his interview with Mrs. Tennyson. She had typed no letter of resignation herself and no one had asked her to do such a thing. Wendy Williams she had known for years, though her acquaintance with Rodney had been slight. Their daughters were the same age, were at school together, were "best friends."

"Could Wendy have typed it?" Wexford asked him. "I mean, could she have had access to this machine? If this killing was premeditated, and it looks as if it was, she could have typed that letter days or even weeks before."

"The Tennyson woman shuts herself up in a room she uses as an office and types for three or four hours a day. As a regular thing she uses the Olivetti and the Remington isn't even kept in there. It's usually in a cupboard in the hall unless the husband Eric wants it or the daughter Nicola uses it to type a school essay. Apparently, they're allowed to do that at the Haldon Finch. Could you credit it?"

"It seems a sensible and harmless practice,"

said Wexford. "Was Wendy ever alone in that house?"

"Early in April she came to call for Veronica, take her home or something. It was dark or late or she was passing. Anyway, the two girls were still out and Mrs. Tennyson was typing something. She left Wendy alone for at most ten minutes, she says, until she finished off what she was doing."

"Wendy would have to know the machine was there. She would have to have paper. But I agree it goes a long way to answering the question of how and where the letter was typed. As to typewriters, what better than to use one that was normally kept shut up in a cupboard? It was by the merest luck that we got on to it." He listened while Burden told him about Ovington. "Is that a motive, Mike? We keep coming back to that, the lack of motive. But if Wendy wanted to marry Ovington . . ."

"Who did Joy want to marry?"

"Yes, OK, I see your point. If they did it they did it together and Joy wouldn't be likely to help murder Rodney so that Wendy could marry somebody else." Wexford brought his fist to his forehead and drummed against it. "I'm a fool! There's no motive. If Wendy knew about Joy she also knew she wasn't married to Rodney, so there was no legal bar to her marrying someone else . . . What about the knife, the weapon we're never going to prove *was* the weapon beyond a doubt? It could have been Joy's or Wendy's."

"Wendy works at Jickie's and Jickie's stock those knives."

"Wendy works there but the whole neighborhood shops there." Wexford thought for a moment. "Among the stuff we found in Rodney Williams's bedroom in Liskeard Avenue," he said, "was an estimate from a firm of decorators for painting Wendy's living room. When we saw that room it had obviously been painted very recently. By that firm? By another? By Wendy herself? I think we ought to find out, don't you?"

Burden looked at him. They were both thinking that Rodney Williams had been stabbed to death. One of the knife thrusts had pierced the carotid. "Yes, I do," he said.

The day was very warm and close, a heavy, sultry, almost sunless day of the kind that only comes as August wanes. For the few moments he and Burden were in his office, the window open and the half-closed blinds swaying slightly in a hint of breeze, he had kept his jacket off. Now he put it on again and went back downstairs to the interview room where the two women were.

17

A picture of Joy and Wendy leaving Kingsmarkham Police Station was on most front pages of the national press next day. The more sensational of the newspapers managed to give the impression that they were not leaving but entering and that readers would not be too wide of the mark in concluding they had never left. Joy had her hand up over her face, Wendy looked piteously into the cameras, a distraught waif in her little-girl smock. The ladder in her tights was cruelly evident. Burden stood by, cool and rather aloof in a newish suit.

"You look young and handsome," said Jenny at the breakfast table. "You look so thin!" She shifted her huge weight, pushing back her chair.

"It's the worry."

"I expect it is, poor Mike." She put up her

arms and hugged him. It was now possible for her to do this only while sitting down. He held her and thought, It may still be all right, we may still survive.

He went out before nine into a morning that was anything but fresh, a gray, sultry, sticky day. The sky was flat, very pale gray with the sun a puddle of white glowing through it. This was the kind of day, he thought, that only England knows. Fifty of them can compose a summer.

How many builders and decorators were there in Pomfret? In Kingsmarkham? Not just the established firms but the one-man bands, the man who works in his spare time for money in the back pocket? With luck the Pomfret Williamses had availed themselves of the services of the firm who sent Rodney the estimate.

He didn't go to the police station first, so he was not present when Hope Harmer phoned to say her daughter was missing, had not been home all night or reappeared that morning.

John Harmer was in his dispensary and business was as usual. That is, when customers wanted soap or disposable razors instead of a prescription made up he came out and served them. He refused to believe anything had happened to his daughter. She was a grown woman well able to take care of herself, as her prowess at that judo stuff evinced. Her absence probably had something to do with this women's movement nonsense.

Paulette's mother had come to work, but only perhaps because of the pressures put on her by her husband. It was from there that she had phoned, the culminating act of a scene between them, Wexford guessed. She was in a piteous state. Hope Harmer was a woman whom it suited only to be happy. She was easily content and in contentment her plump, fair good looks bloomed. Unease affected her as it does an animal, drawing her face, freezing her features, mysteriously making bright hair lank and placid eyes stark with fear.

Wexford had Martin with him, the two of them top brass for the mere matter of a missing girl – but circumstances alter cases.

"My husband says what do I expect when I let her go out with her boyfriend at all hours and stay the night at his place. But they all do it these days and you can't be different. Besides they're engaged and I always say if you really love each other . . ."

She was talking for the sake of talking but her voice faltered. She began twisting her hands.

"Did Paulette go out with her fiancé last night?"

"No, he's in Birmingham. He had to go to Birmingham for his firm."

Not for the first time Wexford marveled at how illogical human thinking can be.

"But she did go out? Where did she go?"

"I don't know. She didn't say. She just went out at about seven."

Martin said, "You didn't want to know where she was going?"

"Want to know! Of course I wanted to know. If I had my way I'd know where she was every minute of the day and night. I mean I didn't ask her, I'd forced myself to that. When she was younger her father used to say: I want to know where you're going and who with but once you're eighteen you're legally grown-up and you can do what you like. Well, she's eighteen and she remembered that and my husband remembers it and he stops me asking and Paulette wouldn't answer anyway."

The poor woman was wretchedly caught between husband and daughter, and bullied, doubtless, by both – or had she been happy to have decision-making taken out of her hands?

"Tell me what happened later on. Of course you didn't wait up for her?"

"I would have. I knew Richard was in Birmingham, you see. John said he wasn't having me get in a hysterical state. He took a sleeping pill and he made me take one."

Presumably sedatives were unlimitedly on tap *chez* Harmer . . .

"This morning I – well, I left her bedroom door open before I went to sleep. That way – if it was shut, you see, I'd know she'd come in. I – I had to make myself open my own bedroom door and look. Her door was still open, it was such a shock, I . . . Well, I went to look, in case she'd come in and left her door but, of course, she hadn't. John still wasn't alarmed. Somehow I couldn't make him see that if Richard was in Birmingham Paulette couldn't have been with him . . .

Mrs. Harmer burst into raging tears. Instead of falling forward on to her arms to cry she lay back, let her head hang back, and wailed. Martin went into the dispensary and fetched John Harmer. He came in looking cross and harassed. The noise his wife was making had the effect of causing him to put his hands over his ears in the manner that does nothing to block out sound but indicates that the sound is in some way distasteful or irritating.

"She'd better have a Valium. That'll help her pull herself together."

"What she had better do, Mr. Harmer," said Wexford, "is get off home. And you had better take her. Never mind the shop."

Godwin and Sculp had not done Wendy Williams's decorating but they knew who had – a man who had once worked for them, who had left to set up in business on his own, and who undercut them, Burden was told, at every opportunity. Running Leslie Kitman to earth was less simple. He had no wife and his mother was no Mrs. Milvey to have his precise location at her fingertips. She gave Burden five possible addresses at which her son might be found: a farmhouse between Pomfret and Myfleet, a block of flats in Queen Street, Kingsmarkham, a cottage in Pomfret, and two houses on new estates outside Stowerton. Kitman was at none of them, but the second Stowerton household told Burden he might just be lucky and find him in – Liskeard Avenue.

And it was there, three houses away from Wendy Williams's, that Burden discovered Kitman on top of a ladder. The house was like Wendy's – gray bricks and white weatherboard and picture windows. Kitman was painting a top-floor window frame when Burden, standing at the foot of the ladder, shouted up who he was. Kitman launched immediately into a catalogue of reasons for not renewing his car tax. Burden hadn't even noticed his car, still less that the tax disc showed an expiry date of the end of June. At last, though, Kitman was made to understand and he came quickly down the ladder, his brush dripping white paint onto the lawn beneath.

The evening before Wendy Williams had spent in bed, where she had retired, worn out, as soon as she returned from the police station. Veronica had brought her tea and bread and butter. It was all she ever seemed to fancy when upset. Joy Williams had also been at home with her daughter. At any rate they had been in the same house, Sara in her room as usual, Joy watching television and intermittently struggling to complete the form of application for a grant that would take Sara through medical school. And although it was a Thursday evening there had been no phone call from Kevin, who extended this courtesy to his mother only when he was at college and not while junketing around holiday resorts.

These were the alibis Wexford was given by his two principal suspects. Richard Cobb came back from Birmingham in the course of the afternoon and furnished Wexford with a very detailed and apparently satisfactory account of where he had been the night before. Police in Birmingham would help with a check on that.

By six Paulette hadn't come home and Wexford knew she never would, he felt in his bones she wouldn't.

The day was sultry and overcast. For hours the thunder had been growling and rumbling, and gradually a wind had risen, a dry gusty wind that did nothing to lower the temperature. It still remained hot and stuffy. Wexford and Burden sat in Wexford's office. A search for Paulette hadn't begun yet. Where would one search?

"The lines I'm thinking along," said Wexford, "are that Paulette Harmer procured the Phanodorm with which Rodney Williams was sedated. She was in a position to do that, she could easily have done it. I'm wondering if she lost her nerve and told someone – well, Joy – she was going to admit it before we found out."

"Of course, there's another possibility . . ." Burden left the suggestion suspended.

Wexford looked abstractedly out of the window. It was time to go home but he had no inclination to go. The weather, the atmosphere, the late day, hung heavy with expectation. The thunder, of course, was a threat in itself, a sign of imminent storm, yet it seemed to contain some kind of emotional menace as well, as of looming tragedy.

"Tell me about Kitman," Wexford said. "In

detail." Burden had already given him an outline of his talk with the painter.

"He started doing that job for Wendy on April the fourteenth. There was paper on the walls, he said, and he had a job stripping it off. He was still doing it all through the fourteenth and fifteenth and he still hadn't finished by the time he knocked off on the fifteenth."

"Should have used Sevensmith Harding's Sevenstarker, shouldn't he?" said Wexford quoting, " 'The slick, sheer, clean way to strip your walls.' "

"Maybe he did. He says the room was still furnished, but he had covered the pieces of furniture up with his own dust sheets. When he came back in the morning – the morning of Friday the sixteenth, that is – some of the sheets were off and folded up. But that was also on the morning of the fifteenth and other mornings, I gather. Wendy and Veronica were to some extent still living in that room."

"Did he notice anything else that Friday morning?"

"A stain on the wall is what we want, isn't it? A great bloodstain? And blood all over his dust sheets? There wasn't anything like that, or if there was he didn't notice or can't remember. The walls were splashed and marked and patchy anyway, you can imagine. And on the sixteenth he covered up whatever might have been there by putting his first coat of paint on. Sevenstar emulsion, no doubt. One thing he did notice, though, and I didn't ask him about this, he volunteered it. Apparently it's been vaguely preying on his mind ever since. One of the dust sheets wasn't his."

"What?"

"Yes. I thought that'd make you sit up. He has a few dust sheets he takes about with him. Some of them are old bed sheets and there are a couple of curtains and a candlewick bedspread too. Well, according to him, when he left on the fifteenth all seven of his sheets were covering the furniture and part of the carpet. Next morning he came in to find that three of the sheets had been taken off the furniture and were folded up on the floor. He thought nothing much of it but later he noticed that one of the folded sheets wasn't his. It was newer than his and in better condition."

"Did he ask Wendy about it?"

"He says he did. On the Saturday. She told him she knew nothing about it. And what did it matter to him, after all? He had the right number of dust sheets. You don't go to the police because someone has taken one of your dust sheets and substituted another. But he wondered about it, he said. It niggled him is the way he puts it. Are we going to have those two women back?"

"Of course we are."

It was Friday, the last Friday of the month. ARRIA met on the last Friday of the month, Wexford thought. No, the last Thursday. It was two months ago yesterday that he had gone to the Freeborns' house and interrupted a meeting.

He picked up the phone and spoke to John Harmer. Paulette's father was anxious now, no longer calm and scathing. He said his wife was asleep. Heavily sedated, Wexford guessed.

"The place is crawling with police," said Harmer.

Wexford replied dryly, "I know."

He thought it an unfortunate way of describing the initial search he had mounted in the environs of the Harmers' home. The man's breathing at the other end of the line was audible. His voice had been rough and shaky. If insulting the police helped him, well . . .

"I can't tell you I don't think this a serious cause for concern, Mr. Harmer. I'm very sorry. I think you should prepare yourself for bad news. Perhaps it would be best to say nothing to your wife as yet."

"I'm not likely to wake her up and tell her you think her only child's dead, am I?"

Wexford said a polite goodbye and rang off. Harmer's rudeness gratified him a little. It was more than excusable in the circumstances and at least it showed Harmer wasn't the unfeeling husband he had thought him. Tomorrow morning they would widen the search for Paulette. By then he might have some idea of where and how to widen it.

A few drops of rain struck the windows, needles on the glass. The thunder thudded and cracked over Myringham way. Martin and Marion Bayliss brought the two Mrs. Williamses in and Wexford went down to the interview room to confront them. Wendy in her Jickie's suit, hair freshly set – in Jickie's hairdressing department? – was in tears, dabbing at her eyes with a pink tissue. Joy had never looked so down at heel, broken sandals on her bare feet, a button missing from her creased cotton dress, a scarf tied round her head. She looked like a refugee, such as have passed in streams across Europe at frequent times in modern history. Her face was gray and drawn.

Burden came in and sat beside him. The room had got so dark they had to have the light on. Still it wasn't really raining. When no one attempted to comfort Wendy and no offers of cups of tea were made she stopped crying. Rather defiantly, she produced the box of pink tissues from her bag and set it on the table in front of her.

"Was Paulette Harmer the girl your husband was seeing?"

Wexford addressed the question to both women. It was awkward. It seemed to treat polygamy as a legal state. Joy gave a dry cackle, more than usually scornful. Wendy said she didn't know who Paulette Harmer was, she had never heard of her.

"Who was it, then?"

"He didn't have a young girlfriend," said Joy. "He didn't have any girl." She nodded at Wendy. "Unless you count her. And that's not the word I'd use for her."

Wendy sniffed and pulled a tissue out of the box.

"Well, Mrs. Williams?" Wexford said to her.

"I told you, I don't know."

"On the contrary, you told me you knew there was one. This very young girl living around here with her parents – you never heard of her, she doesn't exist?"

Wendy looked at Joy. Their eyes met. For the first time Wexford thought he sensed a rapport between them. Then Wendy turned sharply away and shook her head violently.

"Rodney Williams was attracted by young girls," Wexford said. "You're an example yourself, Mrs. Williams. How old were you when you and he met? Fifteen? Is that why you invented a young girlfriend for him? You knew it was in his nature?"

"I didn't invent it."

He was suddenly aware of a change taking place in Joy. She was shaking with emotion. Her hands held the table edge. Rain had begun to patter on the windows. Burden got up and closed the fanlight. Joy leaned forward.

"Has Sara been talking to you?" she said.

It was on the tip of his tongue to say he would ask the questions. But he didn't say it. He felt his way. "It's possible."

"The little bitch!"

How was it he sensed that the two women were at last united by some common bond? And that bond wasn't the dead man. The noise of the rain was intense now, a crashing cloudburst. He thought, they did know each other. The Klein girl was telling me the truth. They were close in a conspiracy and they're back in it again, the acting is over . . . He turned to Joy and it was as if his approaching, ultimately fixed gaze lit the fuse.

She spoke in a raucous, throaty voice.

"You may as well have it. It wasn't young girls he was attracted to, not *any* young girls. It was his own daughter."

18

It happened, it wasn't even uncommon. Lately it had been the modish subject for the pop sociology paperback. Yet that father-daughter incest might be a motivating factor in this case had not crossed Wexford's mind. Afterwards he was to ask himself *why* it hadn't crossed his mind, knowing his mind and the way it worked, but now in the interview room with the two women across the table from him he could only recall *The Cenci* and Beatrice – his own daughter playing Beatrice – running onto the stage crying:

"O world! O life! O day! O misery!"

That should have told him. Wendy had covered her face with her hands. Joy stared at him, her lips sucked in. A bead of saliva had appeared at the left corner of her mouth. She put her hand out for one of Wendy's tissues, tentatively, cautiously, watching Wendy, like an old dog approaching the food bowl but uncertain as to what the young dog will do. Wendy took her hands down. She didn't speak. She gave the tissue box a little push in Joy's direction. Burden sat, wearing his stony, contemptuous look.

Wexford was framing a question. Before he could utter it Joy spoke.

"She came and told me. Her own mother! His own wife! She said he'd come into her bedroom in the middle of the night. He said he was cold, he never seemed to get warm since we'd slept in twin beds. That's what he said to her. He said she could make him warm. Why didn't she scream out? Why didn't she run away? He got into bed with her and did it to her. I'm not going to repeat the word she used, they all use it for *that*. It was while I was asleep. I was asleep and he was doing that with his own daughter."

She laughed. The sound was drier than ever, with more of a rattle in it, but it was a laugh. She looked at Wendy and directed the laugh at her. And, Wexford thought, she may have been in cahoots with her, she may have told her all this before in womanly confidence, in sisters-under-the-skin conspiracy, but she enjoys telling it now – in our presence, a public triumphant put-down.

Like the therapist to whom he had compared himself, he would let her talk without interruptions, without breaking in to question. If she would talk. The pause endured. Wendy looked away and at the screen of water, curiously claustrophobic, the rain was making down the panes. She had pushed her fingers so hard into the skin of her face that they left pink pressure marks. Without prompting, Joy went on.

"She waited till he'd gone to work and then she told me. I was ironing her a blouse for school." Insult had been thus added to injury, she implied. The father's rape would have been less offensive to the mother if the news had been imparted to her while she was ironing a shirt for Kevin. "She burst right out with it. There wasn't a question of being tactful, mind, of – well, breaking it gently. He was only my husband. It was only my husband she was telling me about being unfaithful to me." The laugh came again, but a ghost of it this time. "I wouldn't listen to her. I said, don't tell me, I don't want to hear. I put my hands over my ears."

A rejecting gesture not unknown in the Harmer-Williams families, Wexford thought.

He nodded at Joy, feeling it was necessary to give some sign.

"I put my hands over my ears," she said again. "She started shouting at me. Didn't I care? Wasn't I upset? I answered her then. I said of course I was upset. No mother wants to hear her daughter's like that, does she? I said to her, You spread that about and you'll split us all up, your father'll go to prison and what are people going to think of me? What's Kevin going to say to them at college?"

Burden said quietly, "What did you mean by that, Mrs. Williams, your daughter was 'like that'?"

"It's obvious, isn't it? I'm not saying he wasn't weak." A glance for Wendy and a quick withdrawal of the eyes. "Well, we know he was. But he'd never have done that without . . ."

She stopped and looked at Wexford. He remembered when he had first talked to Sara and her mother had sent him up to her bedroom saying she wouldn't object – "Rather the reverse if I know her."

"Encouragement?" he said flatly.

She nodded impatiently. "Putting her arm around him, trying to get his attention. She wasn't *ten*. I said to her, you're not ten anymore. Sitting on his knee – what did you expect? Now the least you can do is keep quiet about it. I said, think of my feelings for a change."

"When did all this happen?"

"It was before Christmas. I know it was because I remember saying that she'd picked a fine time, hadn't she, just when we were all going to be together for Christmas."

Wendy, whose face had been impassive, winced slightly. Had she realized at last where and how Rodney Williams spent his Christmases? It was soon after that, probably in the first week of January, Wexford recalled, that Edwina Klein had seen the two women together.

"Did you tell anyone?" Burden asked.

"Of course I didn't. I wasn't going to broadcast it."

He turned on Wendy. "When did she tell you? Or should I say warn you?"

Wendy had looked shocked by none of this. Not even surprised. But she shook her head. "She never did."

"Come on, Wendy . . ." Wexford had solved the names problem at last. "Joy found out you existed, sought you out especially to tell you what Rodney was really like. To tell you, in fact, to have a care to your own daughter."

"Tell her?" said Joy. "Why should I care?"

"Wendy," Wexford said more gently, almost

insinuatingly, "you're not going to tell us you didn't know about Rodney and his daughter Sara. You're not going to make believe what we heard just now was all news to you. You couldn't have looked less surprised than if I told you it was raining. Joy came into Jickie's, didn't she, and told you who she was? I'll make a guess at the week before Christmas. How did she know who you were? She'd seen Veronica in the street and spotted the resemblance to Sara – a likeness no one could mistake . . ."

That they were surprised now, both of them, he couldn't doubt. He had been wrong there then. Never mind. There were other ways – following Rodney, seeing him and Wendy together, a host of ways.

"You met at Jickie's, went on to meet again after Christmas. No doubt there were many meetings . . ."

Wendy jumped up, eyes full of tears, grabbing a handful of tissues.

"I want to talk to you alone! Just you and me quite alone!"

"Surely," said Wexford.

He got up. Burden didn't wait for them to leave the room before starting on Joy with his questions. When did she first suspect Rodney had a second home? Did she ever ask him? Joy was laughing at this second suggestion when

Wexford closed the door. He took Wendy upstairs to his own office. The rain had abated, was now merely a trickling, slipping, spilling, down the washed gleaming glass. Twilight hadn't yet begun and the sky was a clear gray, light from cloud-coated sunshine. Wendy stumbled a little going into the room. He thought it might be unwise to touch her, even to the extent of steadying her. She held on to the door frame and shot him a look of grievance.

In the chair he held out for her she sat down gingerly, treating herself as if she had become fragile. She had turned into a convalescent, tentatively putting out feelers to the world. Her shoulders she was keeping permanently lifted.

"What did you want to say to me, Wendy?" He had dropped the "Mrs. Williams" altogether now.

She whispered it, sustaining the invalid image, a broken woman, wan-faced, such as might fittingly inhabit the Castle of Petrella and be called Lucretia.

"The same as what she said."

"I'm sorry, Wendy. You must make yourself plainer than that."

"It was the same for us. The same as what she said. Or – well, it would have been. I mean, he would have done but he went away and got himself killed."

Light penetrated. "You mean Rodney also made advances to Veronica? Only, if I interpret what you're saying correctly, it was merely advances?"

She nodded, tears splashing now, wads of tissues held to her eyes like swabs.

"Before Joy warned you or afterwards?"

A shrugging, then a shaking, of the whole body. Make-up scrubbed off with that cheapest and most readily available cleanser, tears, Wendy presented to Wexford a youthful, naked, desperate face.

"He had been a little more attentive to her, had he, than we in our society expect of a father to a teenage daughter? Did she tell you or did you see? Kissed her and said it was good to be alone with her and you out of the way?"

She jumped up. "Yes, yes, yes!" she shouted.

"So on April the fifteenth, although you didn't think there was much chance of Rodney coming back, you encouraged your daughter to go out so as not to be alone with him? You told her not to run the risk of being alone with him but to stay out until you came home?"

Guilt was heavy on her face now, driving away indignation. He felt she was on the brink of a confession.

"Or did you send her out so that *you* could be

alone with Rodney – you and Joy?"

The air was sharply clear, the rain passed, the sky two shades of blue, a dark clean azure and the smoky blue of massed cloud. Nine o'clock and growing dark. Water lay in glassy pools, reflecting the sky. There was an unaccustomed coolness, almost a nip, in the temperature. Before morning there would be more rain. Wexford could see it in the clarity and smell it in the atmosphere. He walked from the police station and kept on walking, just to get away from the enclosing four walls, the stuffiness, the millions of uttered words, the weariness of lies.

People used to tell him when they needed an alibi – now they cited television – that they had been for a walk. They didn't know where, just for a walk. He hadn't believed them. Everyone knew where they had been on a walk. Now he thought he might not be able to say where he had been tonight. His progress was aimless, though not slow, a fairly brisk marching in the fresh, cold air, a thinking walk to dwell on what had passed.

So inconclusively. So unsuccessfully. He had wrung those two women, turned the handle, and ground them through the rollers. Joy had laughed and Wendy had wept. He had kept on repeating over and over to himself: Edwina Klein saw them together. Why should she lie? Why should she invent? He had to let them go at last. Wendy was near collapse – or feigning it beautifully.

It was clear, the whole case, Burden said. A motive had at last emerged. Joy killed out of bitterness and jealousy, Wendy out of fear Rodney would serve Veronica the same way as he had served Sara. An unfortunate verb in the circumstances, but perhaps not inept . . . A conspiracy laid just after Christmas, brooded over through the early spring, hatched out in April. Murder in the room that would be decorated tomorrow. Stanch the blood with Kitman's dust sheet, realize too late what you have used.

It must have happened that way, there was no other. Perhaps they hadn't intended to kill, only confront him jointly, threaten and shock. But the French cook's knife had been handy, lying on the table maybe. That didn't explain drugging him with Phanodorm. The knife Milvey had found? Its blade matched the width and depth of the wounds. So would a thousand knives.

He was in Down Road, under the dripping lime trees. Perhaps, all along, he had known he was making his way there. The big old houses,

houses that could justly be called "piles," seemed sunken tonight in dark, still, sodden foliage. A dark green perfume arose from grass and leaf and rain-bathed flowers. Somewhere nearby a spoilt dog, left alone for the evening, vented its complaints in little bitter whimpering wails. Wexford opened the gate to the Freeborns' house. Lights were on, one upstairs and one down. The dustmen had been that morning, long before the rain started, and left the scattering of litter they didn't bother to remove from the places where the occupants failed to tip lavishly. A sodden sheet of paper, pasted by rain onto the gravel, bore the ARRIA logo and a lot of printing it was too dark to read.

Both twins came to the door. He approved their caution. Once more they were alone in the house, left to their own devices, the switched-on parents far away at some veteran hippies' haunt. Both had pale blue hair tonight, pink stuff on the eyelids; otherwise the nearly identical faces were bare. And identical on both faces was dismay at the sight of him. Eve spoke.

"Do you want to come in?"

"Yes, please." The house no longer smelt of marijuana. That was one thing he had achieved, a dubious success. The girls seemed not to know where to take him. They stood in the hall. "There was a meeting of ARRIA last night," he said. "Where was it? Here?"

"They're mostly held here," said Amy.

"And it was here last night?"

"Yes."

He pushed open a door and switched a light on. It was a huge living room, floor cushions making islands on parquet that hadn't been polished for two decades, a divan with thrown over it something that might have had its origin in Peru, the only chair a wicker hemisphere hanging from the ceiling. French windows, uncurtained, gave on to what seemed an impenetrable wood.

He sat in the hanging chair, refusing to be alarmed by its immediate swinging motion.

"Who was at the meeting?"

They exchanged glances, looked at him. "The usual crowd," said Amy, and conversationally, "It's always the same lot that turn up, isn't it?"

The names he ran through got a nod at every pause. "Caroline Peters? Nicola Anerley? Jane Gardner? Paulette Harmer?" Eve nodded. She nodded in the same way as she had at the other names. "Edwina Klein?"

There must have been a note of doubt in his voice.

"Yes, Edwina was here. Why not?"

"Why not indeed. And why not Sara Williams, come to that?"

"Sara didn't come," said Amy. "She had to stay home with her mother."

So John Harmer hadn't been so far out when he suggested his daughter's disappearance had something to do with this "women's movement nonsense."

"What time did the meeting end?"

"About ten," said Amy. "Just about ten." She had forgiven him if her sister never would. She had altogether put off that distant manner. "Someone told me today that Paulette didn't go home all night and . . ." She left the sentence hovering.

"You never told me," Eve said sharply.

"I forgot." Amy turned her eyes back on Wexford. "She was a bit late. She didn't say why. Edwina brought her aunt – not to join, just to see what went on, though she's eligible of course, never having married. It was good seeing someone old who'd had principles and stuck to them."

"I have fought the good fight," said Wexford. "I have run a straight race. I have kept the faith."

"That's right. That was exactly it. How did you know?"

He didn't answer her. The Authorized Version was unknown to them, lost to their generation as to the one before, a dusty tome of theology, in every way a closed book.

"Was Paulette alone when she left?"

"The meeting was upstairs." Eve was chilly and unbending, but she had spoken. "We didn't see people out. They went downstairs and let themselves out. Paulette left with Edwina and her aunt."

"They may have left together," said Amy, "but they didn't go off together. I looked out of the window and saw Edwina and her aunt getting into the aunt's car and Paulette wasn't with them."

"What's out there?" Wexford said abruptly. He pointed at the long windows beyond which was visible only a mass of foliage.

"The conservatory."

Amy opened the doors, swung them open, and put her hand to a switch. Unconventional the Freeborn family might be; they were not feckless. The old domed conservatory, its upper panes of stained glass, claret and green in an Art Nouveau design of tulips, was full of dark green leafy plants, some of which look subtropical, all demanding ample water and getting it. It must cost a fortune to heat in winter, Wexford thought, coming closer, entering the conservatory, and spotting an orchid or two, the velvety mauve trumpet of a *Brunfelsia*.

Eve, without being asked, flooded the garden beyond with light. Touching another switch brought on arc lamps, one on the conservatory roof, another in the branches of an enormous ilex. The garden, so called, hardly deserved floodlighting. It was a wilderness of unmown grass, wild roses, brambles, the occasional hundred-year-old tree. And it was huge, the kind of garden whose owners might justly say they were never overlooked. Shrubs that appeared dense black at this hour made an encircling irregular wall round its perimeter.

"We don't any of us go in it much," said Amy. "Except as a shortcut to the High Street. And when it's muddy or whatever . . ." Another sentence was left hanging. She went on vaguely, "Dad's keen on the conservatory. It's him that grows the plants."

The *Cannabis sativa*, thought Wexford, but hardly in here. You needed infra-red light for that and plenty of it. He opened the door into the garden, a glass door of slender green and white panels. The cold, damp air breathed water in suspension at him. He noticed a path among the grass, pieces of crazy paving let into what had once been turf, was now wet hay. The girls weren't coming with him. Eve wound her arms round her body, hugging herself against the cold. Amy breathed on the glass and with her fingertip began drawing a raven with a woman's face. Wexford went down the path. The arc lamps reached no further than thirty feet or so. He took his torch out of his pocket and switched it on.

The path led to the gate in the far fence, he thought. That was what Amy meant by a shortcut to the High Street. First it wound through a copse of dark shrubs, laurels and rhododendrons, all glistening and dripping with water. He was curiously reminded of walking in a cemetery. Cemeteries were like this, untended often, places of ornamental shrubs, funereal trees, like this without flowers, unlike this with gravestones.

He came upon the fence and the gate quite suddenly, almost bumping into the gate, which was in a break in the untrimmed hedge that followed the line of the close-boarding. From here the backs of other big houses could just be seen, two of them with yellow rectangles on black that were lights in their windows. The light didn't reach here and no moon had appeared. The path curved its way all round the garden. He followed its ellipse, returning on the right-hand side. Bamboo here, half dead most of it, a mass of canes. Then something prickly that caught at his raincoat. He pulled and heard the tearing sound. Turn the torch on it to see what had happened . . .

Turn the torch into the midst of this circle of briar roses, brambles with wicked thorns – onto an outflung arm, a buried face, a logo and acronym, red on white cotton – ARRIA and the raven-woman.

It was more like a cemetery here than he had supposed . . .

19

The scene-of-crimes officer. Dr. Crocker. Sir Hilary Tremlett fetched out of his bed and wearing a camel-hair coat over pajama top and gray slacks. Burden as neat and cool as at mid-morning. And the rain coming down in summer tempests. They had to rig a sort of tent up over the body.

She had been strangled. With a piece of string or cord perhaps. Wexford himself could see that without reference to Dr. Crocker or Sir Hilary. The photographer's flash going off made him blink. He didn't want to look at her any more. It sickened him, though not with physical nausea, he was far beyond that. No pharmacology degree now, no marriage to Richard Cobb, no full flowering of that strange beauty that had been both sultry and remote.

The girls worried him. Eve and Amy, alone

in that house with a young girl, a contemporary, dead in the garden. Marion Bayliss had tried to reach their parents but they were at none of the phone numbers the twins could produce. Neighbors shunned the Freeborns. With the families immediately next door they weren't even on speaking terms. Eve thought of Caroline Peters and it was she who came to the house in Down Road and stayed for the rest of the night. Wexford crawled into bed at around three. There was a note for him from Dora which he read but did not mark or inwardly digest: "A man called Ovington keeps phoning for you." She was deeply asleep and in sleep she looked so young. He lay down beside her and the last thing he remembered before sleeping himself was laying his hand on her still-slender waist.

"She'd been dead about twenty-four hours," said Crocker, "which is about what you thought, isn't it?"

When you don't get enough sleep, Wexford thought, it's not so much tired that you feel as weak. Though perhaps they were the same thing. "Strangled with what?" he asked. "Wire? Cord? String? Electric cable?"

"Because it's easily obtainable and pretty well impossible to break I'd guess the kind of nylon cord you use for hanging pictures. And where were your suspects –" Crocker looked at his watch "– thirty-six hours ago?"

"At home with their daughters, they say."

Wexford began going through the statement Burden had taken from Leslie Kitman, the painter. A description of the missing dust sheet was gone into in some detail. Useless now, of course. It was four months since that dust sheet, concealed in a plastic bag, had been removed by the council's refuse collectors. And the knife as likely as not with it. Somehow he couldn't believe in Milvey's knife, he couldn't take two Milvey coincidences . . .

The walls had been stained and pitted, Kitman said. He couldn't remember if the stains had looked any different on the morning of 16 April from the afternoon of 15 April. Some of the holes, he thought, might have been filled in by someone else. He had made good some of the cracks and holes with filler, which, when it dried, left white patches. On 16 April and the morning of the 17th he had lined the walls with wood-chip paper and on the Monday following begun painting over the paper.

Was he going to have those women in again? One of them had killed the girl the night before last. To keep her from confirming their guilt in the matter of the Phanodorm. Only one of them or both? Joy could easily have known where she would be and that she left by the shortcut to the High Street, where she would catch the Pomfret bus.

Burden was late. But then he too had been up and on the go since early yesterday morning, finally getting to bed even later than Wexford. To be up after midnight, thought Wexford, is to be up betimes. He had always liked that, only no one knew what "betimes" meant any more, which rather spoiled the wit of it. Thinking of going to bed reminded him of Dora's note, and he was about to pick up the phone and get hold of Ovington when Burden walked in.

He didn't look tired, just about ten years older and a stone thinner. He was wearing his stone-colored suit with a shirt the same shade and a rust tie with narrow chocolate lines on it. Might be going to a wedding, thought Wexford, all he needed was a clove carnation.

"Jenny's started," he said. "I took her to the infirmary this morning at eight. There's not going to be anything doing much yet awhile but they wanted her in promptly."

"You'd better start your leave as from now."

"Thanks. I thought you'd say that. I must say these babies do pick their moments. Couldn't she have waited a week? She's going to be

Mary, by the way."

"After your grandmothers, no doubt."

But the coincidence he had related to Wexford had slipped Burden's memory. "Do you know that never crossed my mind? Perhaps Mary Brown Burden then?"

"Forget it," said Wexford. "It sounds like an American revivalist preacher. Keep in touch, won't you, Mike?"

Later in the day, with luck, the pathologist's report on Paulette Harmer would come and also perhaps something from Forensics on the murder weapon. He had Martin go to a magistrate and swear out a warrant to search the Williams home in Liskeard Avenue, and he wasn't anticipating any difficulties in getting it. In the meantime he had himself driven to the other Williams home. He didn't feel up to walking, whatever Crocker might advise.

Sara was mowing the front grass with one of those small electric mowers that cuts by means of a line wound on a spool and are principally intended for trimming edges. As he got out of the car the motor whined and stopped cutting, and the girl, crimson with bad temper, upended the flimsy machine and began tugging furiously at the line. He heard a hissed repetition of the word Joy disliked so much that she had used of her father's assault.

"Fuck, fuck, fuck, fuck!"

"If you do that with the current switched on," Wexford said, "one day you're going to cut your hand off."

She cooled as rapidly as she had become incensed.

"I know. I've promised myself I'll always switch it off before I fiddle with it. But these goddamned things never work for long." She pulled the prongs out of the socket to oblige him and smiled. An ARRIA tee-shirt today, identical to the one on dead Paulette. "This is the fourth of these spools we've had this summer. Do you want to see my mother?"

As yet she couldn't know about Paulette. He remembered her thinly veiled boasting to her cousin on the phone and he didn't think she would much care. Nor would she much care when her mother was arrested for the murder. But perhaps it was natural for victims of incest not to care much about anything. He felt a wrench of pity for her.

"I want to talk to you first."

The garage, now there was no car to occupy it, had become a tool shed and repository for rather battered garden furniture. Sara indicated a deck chair to Wexford. For her part she sat down on an unturned oil drum and set about struggling with the stubborn spool. This looked as if it might go the way of its fellows, three of which lay on a shelf next to a dozen half-used Sevenstar paint cans. He supposed she was busying herself so as not to have to look at him while he talked to her about her father.

At his first mention of incest, a tactful broaching of what her mother had told him, she didn't flush but turned gradually white. Her skin, always pale, grew milk-like. And he noticed a phenomenon, perhaps peculiar to her. The fine gold down on her forearms erected itself.

He asked her gently when it had first happened. She kept her head bent, with her right hand attempting to rotate the spool while with her left forefinger and thumb she tugged at the slippery red line.

"November," she said, confirming his own ideas. "November the fifth." She looked up and down again quickly. "There were only two times. I saw to that."

"You threatened him?"

She hesitated. "Only with the police."

"Why didn't you tell your brother? Or did you? I have a feeling you and your brother are close."

"Yes, we are. In spite of everything." She didn't say in spite of what but he thought he knew. "I *couldn't* tell him." Like a different girl speaking, her face turned away, "I was ashamed."

And she hates her mother, so it was a pleasure to tell *her*? She gave a final tug and the line came through, far too much of it, yards of loosely coiled scarlet flex.

Kevin was indoors, having unexpectedly arrived that morning by means of some comfortless and inefficient transport. He was lying spent, exhausted, dirty, and unkempt, on the yellow sofa, his booted feet up on one of its arms. Joy had answered Wexford's knock with refreshments for Kevin in her hands, a trayful of sandwiches, coffee, something in a carton that was ice cream or yogurt. Wexford shut the door on him, hustled Joy into the kitchen. She was dressed exactly as she had been the day before, even to the headscarf – had she tied it on to run to the shops for Kevin-provender? – and gave the impression of having never taken her clothes off, of sleeping in them. He told her, quite baldly, about Paulette, but she knew. John Harmer had phoned her while Sara was in the garden. Or that was the explanation she gave Wexford for knowing. He said he would want her later at the police station, she and Wendy. He would send a car for her.

"What's my son going to do about his evening meal?"

"Give me a tin opener," said Wexford, "and I'll teach him how to use it."

She didn't observe the irony. She said she supposed he could have something out of a tin for once. At least she didn't suggest his sister might cook for him, which was an improvement (if that was the way you looked at things) on twenty years ago.

The next stop was Liskeard Avenue, Pomfret. Martin had got his warrant and was there with Archbold and two uniformed men, PC Palmer and PC Allison, Kingsmarkham's only black policeman. A tearful Wendy was trying to persuade them it wouldn't be necessary to strip the paper off her livingroom walls.

At the glass table sat Veronica. Evidently she had been at work on the hem of a white garment that lay in front of her but had laid down her needle when the policemen arrived. Wexford thought of the girl in the nursery rhyme who sat on a cushion and sewed a fine seam, feeding on strawberries, sugar, and cream. It must have been her dress which suggested it to him, with its pattern of small wild strawberries and green leaves on a creamy ground. Tights again, dark blue this time, white pumps. Another thing that made those girls look alike was the way neither of their faces showed their feelings. They were the faintly melancholy, faintly smug, nearly always impassive faces of madonnas in Florentine paintings.

Wexford's daughter Sylvia had a cat which uttered soundless mews, going through the mouth-stretching motion of mewing only. Veronica's "hello" reminded him of that cat, a greeting for a lip-reader, not even as audible as a whisper. Wendy renewed her appeals as he came in, now making them to him only.

"I'm sorry, Wendy. I understand your feelings. We'll have the room redecorated for you." Or for someone, he thought but didn't say aloud. "And there'll be as little mess as possible."

And it really was Sevensmith Harding's Sevenstarker they intended to use for the job, four large cans of it, each labeled in red italic script that this was the slick, sheer, clean way to strip your walls. Wexford found himself hoping this wasn't too gross an exaggeration.

"But what for?" Wendy kept saying, at the same time, curiously enough, picking up ornaments and pushing them into a wall cupboard, loading a tray.

"That I'm not at liberty to say," said Wexford, falling back on one of the stock answers of officialese. "But there's plenty of time. Please clear the room yourself if you want to."

In silence Veronica picked up her sewing. She threaded her needle, using a small device manufactured for that purpose, and slipped a pink thimble onto her forefinger.

"She's doing the hem of her tennis dress. She's playing in the women's singles final at the club this afternoon." Wendy spoke in tragic tones, only slightly modified by a faint proud stress on the word "club."

Kingsmarkham Tennis Club, presumably, or even Mid-Sussex. "We shan't stop her." Wexford said.

"You'll upset her." She drew him into the kitchen, through the already open doorway. "You're not going to say anything to her about you-know-what? I mean you're not going to go into it?"

"I'm not a social worker," he said.

"Nothing actually happened anyway. I saw to it nothing happened."

Impossible, though, not to see Rodney Williams, hitherto no more than liar and con-man, as some sort of monster. To make a sexual assault on one daughter was heinous enough, but almost immediately to have designs on her younger half-sister?

"Of course, you wouldn't have suspected anything *might* happen if Joy hadn't warned you."

"How many times do I have to tell you I never saw the woman till you – introduced us?"

"Something you haven't told me is how you knew Rodney made sexual advances to Veronica. He didn't tell you but you knew. Veronica was the young girl living at home with her family you led us a wild goose chase about, wasn't she?" He closed the door between the rooms and leaned against it.

Wendy nodded, not looking at him.

"How did you know, Wendy? Did you see something? Did you notice something in his behavior when he thought you weren't looking? Was that after or before Joy warned you?"

She mumbled, "I didn't see anything. Veronica told me."

"Veronica? That innocent child in there who's more like twelve than sixteen? That child you've very obviously sheltered from every exposure to life? She interpreted her father's affectionate kisses, his arm around her, his compliments, as sexual advances?"

A nod. Then a series of vehement nods.

"And yet you say 'nothing actually happened.' By that I take it you mean there was no more than a kiss and a touch and a compliment. But she – *she* – saw this as an incestuous approach?"

Wendy's response was characteristic. She burst into tears. Wexford pushed up a stool for her to sit on and found a box of tissues, never a difficult task in that house. He returned to the living room, where the carpet was now covered with sheets and from which Veronica had disappeared. Allison was daubing the walls with Sevenstarker, Palmer already at work with a metal stripping tool. The hunch he had about what was under that paper was probably crazy, but besides that it was just possible an analysis of old plaster might show traces of Rodney's blood. And might not. Anyway, it was work for Leslie Kitman. He could come in next week and put it all back again at the expense of the Mid-Sussex Constabulary.

The rain had started again. That would put paid to Veronica's match in the afternoon, as neither the Kingsmarkham Tennis Club nor the Mid-Sussex County at Myringham had covered courts. Wexford, back in his office through it was Saturday, noted the time. Twelve-thirty. Getting on for three hours since Mike had been in and announced the imminence of his new daughter. Well, it was too soon yet to expect much, early days.

Something kept nagging at the back of his mind, something Wendy had said. About the tennis match, he thought it was. But she hadn't said anything except that Veronica would be playing that afternoon. Why did he have this curious feeling then that in what she said lay the whole answer to this case? He often had feelings like that about some small thing when a case was about to break, and the small thing always turned out to be vital and his hunch seldom wrong. The difficulty was that he didn't know what he had a hunch about.

All the available men he had were either at Wendy's taking her room apart or else, the far greater number of them, conducting a house-to-house in Down Road and interrogating every girl who had been at the ARRIA meeting. A mood of loneliness and isolation enclosed him. Dora had gone to London and to stay the night with Sheila in Hampstead. His elder grandson Robin would be nine today, his birthday party due to begin three hours from now, Crocker played golf all day on Saturdays. Wexford would have liked to sleep, but he found it hard to sleep in the daytime. What the hell was it Wendy had said? What *was* it? Tremlett was probably still at work on that poor girl's body . . . She had got Phanodorm for Joy and threatened to tell that she had. Well, not threatened, warned rather that she would have to, she would be scared not to. Joy had given Rodney the Phanodorm, substituting it for his blood-pressure pills, and it took just the time of a drive to Pomfret to act. Follow him by bus to Wendy's. He's asleep when you get there and you look at him and remember what he's done to you by way of what he's done to your daughter. Married another woman too, like a bloody sheikh. And the other wife goes along with you, though you hate her. It's her daughter at risk now since you told her where his tastes lie. Why let him ever wake up again? If there's a mess she says the room's going to be redecorated tomorrow. And if you hide the body for long enough . . .

In the morning phone the office, say he's ill, disguising your voice a bit. She'll type his letter of resignation for you, she's got access to a typewriter in a friend's house that no one's going to trace. You're both in it equally, you and she, the two wives of Rodney Williams, for better or worse, till death parts you. She stabbed him too, though you gave him the sleeping pill. You and she together carried the body down that crackpot spiral staircase, through the doorway into the integral garage. Laid him in the car with his traveling bag. She drove because you never learned, but you did most of the grave-digging. Soiling your hands never bothered you the way it did her. Two wives, in it together equally, and whom murder has joined let no man put asunder.

Wexford had got himself under Joy's skin and he very nearly finished this internal monologue with one of her awful laughs. The chances were Burden wouldn't phone before evening. And then surely he'd phone him at home. He drove to the Old Cellar and had himself a slice of quiche, broccoli and mushroom, a pleasant novelty, one small glass of Frascati to go with it – it was Saturday, after all, though with nothing to celebrate – and then back again to the estate where the streets were named for Cornish towns, Bodmin, Truro, Redruth, Liskeard. A cold gray rain fell steadily. They were back to the weather they had had between Rodney Williams's disappearance and the discovery of his body.

In Wendy's living room considerable progress had been made. Three walls were more or less stripped. It wasn't what Wexford would have called slick, sheer, and clean, but it wasn't bad. Martin had got hold of someone from Forensics, a shaggy girl in navy all-in-ones, who nevertheless had the air of an expert and was painstakingly scraping samples of brownish plaster off the walls.

Wendy was downstairs in her sewing-ironing-laundry room or whatever, cutting patterns out of magazines. For therapy, no doubt. Veronica was with her, Miss Muffet on a velvet pouffe. No match for her today, as he had predicted. He suddenly remembered his threat to send a car for Joy "later" and the crisis over Kevin's dinner this had precipitated. Well, it would have to be much later . . . Or tomorrow. Or every day on and forever. No, he mustn't think that way.

Wendy had changed her dress for a linen suit. Perhaps she had been going to watch her daughter play, for Veronica, as though not resigned to cancellation until the last moment, was in her tennis whites, pleated miniskirt – who could imagine her in shorts? – and a top almost too well finished to be called a tee-shirt.

"I suppose they'll postpone it till Monday night," said Wendy in a high, rather mad voice, "and that means half the spectators won't come."

Down the spiral staircase came the expert with her case of samples, the scraper still in her hand.

"I think I'm going to be sick," whispered Veronica.

Her mother was all care, all solitude, jumping up, hastening her to the ground-floor bathroom.

Wexford went back upstairs. Archbold had

gone. The expert had gone. Martin was drinking tea from a flask and the other two Coke from cans while they waited for the Sevenstarker on the fourth wall to do its stuff. Wexford felt something very near a qualm. The room, which had been a shell-pink sanctuary, was a nasty mess. A shambles, Martin called it, but a shambles, meaning a slaughter house, was just what Wexford thought it had been used for, the reason for this destruction. Suppose he was wrong? Suppose the killing of Rodney Williams had taken place elsewhere?

Too late now.

The police's loss would be Kitman's gain. It is the business of the thinking man, he paraphrased, to give employment to the artisan.

"Let me have one of those, will you?" he said to Martin, pointing to the scrapers. The white patches of plaster among the brown were the areas Wendy herself had filled before Kitman began papering.

It wouldn't budge the white plaster.

"Want me to have a go, sir?" Allison produced what Wexford through might be a cold chisel.

"We'll all have a go."

It made Allison's day. He had never before distinguished himself in any way since joining the force two years before. Sometimes he thought – and his wife – that they had taken him on only because he was black and not because he was suitable or any good. They were inverted race snobs. For weeks everyone had bent over backwards to treat him with more kindness, courtesy, and consideration than they would show, for instance, to a millionaire grandfather on his deathbed. That had worn off after a while. He was a bit lonely too in Kingsmarkham, where only his wife, his kids, and two other families were West Indian like him. But today paid for all that. It was what made him in his own eyes an officer of the law.

"Sir, I think I've found . . ." he began.

Wexford was there beside him like a shot. Under his eyes Allison dug in carefully, thanking his stars he'd remembered to put his gloves on. The object was stuck in the fissure wrapped up in newspaper, plastered over. He chipped and dug and then put his hand to it, looking at Wexford, and Wexford nodded.

The knife didn't clatter out. It was unveiled as reverently as if it were a piece of cut glass. They all looked at it lying there on its wrappings, clean as a whistle and polished bright as a long prism in a chandelier.

20

Wexford had them with him all day Sunday, and Monday morning's papers said an arrest was imminent. But Wexford wanted the two women, not just one, Joy as well as Wendy. Charging Wendy with Rodney Williams's murder was an obvious act. The knife buried in her living room wall had a blade which exactly matched the knife wounds on the body, and it was wrapped in part of the *Daily Mail* of 15 April. Still, he wanted Joy as well and Joy had no apparent connection with the crime. The only evidence he had was a witness who claimed to have seen the two women together and a voice on the phone that was probably hers.

Joy also had an alibi. Wendy didn't. All day long nails were going into Wendy's coffin, or at least the shades of the prison house were closing about her. Until Ovington came. That is, until Ovington's second visit.

Alone in the house, eating a junk-food supper, Wexford got a call from Burden late on Saturday evening. Jenny's labor hadn't exactly been a false alarm but it had gradually subsided during the day. They were keeping her in, though, and considering some method of induction . . .

"You wanted her to wait a week," said Wexford nastily. "You'd better come back to work."

He phoned Ovington first thing in the morning. Never mind about Sunday and all that. By the time Ovington arrived at the police station he and Sergeant Martin and Polly Davies had Joy and Wendy in an interview room, the demented refugee and the broken doll. The curious thing was they had come closer to each other. In appearance, that is. There had been a sort of blending, and he thought of Kipling's hedgehog and tortoise, combining to make an armadillo. Joy and Wendy hadn't gone that far, but anxiety and harassment had done their work on the younger woman and the older had smartened herself up, perhaps because her son was back. At any rate the head-scarf was gone and she had proper shoes on. But Wendy's make-up was stale, she had hairs all over the shoulders of her black cotton dress, and the ladder that sprang in her tights didn't fidget her.

He left them to go and talk to Ovington. Smiling as usual, absurdly ingratiating, he could hardly have persuaded even the most gullible to believe him, certainly not a hard-headed policeman.

"She was with you on April fifteenth?" Wexford said. "She came to your place after work for a drink? Why hasn't she so much as mentioned this to me?"

"She doesn't want anyone to know she was seeing me while her husband was still alive."

That was in character. Wifely virtue was one of the aspects of the image Wendy liked to present. That didn't mean Ovington's story was true. Ovington was trying it on, a kind, stupid man with a misplaced idea of duty. Absently Wexford thanked him for coming. Then, as he was going back to the Williams wives, it occurred to him Ovington might have been in it with Wendy instead of Wendy with Joy. In that case who had made the phone call?

Wendy was crying. She said she was cold. It was true that the weather had turned very cold for the time of year, but she should have been prepared for that, sacrificed vanity, and brought a coat. He thought of all the places in the world and all the policemen in them where

Wendy would have been allowed to shiver, where the temperature would have been lowered if possible, a little hypothermia encouraged. You couldn't call it torture, cooling someone into admissions . . .

"Get her something to put on," he said to Polly.

He took them through the incest again and he got more stories full of holes. Joy hadn't believed Rodney would do that, yet she insisted Sara had led him on, insisted too that he would have gone to prison if she had breathed a word. Wendy now said Veronica had told her Rodney had started coming into her bedroom to kiss her goodnight and it wasn't "nice." That, said Joy, forgetting her former statement, was just how it had begun with Sara. Polly came back into the room with a gray knitted garment, something from Marks and Spencer's range for old ladies – God knows where she found it – which Wendy put on with a show of reluctance.

Sandwiches were brought in to them at lunchtime, one lot corned beef, the other egg and cress. Not exactly the Sunday joint, two veg, and Yorkshire pudding. By that time Wexford had taken them through 15 April and was getting on to last Thursday night. Wendy had forgotten her coat but not her box of tissues, shades of peach this time. She sat sniveling into handfuls of them.

Just before three Joy broke at last. She started to howl like a dog. She rocked back and forth in her chair, howling and drumming her fists on the table. Wexford stopped the proceedings and sent for a cup of tea. He took Wendy into the interview room next door and asked her about Ovington. Rather to his surprise she agreed without much reluctance that she had been in Ovington's flat on 15 April from about 7:45 until about 9:15. Why hadn't she said so before? She gave the reason Ovington had given for her. They had hatched this up together, Wexford thought.

"I thought I might as well tell you," she said with aplomb that almost staggered him. "I didn't before because you've all got minds capable of anything. But there's been so much real dirt dug up I don't think my innocent little friendship amounts to much."

What did any of it weigh against that knife in the wall? Late in the afternoon Burden walked in, looking a hundred years old.

"For God's sake," said Wexford. "I wasn't serious."

The truth was Burden didn't know how otherwise to pass the time. He started on Joy, trying to break her alibi. But the tea had done wonders for her. She stuck to her story about watching television at the Harmers' and after half an hour of that had the brainwave that might have struck her days ago. She didn't have to talk at all if she didn't want to. Nobody had charged her with anything.

Unfortunately, by this time Wendy was back in the room with her and heard what she said.

Through her tears she smiled quite amicably at Joy. "Good idea. I'm not talking either then. Pity I didn't think of it before."

Joy uttered one last sentence. "It was me thought of it, not you."

United in silence, they stared at Wexford. Why not charge them both? With murdering Rodney Williams and, if he couldn't make that stick, with murdering Paulette Harmer? Special court in the morning, a remand in custody . . . Archbold came in and said there were three people to see him. He left the silent women with Burden and Martin and went down in the lift.

James Ovington was sitting there with his taciturn father and an elderly woman he introduced as his mother. Somehow Wexford had never thought of Ovington *père* as having a wife, but, of course, he would have; James Ovington must have come from somewhere. He only looked like a waxwork. More so than ever this afternoon, his complexion fresher, his cheeks pinker, his smile flashing.

"My parents want to tell you something."

That was one way of putting it. They didn't look as if they had any desire beyond that of going home again. Wexford asked them to go up to the first floor with him to his office, but Mrs. Ovington said she'd rather not, thank you, as if any suggestion of going upstairs in the company of men was indecent. They compromised wtih an interview room. Mrs. Ovington looked disparagingly about her, evidently thinking it wasn't very cozy. James Ovington said, "What were you going to tell the chief inspector, Dad?"

Nothing, apparently.

"Now you know you were willing to come here and tell him."

"Not willing," said Ovington senior. "If I must I must. That's what I said."

"Is this something about Mrs. Wendy Williams, Mr. Ovington?" prompted Wexford.

Very slowly and grudgingly Ovington said, "I saw her."

"We both did," said Mrs. Ovington, suddenly brave. "We both saw her."

Wexford decided patience was the only thing. "You saw her, yes. When was this?"

James opened his mouth to speak, wisely shut it again. His father pondered, at last said,

"She's got a car. She'd parked it outside the shop on the yellow line. That don't matter after half six. We never saw her go in."

Silence fell and endured. Wexford had to prompt.

"Go in where?"

"My son's place, of course, What else are we talking about? He's got the bottom flat and we've got the top, haven't we?"

"Up four flights," said his wife. "Wear the old ones out first, that's what it is."

"We saw her come out," said Ovington. "Out of our front window. Round a quarter past nine. Tripped over and nearly fell in them heels. That's how Mother come to see her. I said, Here, Mother, look at this, them heels'll have her over."

"It was April the fifteenth!" said James, unable to contain himself any longer.

"I don't know about that." His father shook his head. "But it was the first Thursday after Easter."

That night he went to bed early and slept for nine hours. He didn't let himself think about the two women, Joy with no evidence against her, Wendy exonerated by the Ovingtons. They had been sent home with the warning that he would very likely want them back again on

Monday morning. Old Ovington hadn't been lying, but still his story didn't militate against the possibility that while Joy had done the deed in Wendy's house, Wendy had later met her in time to help her dispose of the body, the clothes, and the car.

In the morning he awoke clear-headed and calm. Immediately he remembered what it was Wendy had said to him. It had been when she told him Veronica was to play in a tennis singles final. The significance was in what it reminded him of, and now he remembered that too and as he did so everything began to fall gently and smoothly into place, so that he felt like one recalling and then using the combination of a safe until the door slowly swings open.

"But what a fool I've been," he said aloud.

"Have you, darling?"

"If I'd got on it sooner maybe that poor girl wouldn't have died."

"Come on," said Dora. "You're not God."

The phone was ringing as he left the house. It was Burden, but Wexford wasn't there to answer it and Dora spoke to him.

A report on the postmortem, rushed through by Sir Hilary Tremlett, was awaiting Wexford. He went through it with Crocker beside him. Strangling had been with a fine powerful cord, and whatever this was had left a red staining in the deep indentation it had made around the victim's neck.

"The nylon line from the spool of an electric edge trimmer," said Wexford.

Crocker looked at him. "That's a bit esoteric."

"I don't think so. Joy Williams has three such spools in her garage and one of them, unless I'm much mistaken, will be empty."

"Are you going to go there and check that?"

"Not just at the moment. Maybe later. Do you think it wrong to encourage a child to inform against its immediate family?"

"Like what happens in totalitarian societies, d'you mean? Or what I suppose happens. Extremists always believe the means are justified by the end. It depends what you mean by immediate family too, I mean, against a parent is a bit grim. That sticks in one's throat."

"Drugging a man and stabbing him and burying the knife in a wall sticks in one's throat too." Wexford picked up the phone and put it down again. "I've got two women to arrest," he said, "and the way things are I'll never make the charges stand up. When do the schools go back?"

Crocker looked a little startled at this apparent non sequitur. "The state schools – that is, the older kids – sometime this week."

"I'd better do it today if I'm to catch her

without her mother." He lifted the phone again, this time asked for an outside line. It rang for so long he began to think she must be out. Then at last Veronica Williams's soft, rather high voice answered, giving the number in all its ten digits. Wexford spoke her name, "Veronica?" then said, "This is Chief Inspector Wexford at Kingsmarkham CID."

"Oh, hello, yes." Was she afraid, or did she always answer the phone in this cautious breathless way?

"Just one or two things to check with you, Veronica. First, what time is your match to-night and where is it?"

"Kingsmarkham Tennis Club," she said. "It's at six." She gathered some courage. "Why?"

Wexford was too old a hand to answer that. "After that's over I'd like to talk to you. Not you and your mother, just you alone. All right? I think you have quite a lot of things you'd like to tell me, haven't you?"

The silence was so heavy he thought he'd gone too far. But no. And it was better than he had hoped. "I have got things to tell you. There are things I've *got* to tell you." He thought he heard a sob, but she might only have been clearing her throat.

"All right then. When you've finished your match come straight here. D'you know where it is?" He gave her directions. "About ten minutes' walk from the club. I'll have a car to send you home in."

She said, "I'll have to tell my mother."

"By all means tell your mother. Tell anyone you like." Did he sound too eager? "But make sure your mother knows I want to see you alone."

The enormity of what he was doing hit him as he put the phone down. Could anything justify it? She was a sixteen-year-old girl with vital information for him. The last teenage girl with vital information for him had been strangled before she could impart it. Was he sending her to the same death as Paulette Harmer? If Burden had been there he would have told him everything, but with the doctor he had reservations.

"You're not going round then, then?" Crocker said, a little mystified as much by Wexford's expression as by the cryptic phone conversation.

"That's the last thing I must do."

Later, when the doctor had gone, Wexford thought, I hope I have the nerve to stick it out. Pity it's so many hours off. But the advantage of an evening match was that afterwards it would soon be dark . . . Advantage! She would be phoning her mother now at Jickie's to tell her, he thought, and somehow – hopefully – persuading Wendy not to come with her. He would have that girl watched every step of the way.

The phone rang.

He picked it up and the telephonist said she had a Miss Veronica Williams for him. What a little madam she was, giving her name as "Miss"!

"I could come and see you now," the childish voice said. "That might be easier. Then I wouldn't have to upset Mummy. I mean I wouldn't have to tell her I don't want her with me."

He braced himself. He hardened his heart. "I'm too busy to see you before this evening, Veronica. And I'd like you to tell your mother, please. Tell her now."

If she called back, he thought, he'd relent and let her come. He wouldn't be able to hold out. Would she recognize Martin? Archbold? Palmer? Certainly she'd know Allison. But would it matter if she did recognize them? He'd be there himself anyway. There was no way he was going to let her take that ten-minute walk in the half-dark from the club down a lane off the Pomfret Road to the police station, especially in the case of her following his directions and taking the footpath across one and a half fields.

The phone rang again. That's it, he thought. I can't keep it up. I'll go round there and she'll tell me and that'll be evidence enough . . . He picked up the receiver.

"Inspector Burden for you, Mr. Wexford."

Burden's voice sounded strange, not really like his voice at all.

"It's all over. Mother and baby are doing fine. Jenny had a Caesarean at nine this morning."

"Congratulations. That's great, Mike. Give my love to Jenny, won't you? You'd better tell me what Mary weighed so that I can tell Dora."

"Eight pounds nine ounces, but it's not going to be Mary. We're changing just one letter in the name."

Wexford didn't feel up to guessing. Jenny's persuaded him into something fancy against his better judgment, he thought.

"Mark, actually," said Burden. "I'll see you later. Cheers for now."

21

A woman had once been found murdered on that very footpath. They would all have that in their minds, even Palmer and Archbold, who hadn't been there at the time, who had probably still been at school. As Veronica Williams still was. Had she ever heard of the murder? Did people still talk about it?

That woman had lived in Forest Road, the last street in the area to bear the postal address Kingsmarkham. The Pomfret boundary begins there, though it is open country all the way to Pomfret in one direction and nearly all the way to Kingsmarkham Police Station in the other. The tennis club, however, is not in Forest Road but in Cheriton Lane, which runs more or less parallel to it on the Kingsmarkham side. Smallish meadows enclosed by hedges cover the few acres between the club and the town, and the footpath runs alongside one of these hedges, at one point skirting a little copse. It emerges into the High Street fifty yards north of the police station and on the opposite side.

Wexford had Martin and Palmer in a car in Cheriton Lane, would station himself and Archbold in the copse, Loring among the spectators at the match, Bennett to start walking from the High Street end, Allison to follow her at a discreet distance.

"One black man'll look very like another to her, sir," Allison had said. "That mightn't be so in a city but it is out here."

"Don't tell me Inspector Burden and I look alike to you."

"No, sir, but that's a question of age, isn't it?"

Which puts me firmly in my place, thought Wexford. Burden was in his office, sitting beside him, anxious to take part in the protection-of-Veronica exercise. Can't keep away from the place for more than five minutes, Wexford had grumbled at him. At least Burden had supplied a diversion in the lull of the long afternoon.

"I don't understand how they could make a mistake over the sex like that. God knows I don't know much about it, but if a man has an XY chromosome and a woman XX surely they must always have it from embryo to old age?"

"It's not that. It's like this. In an amniocentesis they extract cells from the amniotic fluid the fetus is in. But occasionally they make a mistake and once in about ten thousand times they take cells from the mother, not the child. And even then they aren't always going to know their error. Because if the child does happen to be a girl . . . In this case, though, I gather someone's head is going to roll."

"It caused a lot of unnecessary misery."

"Misery, yes," said Burden, "but maybe not unnecessary. Jenny says it's taught her a lot about herself. It's taught her she's not what you might call a natural feminist and now she has to approach feminism not from an emotional standpoint but from what is – well, right and just. We didn't know, either of us, what a lot of deep-rooted, old-fashioned prejudices we had. Because I felt it too, you know, I also wanted a son though I never said. It's taught us how much we've concealed from the other when we thought we were frank and open. All this has been – well, not far from – what does Jenny call it? – Guided Confrontation Therapy."

With difficulty Wexford kept a straight face. "So long as now you've got a son you don't wish it was a girl." He said "you" but he meant Jenny, whom he thought the kind of woman for whom the unattainable grass might always be greener.

"Of course not!" Burden exclaimed, looking very sour. "After all, as Jenny says, what does it really matter so long as it's healthy and has all its fingers and toes?"

This was a cliché Wexford didn't feel he could compete with. Now Burden was here how would he feel about taking part in the Veronica watch? Not much, said Burden, he had to be back at the hospital. Then Wexford thought it might start raining. If it rained the match would be canceled, and in all probability Veronica would simply take the bus to the police station from Pomfret.

But the sky lightened round about 5:30. He wondered what those two women were thinking. How had they reacted to being left all day to their own devices? Unless the match was over in two straight sets Veronica could hardly expect to leave the club before seven. Should he fill in the time by seeing what he could get out of Kevin Williams? But he didn't really want to get anything out of him. He knew it all already. Why not simply go and watch the match?

It hadn't occurred to him to ask himself – or anyone else for that matter – if the tournaments of the Kingsmarkham Tennis Club were or were not open to the public. And it wasn't until he walked through the doors of the clubhouse that the question came into his mind. But a hearty elderly man with the air of a retired Air Force officer who said he was the secretary welcomed him with open arms. They loved spectators. If only they could get more spectators. It provided such encouragement for the players.

He had already spotted Martin and Archbold sitting in the car a discreet distance from the gates. Now if Veronica saw him, as it was most likely she would do, his best course would be to leave. Then, later, she wouldn't fail to follow. The great thing was not to give her a chance to speak to him. Therefore, to the bar, a refuge which was also the last place to which a sixteen-year-old competitor was likely to retreat before a match. The secretary, seeing him headed in that direction, trotted up to say that as a non-member he wasn't allowed to purchase a drink, but if he would permit a drink to be bought *for* him . . . ? Wexford accepted.

The bar was semicircular, with a long, curved window offering a view of three of the club's nine hard courts. Wexford had a half-pint of lager, the club like most places of its kind being unable to provide any sort of draft beer or "real ale." The secretary talked rather monotonously, first about the bad public behavior of certain international tennis stars, then their own disappointment at Saturday's rain and the enforced cancellation of this singles final. There would have been more spectators on a Saturday, he said sadly. In fact, nine people had actually come along – he had counted – but had had to be turned away. Of course, they were most unlikely to come back tonight. Wexford had the impression that if any of them had turned up the secretary would have bought them drinks too.

It got to six, to ten past. She's not going to come, Wexford thought. Then an umpire arrived and climbed up into the high seat. Five canvas chairs and a wooden bench had been arranged for a possible audience. It looked as if they would remain empty, but after a while two elderly women with white cardigans over their tennis dresses came and sat down and at the same time, approaching by the path that led from the farther group of six courts, Loring sauntered up. In sound English fashion he women sat in the canvas chairs on the left-hand end of the row and Loring at the extreme right-hand end of the bench. Colin Budd should have been so wise.

Veronica and a taller, older, altogether bigger girl appeared outside the court and let themselves in by the gate.

"Well, best get out there and give them some moral support," said the secretary, rubbing his hands together.

It was certainly cold. A gust of wind whipped across the court, tearing at Veronica's short, pleated skirt. In classic style they began with a knock-up.

"I don't think I will," said Wexford. "D'you mind if I watch from in here?"

The secretary was terribly disappointed. He gave him a look of injured reproach.

"You mustn't buy any drinks, you do know that, don't you? And you're not to serve him, mind, Priscilla."

Loring, his jacket collar turned up, was smoking a cigarette. The secretary appeared, running up to the two women, and sat beside them. The knock-up, in which Veronica had had the best of it, was over and the match began.

Dark would come early because the day had been so dull. Wexford wondered if the light would hold long enough for the match to be played to the finish. Veronica, whose service it was, won the first game to love but had a tougher time when her opponent came to serve.

"You can have a drink if you like," said

Priscilla. "I work it like this. I give it to you for free and next time a member buys me a drink I'll charge yours up to him. I'm a total abstainer actually, but I don't let on to this lot."

Wexford laughed. "Better not, thanks all the same."

"Suit yourself." She came over and stood beside him and watched.

Three games all. It looked as if it would go on and on and then quite quickly it was all over, Veronica having won her own two service games and broken her opponent's.

"She's a little cracker, that kid," said Priscilla. "Strong as a horse. She's got arms like whip-cord."

It was twenty to seven and the edge of dusk. Veronica won the first two games but the other girl was fighting back for all she was worth. Perhaps she had never played against Veronica before. At any rate, it had taken her all this time to find her weakness, but she had found it at last. Veronica couldn't handle long, swift, diagonal drives to her forehand, though back-hand presented her with no problems. It was half a dozen of those forehands that won her opponent the next game and the next and the next two until she was leading 4 – 2. The light had grown bluish, but the white lines on the court were still clearly visible, seeming to glow with twilight luminosity.

And then it was as if Veronica mastered the craft of dealing with those hard cross-court strokes. Or, curiously, as if some inspiration came to her from an external source. Certainly it was not that she had spotted him or had recognized Loring, whom she had never previously seen. But a charge of power came to her, a gift of virtuosity she had not known before. She had never before played like this, Wexford was sure of it. For a brief quarter of an hour she played as if she were on the center court at Wimbledon and was there not by a fluke but by a hard-won right.

Her opponent couldn't withstand it. In that quarter-hour she gained only four points. Veronica won the set by 6 games to 4 and thus secured the match. She threw her racket into the air, caught it neatly, ran to the net, and shook hands with her opponent. Wexford said good night to Priscilla and left the way he had come, having watched the players go into the pavilion where the changing rooms were. Loring was still sitting on the bench.

Allison he spotted as soon as the footpath entered the field. He was lying very still in the long grass by the hedge and mostly covered by it. But Wexford saw him without giving any sign that he had done so. He was pretty sure

Veronica wouldn't. The path wound on parallel to the hedge, then began to skirt the copse.

The false dusk hung still, suspended between light and dark. If it had been much darker no prudent young girl would have dared walk this way. Veronica Williams, of course, in spite of the impression she gave, was not a prudent young girl.

The air was still and damp and the grass moist underfoot. Wexford made his way along the path, under the high hedge, certain as he had been all along that Veronica's assailant would wait for her in the copse. Archbold had been there since 5:30 to be on the safe side. It was too late now for Wexford to join him without taking the risk of being seen. As it was, by staying to watch the match, he was taking a chance of spoiling the whole plan. Ahead of him a maple tree in the hedge spread its branches in a cone shape, the lowest ones almost touching the ground. He lifted them, stood against its trunk, and waited.

By now it was 7:30 and he had begun to wonder if she would come after all. Though members had been thin on the ground there might have been some plan to fete her in the clubhouse. Hardly with drinks though. And she would have got out of it, she needed to see him as much as he her. Then he remembered she was her mother's daughter; it would take her longer than most girls to change her clothes, do her hair. She might even have a shower. Wendy was the sort of woman who would get a dying person out of bed to change the sheets before the doctor comes.

He stood under his tree in the silent dusk, which was growing misty. Occasionally it was possible to hear in the distance a heavy vehicle on the Kingsmarkham to Pomfret road. Nothing else. No birds sang at this season and this hour. He could see the path about ten yards behind only and perhaps fifty yards ahead, and it seemed to him then the emptiest footway he had ever contemplated. Allison would get rheumatism lying there on the damp ground, the cold seeping into his bones. Archbold, wrapped in his padded jacket, had probably fallen asleep . . .

She appeared quite suddenly. But how else could she have come but noiselessly and walking quite fast? She didn't look afraid though. Wexford saw her face quite clearly for a moment. Her expression was – yes, innocent. Innocent and trusting. She had no knowledge that there was anything to fear. If Sara, her half-sister, was a Florentine madonna, she was a Medici page, her small face grave and wistful in its gold-brown frame of bobbed hair and fringe. She wore her pink cotton jeans, beautifully pressed by Mother, her pink and white running shoes, a powder blue and white striped anorak that hung open over a white fluffy pullover, and she was carrying her tennis racket in a blue case. Wexford took all this in as she passed him, walking quickly.

He didn't dare come out. She might look back. Instead he dropped down into the field at the other side of the hedge. There had been a crop growing here, wheat or barley, but the grain had been cut and all that remained was a stubble that looked gray in this light. He ran along the hedge side, some few feet above the footpath. A long way ahead now he could just see the top of her head bobbing along. She had reached the corner of the copse.

There was a barbed-wire entanglement here that threatened to bar his passage, the spaces between the wires too narrow to squeeze through, the top wire too high to sling a leg over without terrible detriment to trousers. There was nothing for it but to retrace steps, pass through the hedge, and clamber up the bank onto the footpath. She was too far away to see him even if she did look back. He jumped down, rounded the bend in the path, but now, though the copse was in full view, he couldn't see her at all.

His heart was in his mouth then. If she had met her assailant and gone into the wood, if Archbold truly had gone to sleep . . . He left the path and plunged into the copse. It was dark and dry in there, a million needles underfoot from the firs and larches. He ran through the trees and met Archbold head on.

"There's no one here, sir. I haven't seen a soul in three hours."

"Except her," said Wexford breathlessly.

"She just walked past. She's on her own, heading for the High Street."

He came out of the wood on the Kingsmarkham side, Archbold behind him. She was nowhere to be seen, the hedges too high, the foliage on the trees too thick and masking. And then he forgot discretion and catching a murderer and ran along the path in pursuit of her, afraid for her and for himself. A moment before he had been praying Bennett wouldn't appear, walking from the Kingsmarkham end, and spoil it all. Now he hoped he would.

There was one more field and that low-lying, the path passing diagonally across it and then running beside a hedge at right angles to the road. No sign of Bennett. Because he had seen her? Or seen her attacker? Would he be capable of that in this fast-fading light? The meadow was gray and the hedges black and the air had the density of fallen cloud. Through the mist you could just see a light or two from cars on the Pomfret road, behind that an irregular cluster of pale lights that was probably the police station.

She was nowhere. The meadow was empty. There was a movement just discernible on the far side of it, where the path met the hedge. She had crossed the diagonal and come to the last hundred yards, her pale clothes catching what light there was so that she gleamed like a night moth. And like a night moth fluttered along against the dark foliage.

Wexford and Palmer didn't take the diagonal. They dared not risk being seen. They kept to the boundary hedge, though there was no path here, and Palmer, who was thirty, outran Wexford who felt that he had never run so hard in his life. All the time he could see the pale, fluttering moth moving down there, homing on the stile that would bring her to the wide grass verge of the Pomfret road.

She never reached it. The fluttering stopped and there was something else down there with her at the bottom of the field where the dead elms stood, their roots a mass of underbrush, of brambles and nettles and fuzzy white clematis. The something or someone else had come out of that and barred her way. He thought he heard a cry but he couldn't be sure. At any rate it was no scream but a thin shriek of – surprise perhaps. He cut the corner, running hell for leather, his heart pounding fit to burst, running the way no man of close on sixty should run.

And Archbold got there only just first. It was strange that the knife should catch a gleam on it even in this near darkness. Wexford saw the gleam and then saw it drop to the ground. Archbold was holding Veronica, who had turned her face into his chest and was clinging on to his coat. He went up to the other himself. She made no attempt to run. She clasped her hands and hung her head so that he couldn't see her face.

In that moment Bennett materialized, so to speak. He came out of the dark, running. Sara Williams looked up then with an expression of faint, dull surprise.

"Take them both," said Wexford. "They'll be charged with the willful murder of Rodney Williams."

22

"It was they, not their mothers, who knew each other," Wexford said. "Edwina Klein told me but I misinterpreted what she said. 'Those two women know each other,' she said to me. 'I saw them together.' I took her to mean Joy and Wendy. Joy and Wendy were women and Sara and Veronica were girls. Except that to a militant feminist founder member of ARRIA all females are women. Just as they are," he added, "to organizers of sports events. It's the women's singles even if both players are fifteen."

Burden and the doctor said nothing. They were all sitting in Burden's grass widower's house, drinking Burden's grass widower's instant coffee. It was over. A special court for one and a special juvenile court for the other and the two girls had been committed for trial.

Afterwards the press had caught Wexford, a camera crew springing out of their van with the agility of the SAS, and once again he would be on television. Looking a hundred years old, he thought, after being up half the night talking to Sara Williams. People would phone in suggesting it was time he retired.

"They met at a tennis match, of course. The second time I met Sara I noticed she had a tennis racket up on her bedroom wall. She wasn't anywhere near Veronica's standard, not in the high school's first or second six. She just scraped into their reserve. Still, one day she was called on to play and she met Veronica as her opponent. What happened then? I don't know and she hasn't told me. I'd guess that one of the other girls there commented that they looked alike and, seeing they had the same surname, were they cousins? It was up to one of them to probe further and one of them did. Sara, probably. After that it wouldn't have been hard to find out, would it? 'Look, I've got a photo, this is my mum and dad . . .' "

"Something of a shattering experience, wouldn't you say?" said the doctor.

"Also I think an exciting one."

"That's a superficial way of looking at it," said Burden. "I'd almost say unfeeling. Both these girls were lonely, Veronica sheltered and smothered, Sara neglected, no one's favorite. Wouldn't it have been both shattering and immensely *comforting* to find a sister?"

The sensitivity which had developed in Burden late in life always brought Wexford a kind of affectionate amusement. It was so often misdirected. It resembled in a way those good intentions with which hell is paved.

He picked his words carefully. They were strong words but his tone was hesitant.

"Sara Williams doesn't have normal feelings of affection, need for love, loneliness. I think she would be labeled a psychopath. She wants attention and she wants to impress. Also she wants her own way. I imagine that what she got from her half-sister was principally admiration. Sara has an excellent brain. Intellectually, she's streets ahead of Veronica. She's a strong, powerful, amoral, unfeeling solipsist with an appalling temper."

Crocker's eyebrows went up. "You're talking about an eighteen-year-old who was raped by her own father."

Wexford didn't respond. He was thinking about what the girl had said to him, presiding at the table in the interview room with Marion Bayliss at one end, himself opposite, and Martin facing Marion. But Sara Williams had presided, holding her head high, describing her feelings and actions without a notion of defending herself.

"My sister looks just like me. I used to feel she was another aspect of me, the weaker, pretty, feminine part, if you like. I wanted ultimately to be rid of that part."

Solipsism, according to the Oxford dictionary, is the view or theory that self is the only object of real knowledge or the only real thing existent.

"Why didn't you tell your parents you and Veronica had met?"

"Why should I?"

Her cool answers took the breath away.

"It would have been the natural thing to confront your father with what you had found out."

She was honest in her way. "I liked having the secret. I enjoyed knowing what he thought I didn't know."

"So that you could hold it over him?"

"Perhaps," she said indifferently, bored when the discussion was not totally centered on herself.

Was that what she had had to threaten him with in the matter of the incest? Was that how she had stopped it?

"You prevented Veronica from telling her mother?"

"She did what I told her."

It was uttered the way a trainer speaks of an obedient dog. The trainer takes the obedience for granted, so effective are his personality and technique, so unthinkable would an alternative reaction be. Wexford thought Crocker and Burden would have had to hear and see Sara to appreciate all this. He couldn't even attempt to put it across to them. "The two girls met quite often," he went on. "Sara even went to Veronica's home when Wendy was at work. Veronica came to admire her extravagantly. She followed her, she would have obeyed her in anything."

"Would have?"

"Did. Psychiatrists call what overtook them *folie à deux*, a kind of madness that overtakes two people only when they are together and through the influence of each on the other. But in all such cases you'll always find one party who is easily led and one who is dominant." Wexford digressed a little before returning to the point. "Looking back, I don't think Sara Williams has ever addressed a sentence to me that didn't begin with 'I' or wasn't about herself."

He went on: "The coming and going between the Williams homes led to a pooling of information. For instance, Sara had believed her father was a sales rep with Sevensmith

Harding for the Ipswich area. Veronica thought he was a rep with a bathroom fittings company. They took steps to find out the truth and did. It's over a year now since they found out what Rodney really did, what his position was, and discovered – via some research into marketing managers' earnings on Sara's part – what his actual salary was.

"Sara also warned Veronica of their father's – proclivities. That, of course, is how Wendy came to fear an incest attempt. Not because she witnessed anything herself or because Veronica put two and two together from a kiss and a cuddle but because Sara told Veronica what to expect and Veronica passed it on without disclosing her source. One way and another Sara made Veronica into a very frightened girl. A very bewildered and confused girl. Think of her situation. First she discovers her father has a legal wife and a grown-up family, next that he could never have in fact married her mother and she must be illegitimate. Necessarily, therefore, he's deceitful and a liar. He doesn't even have the job he says he has. Worst of all, he has raped his other daughter and will certainly have the same designs on her. No wonder she was frightened.

"Telling Wendy her fears of a sexual attack had the effect only of causing trouble between her mother and father. Did Wendy accuse Rodney and Rodney hotly deny it? Almost certainly. The quarrel was at any rate bad enough to make Wendy believe Rodney would leave her but fear that if he did Veronica would be in danger. So we see that the reason she didn't want Veronica to stay in on the evening of April the fifteenth was that if Rodney did come back she would be alone with her father – and this would be the first time she would be alone with him after the disclosure was made.

"But Veronica had another confidante and friend now, apart from her mother. She had Sara. And Sara absolutely justified the faith she put in her. Sara had a good idea for diverting Rodney's attention from his daughter, diverting his attention from everything, in fact. Substitute sleeping pills for his blood-pressure tablets. It was something that could be done only once though and in an emergency.

"Now on April the fifteenth, however much their mothers may have been in ignorance, Sara and Veronica knew that when Rodney left Alverbury Road he would drive straight to Liskeard Avenue. So Sara herself made the exchange of tablets, two only remaining in the container. Don't forget we found an empty Mandaret container in Alverbury Road and a half-full one in Liskeard Avenue. Rodney took his two Mandaret as he thought, leaving the empty container in his bedroom, and drove to Pomfret. No doubt he began to feel drowsy on the way."

"But these were Phanodorm, supplied by Paulette Harmer?" said the doctor.

"I suppose they were supplied by her. It seems most likely. But Paulette didn't die because she illicitly provided a sleeping drug. She died because the turn events were taking made her concentrate her mind on the evening of April the fifteenth, made her remember in fact what had really happened. What she remembered was her mother speaking to her aunt Joy on the phone that evening and making some remark about being glad Kevin had settled in back at college. And she was going to tell us because she knew from the papers and television and her parents' conversation how strong was the suspicion against her aunt. She knew very well her aunt had been at home that evening, in at eight to receive Kevin's phone call and still in at eight forty-five to receive her mother's."

The girl should have been strewing flowers or rising from the waves in a cockleshell. The face was bland, innocent, and somehow secretive. Even now there was a tiny, self-satisfied smile. Her hair was scraped back tight from that high forehead, but wisps had come free and lay in gold tendrils on the white skin.

"I got a phone call from Veronica. It was just to tell me he'd gone to sleep like I said he would. I said I'd come over."

He had interrupted her to ask why.

"I just thought I would. I wasn't going to get a chance like that again, was I?"

He stopped himself asking her what she meant. Her eyes seemed to enlarge, her face grow blanker.

"I saw him sleeping there and I thought, I've got him in my power. I thought of the power he had over *me*. I started to get angry, really angry."

"And Veronica?"

"I didn't think about Veronica. I suppose she was there. Well, I know she was. I said to her, 'We could kill him and stop all of it.' I told her to get me a knife. I wasn't serious then, it was fantasy. I was angry and I was excited – high like when you've had a drink."

Folie à deux. Was Veronica excited too? He wouldn't get much about another's feelings out of this girl.

"I took the knife out of her hands and took off the cardboard guard that was on it. I went up to my father, who was lying on the settee, and I started playing around, waving the knife over him, pretending to stick it in him. I could tell he was sound asleep. I was making Veronica laugh because I was doing all this stuff and he was just oblivious of it. I don't remember what made me stop playing. I was so excited and high I don't remember. But that's how it was. One minute it was fantasy and the next it was for real."

She looked down the table at Marion and then the other way at Martin. It was as if she were gathering the attention of her audience. Once more her eyes met Wexford's in a steady gaze.

"I raised the knife and stuck it in his neck, right in hard with both hands. I'd made him wake up then and make noises, so I stabbed him a few more times to stop the blood spraying like that. I'm going to be a doctor so I knew the blood would stop when he was dead . . ."

It took Wexford, hardened as he was, a moment or two to collect words.

"Did Veronica stab him?"

"I gave her the knife and told her to have a go. I'd made a big wound in his neck and she stuck it in there and then she went off and was sick."

"Completely mad," said Burden. "Bonkers."

"Perhaps. I'm not sure. Let's not get into defining psychosis."

"What happened next?" said the doctor.

"The room was covered for the most part in dust sheets. Rodney had come in half asleep, climbed the stairs, and lain down on the settee, which had a dust sheet over one end. The end, incidentally, where he laid his head. It was this sheet, the property of Leslie Kitman, which received most of the blood. Some went on to an area of wall from which the paper had been stripped that day. Sara washed the wall and wrapped Rodney's head up in the dust sheet. Veronica, recovered and very much under orders from Sara, washed the knife and then had the idea of plastering it into the wall. This was the first weird too-clever thing the girls did. There were others. There were fissures in the walls needing to be filled in and in the garage was a packet of filler. Also in the garage was Rodney's car, Greta the Grenada, which Sara, though not Veronica, was able to drive. They rolled up the dust sheet and wrapped one of Wendy's Marks and Spencer's tea cloths round Rodney's neck. Having cleaned up the room, they carried Rodney down the spiral staircase, through the door from the hall into the garage, and put him into the boot of the car. On their way out in the car they deposited the dust sheet in the dustbin. It was about seven-thirty."

"Then," said Burden, "how did Kevin manage to speak to his sister when he phoned Alverbury Road at eight o'clock?"

"He didn't. He spoke to his mother. And, of course, he and Joy were both well aware it was his mother he had spoken to. They lied to protect Sara. Oh, I know Joy hasn't much affection for Sara, but she was her daughter. Once she began to think about it she saw that Sara might have had something to do with Rodney's disappearance. At first she genuinely thought he had left her and she got me in to advise her. But then things changed. I think I know why. On my advice, she phoned Sevensmith Harding and they told her *she* had spoken to them on Friday, April the sixteenth, to explain Rodney was ill. Now Joy no doubt at first thought this a mere mistake, but they had been so sure it was her voice. Joy knew someone whose voice sounded very like hers – her own daughter."

"Don't forget that she knew how Sara felt towards her father on account of the incest. She also knew Sara had been out of the house for hours on the evening of April the fifteenth. So she told us and got Kevin to agree – no difficulty there, he distrusts the police and is close to his sister – that it was she who had gone out and Sara who had been at home to take the phone call. Was there collusion with Sara? I doubt it. There was no real communication between her and her mother. My guess is Joy said it might be wiser to arrange things this way and Sara agreed with just a nod and a 'yes' probably."

"You're painting a picture of a self-sacrificing maternal type," said the doctor, "which doesn't at all accord with our concept of Joy Williams. Rather like the old story of the mother pelican tearing at its own breast to feed its young – and just as much of a myth."

"No. Joy quite rightly believed there was no real risk in it for her. She thought it impossible we could arrest the wrong person. Her trust must have been sorely put to the test these past few days."

Always happier on circumstantial details, Burden said, "So the two girls took Williams's body up to Cheriton Forest and dug a grave for him with his own snow shovel?"

"A shallow grave because, having killed him, Sara didn't want it to be too long before the body was discovered. She wanted a couple of weeks to pass only, rightly believing that this was the sort of time which would be just about right to blur the evidence. In fact, things didn't go her way and it was two months before the body was found.

"I turned over and over in my mind the complication of the Milvey coincidence. But now it has come out quite clearly. There is no coincidence. Sara and Veronica hid Rodney's traveling bag – in the forest probably – hoping it would be found within, say, the next few days. But as it happened, no one found it. Then one day Mrs. Milvey happened to say to Joy in Sara's hearing that Milvey would be at Green Pond next day, dragging the pool. Sara retrieved the bag and dumped it in the pool in time for Milvey to find it next day."

"But why did she want the body found? What difference could it make to her?"

"I'll come to that later."

"I don't see why go to all the trouble of phoning Sevensmith Harding and forging a letter to delay discovery, and then later try to accelerate it. Incidentally, I take it it was Sara who made the phone call? Her voice is very like Joy's."

"She made the phone call and Veronica typed the letter. At her friend Nicola Tennyson's house, on Nicola's mother's typewriter.

"They buried the body, hid the traveling bag, and Sara drove Veronica back to Pomfret to be sure she got home before Wendy did. That was at about nine. Wendy, of course, didn't get home until nine-thirty, being out doing some mild courting with James Ovington. Sara drove to Myringham and dumped the car in Arnold Road, where no more than half an hour later it was seen and indeed bumped into by Eve Freeborn. If Sara had been a bit later and Eve a bit earlier those two members of ARRIA would have encountered each other and made our task a lot easier. But by the time Eve came Sara was on the bus for home.

"In the morning she shut herself in he living room and made the phone call before she went to school. Of necessity it was a very early call and she was lucky there was someone there to receive it. And that, I think, accounts for all the circumstances of the murder of Rodney Williams."

Burden picked up the tray.

"Does anyone want more coffee?"

Neither did. Wexford said it was nearly beer time, wasn't it? The doctor frowned at him and he deliberately looked away, out into Burden's bright, neat garden, the flower borders like chintzy dress material, the lawn a bit of green baize. The sunshine was making Jenny's yellow chrysanthemums nearly too bright to look at. Burden opened the French windows.

"The sad thing," said Crocker, "is that all this

is going to make it next to impossible for Sara Williams to make a career in medicine."

Burden looked at him. He said sarcastically, "Oh, surely St. Biddulph's will overlook a little matter like stabbing her father to death with a carving knife."

"You don't think it justification then, and more than justification, for a girl to make a murderous assault on the father who has raped her and shows signs of meting out the same treatment to her younger half-sister? Don't you think any judge or jury would see this as an extenuating circumstance?"

It was Wexford who answered him. "Yes, I do."

"Right, then there's not going to be any question of imprisonment, is there? She'll never have the dubious distinction of being a GP like your humble servant here, but at least there won't be punishment in the accepted sense."

"I wouldn't be too sure of that."

"On account of the planning and the covering of tracks, do you mean?"

"She killed Paulette Harmer," Burden said.

"She did indeed, but that wasn't what I meant. You see, Rodney Williams never committed incest with his elder daughter. He never showed signs of committing incest with his younger daughter. And I very much doubt if he ever sexually assaulted anyone, even in the broadest meaning of that term."

23

Crocker had caught on quickly. Wexford left it to him to explain. The doctor began outlining Freud's "seduction theory" as expressed in the famous paper of 1896.

Thirteen women patients of Freud claimed paternal seduction. Freud believed them, built on this evidence a theory, later abandoned it, realizing he had been too gullible. Instead, he concluded that little girls are prone to fantasize that their fathers have made love to them, from which developed his stress on childhood fantasy and ultimately his postulation of the Oedipus complex.

"You're saying it was all fantasy on Sara's part?" Burden said. "She's not exactly a *little* girl."

"Nor were Freud's patients little girls by the time they came to him."

Wexford said, "I think Sara had a daughter's fantasy about her father. When she was older she read Freud. She read books on incest too – they're all there in her bedroom. There's a mention of father-daughter incest in the ARRIA constitution. Did she read that too or did she write it? At any rate, *in her mind* she was heavily involved with her father, far more involved with him than he was with her."

"How do you know the seduction didn't really take place? Men do commit incest with their daughters. I mean, how could Freud have known one of those thirteen wasn't fantasizing but telling the truth?"

"I can't answer that," Wexford said, "but I can tell you it never happened to Sara. She isn't the kind of girl to whom it happens. She isn't ignorant or obtuse or cowed or dependent. This seduction, or apparent seduction, followed a classic pattern as laid down in the books. The girl doesn't struggle or fight or scream. She doesn't want to make a disturbance. At the first opportunity she tells her mother and mother reacts with rage, reproaches, accusations of the girl's provocative behavior. Now Joy, as we might expect, fitted beautifully into the classic pattern. But Sara? If it had really happened wouldn't Sara, a leading member of ARRIA, a militant feminist, have fought and screamed? She was very handy with a knife, wasn't she? And she's the last person to care about making a disturbance in a household, either emotional or physical. As for telling her mother – Sara tell her mother? There's been no real communication between them for years. She despises her mother. If she'd told anyone it would have been her brother Kevin. No, there was no seduction, for if there had been she would have kept the experience secret to use against her father, not come running with it to Joy.

"It was Sara who stabbed Colin Budd, of course. It happened, if you remember, the night before Milvey started dragging Green Pond. Sara retrieved the bag after dark, went up to the forest to do it, and put the bag inside a plastic sack. When Budd came along she was waiting to catch the bus that would take her to the other end of Kingsmarkham, near enough to the Forby road and Green Pond Hall. The last thing she wanted was Budd taking an interest in her. Besides, she had indoctrinated herself to be always on the watch for sexist approaches. What was she doing but going about her private business? And this man has to treat her as if her primary function in this world was to be an object for his diversion and entertainment. No doubt she also lost her nerve. She stabbed him with a penknife."

"If it was all fantasy," said Burden, reverting to the analysis of Sara Williams's character, "why did she warn Veronica? Why warn her of something that would never happen?"

"You're supposing fantasy is something 'made up,' so therefore something the fantasizer herself doesn't believe in?"

"Well, does she? Did Sara convince herself?"

"Yes and no. She's admitted to me nothing ever happened. On the other hand, I wouldn't be surprised if tomorrow she says it did and believes it herself. Having this secret to communicate, this awful and horrifying secret, must have much increased her ascendancy over Veronica. It enhanced her power. Veronica was very frightened of her, you see, full of admiration, awe almost, but even before the killing of Rodney becoming unnerved by the whole set-up."

Wendy had been sent for and for once had been calm, sensible, steady. He had considered the atmosphere of his office more relaxing than one of those stark interview rooms. Marion and Polly were seated side by side and Veronica a little apart from everyone until Wexford came in. Little Miss Muffet and the great spider who sat down beside her. Only there was no frightening her away. It would be a long time now before Veronica Williams could get away.

She was very pale. Her hair, he noticed, was a couple of inches longer than when he had first seen her, six inches longer than the crop of the beach photograph. Had she been growing it in imitation of her idol and model, Sara? He had asked her when she first met her half-sister.

"It was September." Her voice was so soft he had to ask her to repeat it. "September – a year ago," she said.

"And you met how often after that? Once a week? More?"

Very quietly, "More."

He extracted from her the information that they constantly spoke on the phone. It was like a game sometimes, Sara phoning and saying she would be in Liskeard Avenue in five minutes, she phoning Sara to say if Sara was careful not to be seen she could come and watch Rodney and Wendy watching *her* play tennis.

"It stopped being a game, though, didn't it? On April the fifteenth it stopped?"

She nodded and her body convulsed in an involuntary shiver. Wendy said, "Why did you always do everything she said? Why did you tell her everything?"

How could she answer that?

"You told her you were coming here to confess your part in it, didn't you, Veronica?" Wexford spoke very gently.

Her eyes went to Wendy. "I thought the police would arrest my mother."

A small spark of triumph on Wendy's doleful face. In these unbelievable circumstances her years of devotion were rewarded . . .

Wexford surfaced from his reverie to see Burden depositing three beer cans in front of them from a tray laden with the kind of junk food he lived on while Jenny was away.

"Wake up!"

"Sorry."

"Look, if there was no incest and therefore no renewed assault from Rodney to be feared, if there was no threat to Veronica, what was the motive for killing him? All through this case we could never come up with any sort of solid motive. Or are you saying a psychopath doesn't need a motive – at any rate not a motive understood by normal people?"

Wexford said slowly, "I've suggested to you that there was a good deal of calculation in Sara's behavior, some of it of an apparently incomprehensible kind. Her original concealment of the body, for instance, and later her anxiety for it to be found. I've also made it clear – rather to your joint disapproval, I think

– that I don't feel much sympathy towards Sara. And this is because I feel she had no justification for what she did.

"She had a motive all right, and as calculated and cold-blooded a motive as any poisoner polishing off an old relation for his money."

"But Rodney didn't have any money to leave, did he?" Burden objected.

"Not so's you'd notice, though the manager of the Anglian-Victoria has shown me how a nice little bit was accumulating in the account from which the two joint accounts were fed. Enough, anyway, for him to recommend that Rodney put it into investments. Still, it wasn't for a possible inheritance that Sara killed him, though money was her motive."

"Not a cash gain though, I think," said the doctor.

Wexford turned to Burden. "You raised this very subject not long ago, Mike. That was when you thought you were going to have a daughter – and that's relevant too. You talked about her going to university and applying for government grants. Do you remember?"

"I suppose so. I don't see where the relevance comes in."

"Sara wants to be a doctor," said Wexford. "Well, *wanted* to be, I should say. It was a driving ambition with her. And increasingly hard though this is becoming, she knew she had the ability to get into medical school. Her parents, however, discouraged her. And it must have looked to her at that stage as if this was a classic case of opposition to daughter's ambitions simply because she was a daughter and not a son, because in fact she was a woman. On Joy's part it probably was. Very likely she wouldn't have cared for Sara to achieve greater success and have a more prestigious profession than Kevin.

"At first this parental opposition didn't much worry Sara. I'm speaking of course, about this time last year. Sara remembered her brother getting a place at Keele and the form of application for a grant coming from Sussex County Council Education Committee to her father. At the time she didn't take much notice. Certainly she didn't see the completed form. But she knew that the greater the parental income the smaller the grant would be and that with the form there came a form of certificate of parental employment the parent's employer had to complete, detailing his gross salary, overtime, bonus or commissions, and his taxable emoluments. Now, Mike, you'll recall that certificate in your own case and sending it to the Mid-Sussex Constabulary when you applied for grants for John and Pat?"

Burden nodded. "I'm beginning to see the light here."

"Twelve months ago Sara met Veronica. Gradually, when the shock of that encounter began to recede, when it provided the solution to certain unexplained anomalies, shall we say, Sara saw the cold reality for what it was. Her father might talk about not wanting his daughter to be a doctor for aesthetic reasons, for reasons of suitability, she would get married and her education be wasted, et cetera. He might talk that way, but the reason behind the talk was very different. Finding that he had lied to both her mother and Veronica's about what his position and his earnings were, she had taken steps to discover what he did and what he earned. Now she understood. If he filled in the grant application form for her he would have to declare to the Sussex County Council that his income was not £10,000 a year but two and a half times that, and there would be no way he could deceive the authority as he had deceived her mother, because his employers, Sevensmith Harding, would have to complete the certificate of parental income from employment.

"Now according to the grants department's contribution scales, a parent earning £10,000 per annum would have to contribute to medical school costs only something in the region of

£470, but a parent earning £25,000 a sum of nearly £2000. Rodney had two homes and two families, he was already paying out this sort of sum for Kevin at Keele – remember, he had to tell the grants department the truth, whatever he told his wives – and Sara could see the way the wind was blowing. She could see there was no way he would part with £2000 a year for her benefit. And when she asked him point blank if he would fill in the form when it came, he told her he wouldn't – she would never make a doctor and he was doing her a kindness in not encouraging her."

"What a bastard," said Crocker.

Wexford shrugged. "The mistake is ours when we deceive ourselves about parent-child relationships. When we keep up the belief that all parents love their children and want what's best for them."

"Surely, though, if Sara had talked about this at school or discussed it with some sympathetic officer at the grants department, a way could have been found for her to get a grant, bypassing Rodney? There must be many cases where a parent withholds consent and won't complete a grant application."

"Probably. But Sara is only eighteen. And remember that to have done what you suggest she would have to reveal that her father was a liar and a cheat, that he deceived her mother, that he was a bigamist. And how long would all this take? Would it mean her waiting a year? And what of her place at St. Biddulph's, a teaching hospital where places are like gold dust and where they keep a reserve list bursting with applicants dying to be accepted? What she decided on instead was, first, persuasion, and if that failed, blackmail."

"She told him that if he didn't consent to fill in the form she'd tell Joy about Wendy and get Veronica to tell Wendy about Joy?"

"She was *going* to tell him that. She had a bit of time though. She hadn't even sat her A-levels. The grant form wouldn't come till July. And she also had the incest. Of course, it had never taken place but Joy thought it had, Veronica was scared stiff it had. If all else failed she might be able to use it as another weapon in the blackmail stockpile. That was why she was pleased to see how effective her warnings had been in Veronica's case. Veronica was beginning to be afraid of the affectionate attention Rodney paid her. Veronica didn't want to be alone with him, and if she had to be she wanted him disarmed and immobilized. Sara saw to that with the Phanodorm, and increased Veronica's fear by the seriousness of taking such a step.

"But how much simpler, after all, to kill him! And there he was, lying asleep, the potential destroyer of her future. Kill him now, in this room which will soon be made pure and immaculate, cleansed of all signs of violent death. Rid the world of him, seize your opportunity. And perhaps it would also be a heroic act. Hadn't there almost been a clause in the ARRIA constitution demanding a man's death as qualification for entry? Veronica will help because Veronica also hates him now and is mortally afraid of him . . .

"But suppose they never find the body? Suppose the weeks go by and July comes and August and with them the grant application and you can't fill in the section that says 'Father, if deceased the fact should be stated . . .' because only you and Veronica know he is deceased? You have finished your A-levels and the time is going by – the moment has come to take steps for that body to be found without more delay."

"You might say," said Crocker, "that the murder was both coolly premeditated and carried out on an impulse."

"You might. Because of what Sara is, a highly complex personality, this was all kinds of a murder. A ritualistic killing – remember that Veronica was required to stab him too. A revenge killing – Sara had more than half-convinced herself and wholly convinced Veronica of the reality of the incest. When she stabbed Rodney she was a woman out of classical myth, she was Beatrice Cenci. It was an *experimental* killing, a kind of vivisection, carried out by Sara the scientist, to see if it would work, to see if it could be done. It was murder from disgust, from disillusionment. Rodney, whom she had once worshipped, was just a squalid bigamist with another daughter, a copy of herself, he loved as much as or more than he had ever loved her. But above all, in spite of all those other factors, it was murder for gain, carried out so that she might satisfy her ambition at all costs. All in all, I don't think that's the sort of person I'd care to have as my family physician, still less performing surgery on me and mine. So perhaps Rodney was right when he told Sara she was an unsuitable candidate for medical school. Who knows? Perhaps it wasn't simply meanness with him, he wasn't quite the bastard you make out. Perhaps he sensed in that daughter of his, without ever examining his conclusions, traits in her character that were abnormal, that were destructive, and it was to these he referred when he said she would never make a doctor."

Wexford got up.

"I shall call it a day," he said. "I shall go to the wife of my bosom the same as I ought to go."

Burden began tidying the room, putting things on to a tray. "And tomorrow the wife of my bosom comes home to me." He looked pleased, satisfied, hopeful, as if there had been no five months' long disruption of his happiness. "One of her old pupils at Haldon Finch went in to see her and the baby. An ARRIA member. She told Jenny the raven bit means they're cleaning up the carrion men have left behind in the world. We did wonder."

"Ah," Wexford paused in the doorway. "Something I nearly forgot to tell you. About Williams's young girlfriend . . ."

They looked at him. "Williams didn't have a young girlfriend," Burden said.

"Of course he did. She had nothing to do with his death, nothing to do with this case, so she hardly concerned us. But a man like Williams – it was in his nature, inevitable. Both his wives knew it, they sensed it. Probably he'd always had a young girlfriend, a succession of them."

"This one – hers were the other set of prints on the car. No wonder she said her dad didn't want me to take them. They met at Sevensmith Harding, of course. In the office."

"Jane Gardner . . ."

"That's who he had his date with on April the fifteenth in Myringham. Join her for her babysitting, then spend the night together at the Cheriton Forest Hotel. Why else did he have a bag with him with a single change of underwear and a toothbrush and toothpaste? But the sleeping pills overcame him as he was driving through Pomfret, and instead of going on to meet Jane he was just able to make it to his own house. What she thought was that he'd stood her up. Then, when he disappeared, that he'd gone off with another woman. I had a word with her this morning and she admitted it – no more need to conceal it now we'd made an arrest."

"What put you on to her?"

"I don't know. Guesswork. She was the only person I ever spoke to who had a good word for Rodney Williams."

Wexford let himself out, closing Burden's blue front door behind him.

THORNDIKE PRESS HOPES you have enjoyed this Large Print book. All our Large Print titles are designed for the easiest reading, and all our books are made to last. Other Thorndike Press Large Print books are available at your library, through selected bookstores, or directly from the publisher. For more information about our current and upcoming Large Print titles, please send your name and address to: